Business Process Technology

Dirk Draheim

Business Process Technology

A Unified View on Business Processes,
Workflows and Enterprise Applications

 Springer

Dr. Dirk Draheim
Universität Innsbruck
Zentraler Informatikdienst (ZID)
Technikerstr. 23
6020 Innsbruck
Austria
draheim@acm.org

ISBN 978-3-642-01587-8   e-ISBN 978-3-642-01588-5
DOI 10.1007/978-3-642-01588-5
Springer Heidelberg Dordrecht London New York

Library of Congress Control Number: 2010932874

Cover design: KuenkelLopka GmbH

Printed on acid-free paper

Springer is part of Springer Science+Business Media (www.springer.com)

Foreword

In the last decade there has been an explosion of interest in the modeling and automation of business processes, and competence in this area is seen as increasingly critical to business competitiveness and stability. However, this has lead to a parallel explosion in solution approaches and technologies leading to a state-of-the-art that is highly disjointed and confused. In particular, there is a mismatch between business process modeling technologies on the one hand, which focus on allowing domain experts to describe business processes in a graphical, easy-to-use way, and workflow engines on the other hand which focus on automating the enactment of business processes in association with human users. Not only is there little consensus on concepts and terminology, there is also little connection between commercial solutions and established computer science theory. This is where Dirk Draheim's book makes its contribution. First, it clarifies the conceptual differences and similarities between the many different business process technologies available today and lays the foundation for a unified understanding of the field. Second, it explores the relationship between these technologies and traditional principles of computer science such as structured programming. And third, it lays out a vision for the future of business process technology and its optimal use in business process improvement and enterprise systems development.

Most books on business process technology either take a very broad but high-level view of the challenges and solutions in this area or provide a very detailed but narrow view of a specific issue or technology. It is rare to find a book that manages to do both. Dirk Draheim combines his experience with the wide-range of practical technologies currently used to automate business processes with his deep understanding of computing science formalisms to show how the former can be given a stronger theoretical foundation. Finally the best part of the book is saved until the end. In the final chapter Dirk Draheim proposes "Typed Workflow Charts" as a new formalism for modeling and automating business processes. This represents a genuinely innovative step forward which is likely to have a big impact on the way business processes are specified and automated in the future.

Mannheim, July 2010   *Colin Atkinson*

Author's Preface

Is it possible to specify business processes in a technology-independent and executable manner? That is the question this book addresses. There are different communities addressing business processes each with different objectives, tools and terminology – business process reengineering, business process modeling, task modeling, business process management, workflow management. We seek for a unified understanding of the phenomena addressed by these communities. There is a huge potential for automation in today's Enterprises. An integrated platform for specifying and controlling processes in an enterprise would be an enabling technology to use this potential. However, there are severe challenges that must be overcome before such a platform can be designed. First, there are structural frictions in today's business process modeling and today's business process implementations, i.e., lack of operational semantics and lack of a canonical implementation. Second, current business process management (BPM) and workflow technologies are not fully integrated with the application programsthat implement the dialogues of an enterprise application.

Business process models do not have a precise operational semantics in the sense of a fixed set of rules that describe the state changes in the system under consideration. There is no canonical mapping between the activities of the business processes and the dialogues that support these activities. The workflow paradigm in its current form does not really help in this situation. Up to now, workflow technology is only really convincing in the field of document management. Current business process execution and management technologies arose as enterprise application integration technologies and they are still used in this manner. However, workflow technology is not yet a proven concept as a general enterprise resource management technology.

Today's BPM technology is successfully used in enterprise application projects in the following sense. As a first step the system analyst identifies the rules behind the interplay of existing enterprise applications. These rules are then automated by a BPM product. Today's BPM technology controls workflow states. However, it does not control the dialogues that bridge the workflow states – the dialogue states are not seen by BPM technology. This means, most importantly, that the dialogues are also not amenable to advanced BPM tools and techniques like business process simulation and business process monitoring.

Furthermore, if BPM technology is used to build a workflow-intensive system from scratch it is not obvious any more how to design the human-computer interaction. The problem is to fix the right granularity of workflow states versus dialogue states. Despite some heuristics a systematic treatment of this question is still missing. We follow a different, more direct approach: workflow states and dialogue states are unified so that the aforementioned problem simply does not appear any more. This text aims at characterizing and mitigating the mentioned gaps. We target a seamless specification of workflows and dialogues.

Objectives of the Book

We analyze the existing gap between business process modeling, which is a system analysis activity, and business process automation, which is related to system design. We also analyze the gaps and tension between current classes of business process technology, i.e., business process modeling tools, workflow definition, and integrated development environments. We claim that an analysis of the aforementioned gaps and tension is necessary before an integrated business process management platform can be designed. These are some of the discussions, questions, results and contributions of the book:

- We explain that business process management lifecycle models should be understood as pools of systematic activities and argue that they can hardly be interpreted as strictly staged models in Sect. 2.4.1.
- We propose a new model of IT ownership which cleanly separates foreseeable total costs of ownership and assessable total benefit of ownership in Sect. 2.6.4.
- We introduce a spiral quality management system model in Sect. 2.7 which is reductionist in terms of organizational functions but sophisticated in terms of interfaces between organizational functions.
- We identify three distinguishable aspects of component technology in Sect. 3.3, i.e., the sub industry aspect, the infrastructure aspect and the large system construction aspect.
- We explain why today's emerging CSCW tools should be exploited in business continuity management in Sect. 3.4.
- We propose the integration of business processes, production processes and business intelligence by the means of data warehousing technology in Sects. 3.6.2.
- We distinguish between a global view on workflows, which is the view of workflow supervisory, and a local view on workflows, which is the view of the single workers involved in workflow executions, in Sect. 4.1. It turns out that this distinction helps in the understanding of quality of design

of business process specifications and also helps in understanding the gap
between business process modeling and business process automation.

- We report on the informality of business process modeling languages in
  Chapter 4 and why this informality is sometimes needed in projects. For
  example, we report on the semantic inconsistencies of how events are used
  in today's business process modeling languages in Sect. 4.4.
- We discuss the need for a means to specify arbitrary synchronization in
  business process models and workflow definitions in Sects. 4.6 and 9.2.10.
- We coin and define the term of a methodology stakeholder in Sect. 5.1.
  We explain the impact of methodology stakeholders on the software engineering practices of real-world projects.
- Throughout the text we foster a visualization independent viewpoint of
  business process specification and even more, i.e., a syntax independent
  viewpoint or to say it better a concrete syntax independent viewpoint –
  see, e.g., the discussion of abstract syntax in Sect. 5.1.3.
- We describe two different semantics of business processes with multiple
  start and end events in Sect. 5.2.2, i.e., a self-contained semantics and a
  global, context-embedded semantics. We describe that the selection of a
  self-contained semantics has an impact on the flexibility in building hierarchies and try to find an explanation why a self-contained semantics seems
  often to be preferred in practice.
- We identify the reasons why methodology stakeholders stuck to the guideline of single entry or exit points for business process specifications – see
  Sect. 5.2.3.
- A visualization-independent characterization of uniqueness of interface
  points – see Sect. 5.2.4.
- We observe that certain type specifications for data in leveled data flow
  diagrams are control flow constraints in Sect. 5.3.
- We investigate the opportunity of bringing the best practices of structured
  programming to the field of business process specification in Chapter 6.
  This attempt is done in a sophisticated manner. It is accompanied by a
  reconsideration of the arguments of structured programming in that we
  ideally target to identify the scientifically discussable core – in the sense
  of falsifiability [287, 288] – of the structure programming metaphor.
- We explain workflow systems from the viewpoint of human-computer interaction in Sect. 7. We explain workflow systems as three-staged human-
  computer interaction. On this basis we are able to distinguish between
  terminal/server-style and windows-style workflow systems and analyze
  their differences.
- We explain the importance of a general instead of pattern-oriented viewpoint on the assignment of resources to activities in workflow automation
  in Sect. 7.2.3.
- We identify four well-distinguishable visions for service-oriented architecture, i.e., the enterprise application integration vision, the business-to-
  business-vision, the flexible processes vision and eventually the software

productizing vision – see Sect. 8.1. This clean distinction can help in
projects to identify and prioritize more quickly the actual targets of the
different stakeholders who are advocating a service-oriented architecture
strategy.

- We identify two different styles of service-oriented architecture for enterprise application architecture which are basically distinguished from each
other by whether the service tier implements business logic and holds
persistent data and coin the terms fat hub resp. thin hub hub-and-spoke
architecture for these architectural styles – see Sect. 8.2.

- We give a characterization of SOA governance as an approach to massive
software reuse – see Sect. 8.5.2

- We elaborate that software reuse can be distinguished from software use,
i.e., that software reuse is the either a static use of arbitrary software or a
dynamic use of multi-tenant software – see Sect. 8.5.3.

- We introduce the notion of a typed business process modeling. This approach has typed workflow charts as a basis which are integrated with a
hierarchy of typed business process models – see Sects. 9.2 and 9.4. The
analysis of leveled data flow diagrams in Chapter 5 lays the basis for the
design of a concrete integrated typed business process platform.

- We introduce workflow charts and define their semantics in Sect. 9.2.2.
Workflow charts are typed tripartite directed graphs. Workflow charts extend and generalize formcharts with respect to the needs of executable
business process specification. This means that workflow charts resolve the
research question posed in Sect. 3.2. Using workflow charts as a domain-
specific programming language means closing today's gap in workflow definition and application programming.

Acknowledgements

I am grateful to Prof. Dr. Colin Atkinson, Prof. Dr. Ulrich Brüning, and Prof.
Dr. Wolfgang Effelsberg for making this work possible. Thanks to my advisor
Colin Atkinson for his deeply impacting scientific remarks. Thanks to Ulrich
Brüning for introducing me to the University of Mannheim. Thanks to Ulrich
Brüning and Wolfgang Effelsberg for ongoing technical and personal advice.
Thanks to the University of Mannheim for hosting me.
Thanks to Prof. Dr. Josef Küng and Prof. Dr. Gerhard Weiß for reviewing
this text. Their comments essentially improved the text.

Innsbruck, July 2010   *Dirk Draheim*

Contents

List of Figures

Listings

1

Introduction

The topic of this book is the gaps and tensions between the realms of business process modeling, workflow definition and application programming – see Fig. 1.1. The goal is to eventually realize fully integrated executable business process specification. In order to approach this goal, first the gaps and tensions between these three fields must be carefully analyzed. We clearly have a software engineering viewpoint on business processes, as you might guess from our choice of terminology in Fig. 1.1, i.e., business process modeling in favor of business process engineering, workflow definition in favor of the currently widely used term business process management, and application programming instead of enterprise applications. This means we have a focus on notation and its semantics.

But please pay attention! We neither neglect the business-related mission nor the technical issues of enterprise information technology. On the contrary, we believe that each purely language-oriented approach is likely to fail to overcome the problems that you are faced with if you aim to create a next generation business process platform. It is simply not enough to choose a lan-

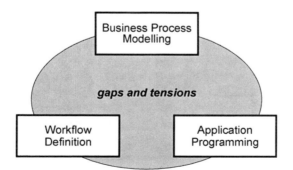

Fig. 1.1. Gaps and tensions between business process modeling, workflow control and dialogue control.

D. Draheim, *Business Process Technology: A Unified View on Business Processes, Workflows and Enterprise Applications*, DOI 10.1007/978-3-642-01588-5_1,
© Springer-Verlag Berlin Heidelberg 2010

guage that seams to be rich enough to describe business process phenomena
and to define a mapping onto components of a programming technology. It is
not enough, because there are plenty of subtle driving forces in the context
that cannot be simply neglected. These driving forces are (i) non-formality of
business process modeling, (ii) a certain kind of design orientation of application programming and (iii) a certain focus of today's workflow technology on
enterprise application integration (EAI).

The activity of business process modeling has a business process optimization facet and a requirements elicitation facet. For neither of these two facets
is specification completeness a necessity, which means, in particular, the business process descriptions in this area are usually far from being executable.
The reason for this is simple: the languages and notations used here are not
formal, i.e., they have no formal semantics as is the case for programming
languages. It is wrong to judge this immediately as a flaw, there is also a
reason for this. The languages and notations need only to be as accurate as
needed for supporting tasks in business process optimization and not beyond.
Note that too much accuracy is simply overhead here and can even hinder
the creative activities in this field. Remember that business process optimization relies on activating and communicating know-how of business process
experts, best-practices like strategic benchmarking or approaches to learning
organizations. The same is true for requirement elicitation, here again complete accuracy is not necessary. This might puzzle you, because, specification
completeness is usually considered an ideal for requirement specification, see,
e.g., the characteristics of a good software requirements specification (SRS)
listed in IEEE standard 830-1993 [169]. However, again completeness does not
mean need for executability or formality. In practice a good, elaborated text
document to which the different stakeholders have committed as a result of a
requirement elicitation process is considered appropriate.

1.1 Relevance of Business Process Technology

Business process technologies are clearly a major issue in information technology projects in today's enterprises. For example, in 2005 business process
management suites were at the peak of inflated expectations in the Gartner
hype cycle report for emerging technologies [126, 125]. Being at the peak is
telling, however, alone the fact that business process management suites are
among the technologies investigated in the report indicates the importance
of the topic for business stakeholders; actually, the technologies considered
in the hype cycle report span a wide range including, e.g., DNA logic and
handwriting recognition.

Moreover, also the topic of business process platforms is among the investigated topics of the hype cycle providing further evidence for the importance of business process management. From a vendor's viewpoint a business process platform is a business process management suite that ships with

commercial off-the-shelf components for a certain domain. From a more conceptual viewpoint business process platform technologies go beyond business process management suites in that they define a component model for hooking workflow-based application parts into a business process management technology, most likely in terms of service-orientation, because service-oriented architecture (SOA) is the current trend of component-orientation in the realm of enterprise computing. So, business process platforms are a vendor's answer to the increased need for flexibility and adaptivity in business process management.

Also, a glimpse at the seventh framework program (FP7) of the European Union [123] shows that the scientific community is also very well aware of the impact of innovative business process management solutions: "ICT in support of the networked enterprise" is an objective of FP7 and one of the target outcomes of this objective are "tools and technologies that enable intra-enterprise collaboration and the definition and execution of tasks and workflows for operation across multiple domains" [123].

On the Role of Business Processes in an Enterprise

Basically, we have seen four large schools of management in the last century. The classic Taylorism [339, 340, 341] was a systematic work-organizational approach, a school of improvement of processes. Taylorism was overcome later by human-resource orientation [19], followed by a mathematical school or operations research [253] and systemics or cybernetics [21, 22, 23, 234] eventually. Business process orientation in its concrete forms of business process reengineering and business process management entered the stage in the 1990s and still has major impact on enterprises and enterprise technologies. So, is business process orientation a fifth school of management or is it only an implementing discipline or even less, just a terminology? Some would say that business orientation is a revival of Taylorism, others would say that it starts where Taylorism has ended an develops it further by bringing a more holistic, organizational viewpoint to it. However, it is a fact that many successful enterprises are oriented towards business processes today. You can find business process orientation implicitly in today's established quality management approaches. You can find business process orientation explicitly in concrete projects that exploit one of the known business process disciplines or technologies.

Excellent enterprises are managed in an excellent way. Management is about strategic planning and the management of operations. Management of operations is about planning, organization, coordination and control [124]. The management of operations is about the management of business processes. Planning and organization provide the resources and create the structures that enable an efficient functioning of the business processes. Coordination and control of daily operations provide business process execution and business process monitoring. Today's quality management systems like ISO 9000 are business process oriented. If a quality management system is well-established in an enterprise it is not just an auxiliary function. A quality management system can become so pervasive in an enterprise that it forms the central pillar of the management system of the enterprise. Quality management systems are based on a notion of business process management lifecycle. The key performance indicators that drive the business process management lifecycle of a quality management system are specified and analyzed in terms of the defined business processes of an enterprise.

The enterprise resources form the hardware of the enterprise. The business processes are the software of the enterprise. The management of an enterprise has a central interest in business process definition. In daily operations the work is not necessarily transparent, i.e., it is not necessarily following fixed rules and processes. Work can be done in an ad-hoc manner, it can be based on routine and word-of-mouth knowledge. It often needs significant efforts to make the functioning of an enterprise more transparent. Business process documentation is the first step in a business process definition project that targets a systematization of daily operations. Actually, business process documentation alone already causes a power shift to the management of an enterprise. Knowledge about how things are done in an enterprise is a crucial element of power. The more the managers know about how employees reach their targets, the more they will conceptually decouple people from their tasks, i.e., the more concrete stakeholders will become substitutable and therefore less important in the company. Therefore, it is often possible to encounter significant resistance when a business process definition project is executed. Often, business process projects must be conducted as change processes with a systematic organizational change management.

Establishing Business Process Technology

Business process technologies comprise tools to analyze, document, specify, monitor, simulate, support and implement business processes – see also Fig. 9.1. It is the role of business processes and process orientation in today's enterprises that makes business process technology so important. Further evidence for the significance of business process technology is given for us by the concrete business process technology related projects that we see in industry, in particular, by our own experience in projects with industrial partners. We guess that business process technology is an issue in one form or another in each enterprise of a certain size. Somehow, industrial stakeholders approach business process technology either top-down or bottom-up. The top-down approach is a rather strategic one. It is driven by the desire for a general, i.e., enterprise-wide information technology reorganization or business process reorganization. The bottom-up approach is usually technology-driven, i.e., the need for local improvements in an enterprise IT landscape force stakeholders to look for appropriate products available to improve the situation. Therefore there are forced to look into state-of-the-art concepts that these products are based on – possibly resulting in a change of mind set. This impact alone but also some tight coupling of the concerned system with other systems of the enterprise can yield to a domino effect onto the surrounding system landscape, likely triggering the decision to proceed rather top-down eventually.

Often, the usage of concrete business process technology emerges step by step over the years by the need of continuous improvement of support for the business processes of an enterprise. Often, there is also need for explicit projects related to business process technology. We have conducted ourselves a couple of such projects, e.g., with logistics providers, banks and insurance companies. Such explicit business process projects can have the task to bring together business process modeling activities with software engineering activities for business-process applications, to select a concrete business process management technology, to test the maturity of a concrete business process management technology, to answer a concrete question in business process definition, to design the human-computer interaction of a workflow-intensive system or to define a software component architecture for a concrete business-process application. The experience from these projects strengthen our opinion that, on the on hand side, business process technology is here to stay and that, on the other hand side, there is still a potential to improve business process technology significantly.

Beyond Business Process Management and Technology

Management is a complex and heterogeneous function in an enterprise. A first attempt at systematization of management tasks is usually to consider different levels of management that somehow correspond to levels in the organizational hierarchy, e.g., a strategic level, a tactical level and an operational level. For the sake of the following discussion we want to draw the reader's attention to three other different categories of management that we see in today's enterprises, i.e., business process management, project management [291] and knowledge management [233, 334]. These three kinds of management coexist in an enterprise. The operational level, i.e., the level of daily operations, is the domain of business process management. The more you move up the levels in the organization chart, the less work will be defined in terms of processes. Also at the lower levels of an organization there is a lot of work that is not amenable to business process management. For example, the work in an R&D department (research and development department) is a creative task that is often hard to define and hard to understand. The correct management approach for a creative R&D department might be what is known as the 'laissez faire' approach to management.

Business process management is about processes that are started over and over again in order to achieve a defined business objective. Like business processes projects are also defined forms of work undertaken by people in an enterprise to achieve a goal. However, projects are temporary and unique. You could say that a project can also be considered as the single instance of a business process. Sometimes, projects are repeated, so then they are actually not really unique any more. But this is only an artificial discussion. Projects are different from business processes. They are planned, staffed and controlled in a different manner. For example, projects are always managed by project managers, whereas there are not necessarily explicit business process managers in an enterprise that runs defined business processes. However, there is a potential for unification of business process management and project management practices and tools in the future. Knowledge management is about the systematization of know-how in an enterprise. Knowledge management is not the opposite of business process management; it is orthogonal to business process management. Business processes also embody a form of knowledge. Defined business processes are accompanied by additional knowledge that might not be amenable to a definition as business processes.

The main topic of this book is the integration of business process modeling, workflow definition and system dialogue programming in future business process management platform. Beyond that, there is a potential in integrating practices and tools for business process management, project management and knowledge management. The proposed exploitation of Web 2.0. technology for business continuity management in Sect. 3.4 and the envisioned integration of production processes, business processes and business intelligence in the domain of manufacturing in Sects.3.5 and 3.6 are instances of this potential.

1.2 Need for Flexible Business Process Technology

Today's enterprises must react to new customer demands in highly competitive markets. Due to the globalization of markets with its new opportunities and threats enterprises must be able to react even more quickly. Information technology plays a pivotal role in making enterprises more flexible. We will talk about information technology as a mission-critical asset also later in Sect. 2.6.

With respect to flexible information technology, there are two sides to the story. You can understand improvements to flexibility as an introduction of new innovative functionality that speeds up the business process management lifecycle – for a discussion of the business process management and the business process management lifecycle, in particular, please have a look at Sects. 2.4 resp. 2.4.1. Capabilities for monitoring and analyzing running processes belong to such functionality that goes beyond IT support for processes of daily operations. And stakeholders feel the same about tools that help to model and execute processes more precisely and faster. This means that in the efforts of top management to make the enterprise more agile, i.e., more reactive, the application of new innovative technology is considered.

However, also the different perspective is important. Often, the IT system architecture in an enterprise is experienced as inflexible, i.e., hard to maintain and change. Sometimes, the processes of an enterprise seem to be hard-wired in the software applications of the enterprise. Often, they are not explicitly documented, but rather given by the way staff works with the software applications that support the business processes. A first step in changing the processes of an enterprise is then an 'as is'-analysis of the IT systems of the enterprise and the way they support the business processes of the enterprise. A concrete problem in large enterprises is that the several functional units, e.g., the several departments of the enterprise, each may have their own specific IT support. Then, support for cross-functional processes is often poor; technologically it is about enterprise application integration. In such cases the flexibility of the overall IT support of the enterprise suffers, simply because of the complexity of the underlying overall system architecture.

1.3 Outline of the Book

In Chapter 2 we set the stage by describing why and how enterprises strive for business process excellence. We explain widely known business process disciplines, i.e., business process reengineering, business process optimization, business process management and business continuity management. We make an attempt to explain the differences and relationships between these disciplines. However, the more important target of Chapter 2 is to strengthen the reader's awareness for business process excellence and its role for today's enterprises. Furthermore, the chapter explains the importance of information technology for achieving business process excellence. The striving for business process excellence and the importance of business process technology is the background against which all the other chapters of the book have to be understood.

There is still a huge potential for research in business process technologies. This is so with respect to R&D, i.e., research and development activities which target new innovative products with as little time-to-market as possible. But it is also true with respect to more basic research activities with long-term research goals. In Chapter 3 we identify and describe two basic fields that open research opportunities in business process technology, i.e., executable specification and component technology. Future business process platforms will combine executable specification with new concepts of component technology.

There are three kinds of management in modern enterprises, i.e., business process management, project management and knowledge management. We believe that there is a potential to design tools that offer integrated support for these different styles of management. In a first step these tools will be no general-purpose tools, but domain-specific. As an example for such integrated management platforms we envision the usage of social software for business continuity management. As another example for this principle we describe the design of an industrial information backbone that integrates the fast production processes with the slower production planning processes and strategic decision processes.

In Chapter 4 we look at the informality of business process analysis and business process modeling. Is the informality of business process modeling a flaw that should be overcome or is it necessary to stay agile in top-level system analysis? Is there a sweet spot between informality and agility? We try to explain why concrete business process modeling language constructs that are widely used today are not formal even if they appear as being formal. With an understanding of informalities in business process modeling pitfalls can be avoided and modeling languages can be used to their best potential without the typical natural diffidence. The insight presented in Chapter 4 can be exploited in projects where general business process models coexist with specific executable business process specifications, i.e., workflow definitions. It can also be exploited in the design of integrated business process platforms. We have a concrete look at the ambiguities of the usage of events in typical, state-of-the-art business process modeling projects. We discuss the need for a mechanism to specify arbitrary synchronization phenomena in business process modeling.

This means that Chapter 4 addresses the vertical gap and vertical tensions between business process modeling, on the one hand, and workflow definition and application programming, on the other hand, that have been illustrated in Fig. 1.1. And so do Chapters 5 and 6. Chapter 5 is about the decomposition of business process specifications. We treat decomposition of business process specifications by considering leveled data flow diagrams. The principles and issues in decomposing business process specifications are basically the same for business process specifications in general and executable business process specifications in particular. A key issue in leveled data flow diagrams is that the operational behavior of a system can usually only be understood by the finest level of diagrams in the hierarchy. There is a loss of information with respect to the operational behavior while moving upwards the hierarchy. This is so for hierarchies built on top of a flat business process analysis model and those built on top of executable business process models. Furthermore, we analyze, on the one hand side, the parallel decomposition of activities, transitions and data and, on the other hand side, the parallel decomposition of activities, transitions and control flow constraints.

In Chapter 6 we investigate in how far a structured approach can be applied to business process modeling. In doing so, we try to contribute to a better understanding of the driving forces on business process specifications. The chapter shows that a structured approach can not be applied to business process modeling without care. Business process specifications are fundamentally different from computer programs. In computer programming the structured approach is well established. The crucial difference is that a computer program can be restructured in order to achieve a better design in whatever sense without changing the semantics of the computer program which is a functional transformation. However, business processes express a behavior and have an observational semantics. Therefore, they do not offer the same degree of restructuring. It is the task of Chapter 6 to characterize this fact and analyze it further.

Chapter 7 and Chapter 8 are about the implementation level of business processes. Chapter 7 analyzes workflow technology. We take a human-computer interaction viewpoint in characterizing workflow management systems. We explain how current workflow technology orchestrates applications and programs that implement system dialogues. This way, the vertical gap between workflow definition and application programming as visualized in Fig. 1.1 is implicitly explained. We also have a look at the assignment of actors to tasks in workflow technologies. Here, we are not interested too much in concrete IT product features and concrete role models. We are interested in a basic understanding of the assignment of actors to tasks. Chapter 8 deals with component technology for programs that implement workflow-based systems. It does so by discussing the emergence of service-oriented architecture. If you do not insist on a concrete definitions of component technology, in particular, on such that need the object-orientated programming paradigm as a basis, it is fair to say that service-oriented architecture is today's leading component approach in the field of business process technology. Again, we have a look at how current workflow technology orchestrates applications and programs in Sect. 8.4.1 – see also Fig 8.5 – this time from the perspective of exploiting concrete web services technologies for building business process management suites.

Chapter 9 provides the conclusion. It summarizes some of the major insights of the book. For example, it once more discusses a distinction between business process modeling and workflow definition languages. However, it goes beyond a mere summary by eventually describing the notion of typed business process modeling and, even more concrete, introducing a three-staged workflow definition language – so called workflow charts. Workflow charts can be exploited as executable business process models; they can be considered the top-level syntactical structure of a domain-specific high-level programming language for business process execution.

Business Process Excellence

Businesses are made of processes. Enterprises strive for excellence in business processes. Different stakeholders perceive the topic of business processes differently. You can approach business processes either from a strategic viewpoint or a technical viewpoint. This, in the first place, means that business processes as an object of investigation are so complex that whole sub communities formed to address the topic appropriately. Strategic issues and IT issues are eventually intertwined if you conduct a business process improvement project. Business processes are supported by IT in today's enterprises, so if your target is to improve business processes of an enterprise you are usually immediately involved in IT issues.

In this chapter we present the strategic view of business processes. We have seen and still see massive business process reengineering efforts in enterprises. Business process reengineering (BPR) [151, 150] is by far not only about business process optimization or business process redesign. It is a management issue, actually, it is a top management issue. Business process reengineering is a paradigm at the level of organizational structure, so it is about business reengineering, and usually about reengineering of large enterprises, i.e., corporate reengineering. After introducing business process reengineering and discussing its intention we will have a look at concrete opportunities to improve processes. Knowing about the motivation of business process improvement and learning about concrete examples of business process optimization is a good start, however, in concrete process improvement projects a systematic approach is needed to proceed successfully. With business process benchmarking we have a concrete approach for this at hand.

A further topic in this chapter is systematic business process management. Business process management is about a group of activities that make the business processes of an enterprise the subject of continuous investigation and improvement – it consists of the definition, execution, monitoring and optimization of business processes. If you set business process management into relationship with business process reengineering, you can see it from two sides. On the one hand, it can be seen as the result of decisions made during

D. Draheim, *Business Process Technology: A Unified View on Business Processes, Workflows and Enterprise Applications*, DOI 10.1007/978-3-642-01588-5_2,
© Springer-Verlag Berlin Heidelberg 2010

business process reengineering being responsible for the fine-tuning of business processes in daily operations. On the other hand, it can be seen as a tool for ongoing, continuous business process reengineering. In practice, taking one of these two viewpoints determines whether business process management has rather a tactical or strategic emphasis in an enterprise. In any case, the analysis of benefits of business process management and possible impacts in general is not part of business process management itself, it really belongs to strategic efforts outside business process management.

Finally we need to discuss the strategic role of information technology (IT). Information technology is at the heart of the modern enterprise. As a crosscutting concern it empowers the enterprise both in house and in its context – the competitive market and the hosting society. Furthermore, there is often potential for improving business processes without exploitation of information technology. But usually concrete improvements are enabled by information technology. Information technology can support business processes directly and indirectly by empowering management and reengineering efforts. Once the importance of information technology for business process reengineering and management is recognized and taken for granted, these topics can be discussed independently of technology. However, eventually when it comes to the implementation of reengineering results and the establishment of business process management, concrete information technology must be chosen.

The explanation of business process reengineering, optimization, benchmarking, management and the enabling IT from a strategic viewpoint sets the stage for the discussion of business process technologies like workflow products and business process modeling languages and tools. Advances in these technologies must eventually address business process optimization. What we are seeking are such advancements that make IT systems flexible and integrative. Here, flexibility means a significant reduction of costs for the redefinition and construction of enterprise IT systems compared to today's technologies, so that there is an observable impact on the reactiveness of business process management. Another strand of advancement is towards pervasive integration, i.e., the availability of all information emerging in an enterprise in all potential processes.

2.1 Business Process Reengineering

In order to give an impression of what business process reengineering is about we explain it from the viewpoint of business reorganization first. Later, in Sect. 2.2 we will discuss typical reengineering patterns. These patterns make clear that business process reengineering is not merely about reorganization; it is about migration to process-oriented structures – having reorganization often as a typical result. In a traditional structure the units of the corporation are functional business units, i.e., marketing, production, procurement, sales, accounting, human resources, research and development. Now, large compa-

nies offer several products and several services. So business processes crosscut
the functional units of a traditional hierarchy. This is where business process
reengineering can start. It is about changing the focus to the business processes. It proposes to ask for new organizational structures that eventually
enable continuous business process optimization. For example, it would be
possible to radically change the organizational structure and make the main
processes the top-level units of the enterprise. Now, the managers of the resulting units are no longer department managers or area managers, instead
they are process managers in charge of the outcome of one process. Before
such a restructuring each of the units was involved in each of the crosscutting
processes. This means responsibility was spread with the risk of overhead and
not exploiting potential specialization.

Now, after making the main processes top-level units, each of the units
reflects the former hierarchical structure inside, i.e., having groups for the
various functions. In this way, the functions can be specialized and optimized
by streamlining them to activities that add value. Such reorganization can
already make sense for small and medium enterprises (SMEs). For example,
imagine a small software development and IT consulting company that is
organized as a number of profit centers. Now, having a top-level sales department neighboring the profit centers would most likely be an anti-pattern.
Usually, it would be more appropriate to have sales persons in each of the
profit centers for obvious reasons. However, in general there is no evidence
that a process-oriented reorganization of an enterprise makes it perform better, because one has to admit that one may also observe counter effects. Before
the restructuring, the process responsibilities were spread over several units,
now responsibilities for the major business functions are spread over different units with potentially similar drawbacks – in a traditional hierarchy the
know-how with respect to a function is gathered and improved over years in
a central unit. At least, it seems to be self-evident that with respect to continuous process optimization the process-oriented organization is the correct
choice.

2.1.1 Strategic Nature of Business Process Reengineering

The business process reengineering paradigm as introduced in [151] was a
radical approach from the beginning, foreseeing a business revolution. For
example, it is emphasized that business process reengineering is not reor-
ganizing, and it is not restructuring. Instead, it is really about creating a
fundamentally new work organization in the enterprise. However, in practice,
process orientation often evolves in enterprises in a step-wise fashion resulting in matrix-like structures having designated stakeholders on a more or less
equal level for both functions and processes. Here, in this book, it is important
to understand that business process engineering is a holistic effort that aims
to empower the enterprise for process improvement.

Business process reengineering can also go beyond the boundaries of the enterprise, then having inter-enterprise processes as its object. A typical example is the optimization of processes between a manufacturer and one of its suppliers. Opportunities are the reduction of reconciliation by reducing the number of contact points or the relocation of responsibilities. Again, information technology has proven to be a key enabler for better performing processes – we have seen the electronic data interchange (EDI) [118] and business-to-business (B2B) initiatives in this field.

In business process reengineering the restructuring goes hand in hand with adopting best business practices in general. Therefore, when talking about business process reengineering to managers usually a group of innovative management practices on different levels come to their minds that are actually cornerstones of other prominent management approaches of the 1990s like total quality management (TQM) [31] or Kaizen [337, 167], e.g., profit centers, outsourcing, the networked organization, the learning organization, the paperless office, customer relationship management, continuous improvement, team work [225].

2.1.2 Power Shifts Triggered by Business Process Reengineering

In the following few paragraphs we try to sketch the tacit understandings of business process engineering. It may explain why some stakeholders in enterprises support it whereas others do not.

Business process reengineering changes the way the business is done. This also has an impact on the group dynamics [216] in the enterprise, i.e., resulting in the redefinition of roles and a new perception of roles. Many of the changes that come along with business process reengineering efforts are, in principle, well suited to empower employees. So is the reduction of control to a reasonable level and the increase of people's responsibility for tasks, which goes hand in hand with the aforementioned reduction of control. So is also with the allowance of more decision making in operational tasks – we will see more examples that prove this statement correct when we discuss concrete patterns of business process reengineering later in Sect. 2.2.

The efficiency of assembly lines in factories of early industries came along with a monotony of jobs and alienation of workers. In a modern factory the degree of automation in the assembly line increases. We have seen a shift from manufacturing – the second sector of industry – to services and organization – the third sector of industry – in societies [129]. But this trend can be observed not only at the level of economies but also in single enterprises, driven by the demand for more sophisticated products and services, on the one hand, and the increased degree of automation, on the other hand. So, the problems that are addressed by business process reengineering in an enterprise stem from a business culture that lags behind – simplifying a bit, it is not appropriate to manage the processes in a modern enterprise in a similar manner as an assembly line. The awareness of this is increasing – people arrived in the information society [229, 26], which clearly goes beyond the three classical industrial sectors.

Business process reengineering is a rationalization approach, it eventually targets cost savings. However, it does so by encouraging people also to consider solutions that overcome the attitude that people usually associate with rationalization, i.e., high specialization and strict separation of duties. The prosperity of employees has early been an objective in approaches to rationalization – in the approach of scientific management [338] there is the fundamental idea that the prosperity of employers and employees are not antagonistic, on the contrary, there is the conviction that the prosperities of employers and employees are mutual dependent in the long run and that the interests of both groups are actually the same. For us, this leads to the following questions.

Does business process reengineering actually empower staff? Does business process reengineering therefore mean that a power shift [252] from the strategic to the tactical level and from the tactical level to the operational level occurs? With respect to the first question: if processes in an inelastic business hierarchy really obey to the imposed rules and control, yes, reengineering is about actually changing things in daily operations. However, there is sometimes a difference between how things are done and how things are explicitly done. Then, reengineering is about internal business transparency.

If there is a difference between processes and the explicitly defined processes this does not necessarily mean that overall efforts are performed suboptimally. Often, some additional processes are necessary that are not under control of the management. Often, it would mean to trap into the anti-pattern of micro management if the management tries to get into control of all these micro processes that make up a successful enterprise. The same is true for responsibility. Typically, people in enterprises often feel responsible for their tasks and beyond, even if they do not have the responsibility formally. Take software project management as an example for these phenomena. Despite the discussion of sophisticated software processes like the iterative approach [303], spiral model [35], the two-dimensional Rational Unified Process (RUP) [209] or the agile software development approach with Extreme Programming (XP) [20] as prominent representative you see a lot of projects in practice that are simply managed with a stage-wise process model [27]. Some of these projects are successful, others are not. In the successful projects there is usually a tacit commitment of all stakeholders that the stage-wise model with its milestones is just the manager's viewpoint on the project, i.e., a foundation for tracking the project proceedings, but does not enforce a strictly step-wise approach to work organization.

Enterprises encapsulate know-how, also process know-how. Sometimes, the knowledge of how things are actually done is not explicitly available in enterprises but distributed over teams and stakeholders. Then business process engineering is also about making explicit the process know-how. This point is important with respect to the second question we posed, i.e., whether business process reengineering enacts a power shift down the enterprise's hierarchy.

Making explicit the process know-how in an enterprise is an important interest of those who have personnel responsibility – beyond the immediate cost
savings that can be gained by business process engineering. In the extreme,
through a rigorous definition processes become a kind of software, they then
exist independently from the persons that run them and the persons that run
them become replaceable.

2.2 Business Process Optimization

The notion of division of labor is central to business process optimization.
Division of labor is at the core of industry. The discussion of division of labor
always has an economics facet, but it does not have to be conducted always
only at the level of economies, where it is about the emergence of professions
or industrial branches. Division of labor can also be discussed at the level of
work organization – see, e.g., [323] – and that is the level of discussion that
interests us here.

Division of labor can save costs, because of the extra dexterity that emerges
from added routine or special education connected to the several branches that
are the result of a division of labor. This effect can be observed on different
levels, ranging from the very macro level of industry sectors to the very micro
level of tasks and operations in a factory. However, division of labor can
also cause additional critical costs, because of overhead for organization and
communication. This phenomenon is very well known from the field of project
management [291]. Project management differs from production management
in that projects are limited in time. The costs saving effects of division of
labor can also be observed in projects; however, that is not the point. Often,
a certain task is distributed over the members of a team without the potential
to exploit specialization. Here, division of labor is just needed to get a job
done by a given deadline. In project management it is known that division of
labor always costs extra resources. You can reduce the project time needed by
dividing work, however, at the same time you increase the work time needed
– due to the extra efforts to manage more people in parallel. It is also known
that, sometimes, the overhead of dividing work can even consume the savings
in project duration. That is what is expressed by Brook's law with respect
to the domain of software project management: "Adding manpower to a late
project makes it even later." [45].

Not neglecting the trade-off between potential cost-savings and potential
costs of division of work is a center pillar of business process reengineering. In
business process reengineering efforts certain patterns of redesigning processes
have been observed [151]:

- Defining a new job by combining several existing ones.
- Performing work in the context where it arises.
- Balancing centralization versus decentralization.

- Allowing decision making at the operational level.
- Allowing process steps to be performed in parallel wherever possible.
- Identifying efficient versions of business processes.
- Reducing control.

These patterns must not be understood as a cookbook or "How To"-guide. They can provide some guidance in business process reengineering efforts, because they are examples of results in successful reengineering projects. However, they do not replace systematic approaches to reach business excellence like the ones described in Sect. 2.3.

The patterns explained in this section have their counterpart discussion in currently emerging business process management technology.

2.2.1 Combining Jobs and Naturally Hosting Work

Combining existing jobs into a new one is at the core of the discussion we just started on the trade-off between overhead and cost savings of division of labor. If a task is distributed over several persons it can be, in principle, led back to a single job done by a single person. What you might loose in doing so is the potential extra specialization. However, you might also get rid of overhead in communication between the people involved in getting the task done. This argument might not work for an assembly line where there is no communication needed between the several steps. However, it becomes more and more important the more complex a task is in terms of the amount of knowledge that emerges in each single instance of the task. Such knowledge must be transferred from one step to another.

The overhead for communication is perhaps the most directly observable cost; however, it is not the only one. Distributing a task over several people might lead to an alienation of the involved personnel. Such alienation might have a cost. For potentially creative tasks it can be a severe problem if people loose a holistic viewpoint. For creative people it may be a problem to be restricted to too specialized operations so that human potential is wasted from a general viewpoint. Furthermore, quality of the outcome might suffer, because everybody is concentrated on the concrete operation he is responsible for, but nobody is responsible for the task as a whole anymore.

We use the term cohesion principle for collecting work pieces that are scattered around organizational units in the enterprise and assigning them to a single organizational unit. The cohesion principle is a general pattern in business process reengineering that can be observed on different levels of granularity. The combination of jobs just discussed is the application of this principle to the organizational level of single employees. It can also be applied to the level of teamwork [225]. Here it means that a task is too complex to be handled by a single person with either respect to work load but more likely with respect to expertise needed to get it done. A notion of team can balance the need for division of labor and the need for responsibility for the task.

Figure 2.1 once more shows the application of the cohesion principle at the level of single employees. Figure 2.1 is also meant to illustrate why we have chosen the term cohesion for the principle. Consider process (i). Assume that somehow the person in business unit (b) is the process owner, i.e., he starts the process, finishes the process and is eventually responsible for the outcome of the process. The majority of the job is done by this person and only some work is done by some others in business units (c) and (f). It is fair to say that process (i) actually resides in business unit (b) and that after the business reengineering in Fig. 2.1 the activities in business units (c) and (f) returned to the context from which they originally arose. Criteria like the location of the main part of a process and the main process stakeholder are all very good, but they are not hard criteria. They can give guidance in reengineering but eventually the question must be answered as to where it makes most sense to perform an activity from an overall cost-savings perspective. Eventually, it is the cost-effectiveness of a process that counts. It could be that there is strong rationale for getting parts of the process (i) in Fig. 2.1 done in some other business units and that it makes no sense to remove them from there. Business process reengineering is just about encouragement – it encourages reconsidering the way a current business is run.

If the cohesion principle is applied to the level of business units it can lead to the discussion about process-oriented business reorganization that we had in Sect. 2.1. At this level the principle can be about reconsidering the existing organizational structure with respect to business process awareness.

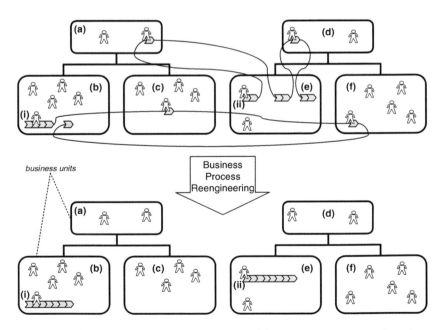

Fig. 2.1. Applying the cohesion principle of business process reengineering.

Reengineering for the purpose of reorganization is often perceived as business process reengineering 'per se', perhaps because of its generally visible impact. Reengineering involving the level of business units can lead to a hard reorganization but it does not have to. Then, reengineering is rather about balancing centralization versus decentralization. The existing business units remain as traditional centers of expertise; nevertheless, some responsibility and know-how is transferred to other business units where the actual processes reside – actually, the processes in Fig. 2.1 are examples of this because the organizational hierarchy is not changed due to the business process adjustments.

2.2.2 Decision Making

A typical application of the described principle of combining work pieces into broader ones that perform more efficiently is to give decision steps in a process to staff at the operational level.

Often, some decision making is given to extra roles just as a matter of principle. Allowing decision making at the operational level can have all of the effects described above, i.e., reducing overhead, reducing alienation, improving responsibility for the task. And perhaps it is even particularly well-suited to foster the effects. However, it is not really justified to consider the pattern of giving decision making from the tactical to the operational level as something fundamentally different as combining work pieces merely from the operational level. From a general viewpoint, and, in particular, from a process-oriented viewpoint it is actually not different – it is just about combining work pieces and the difference is only in the hierarchical level the work pieces stem from. This is illustrated in Fig. 2.1. Here, process (ii) spans two different levels in the organizational hierarchy before reengineering. However, like the reengineering of process (i) it is eventually just about combining work items into a new job.

2.2.3 Parallelism in Business Processes

Exploiting potential parallelism in business processes yields a speed up [112] – see Fig. 2.2. Consecutive dependencies should be limited to causal dependencies. Therefore all of the process and task modeling languages and technologies as well as project planning tools [291] like PERT (Project Evaluation and Review Technique), CPM (Critical Path Method) or the Gantt diagram offer support for the definition of parallel activities. The problem is that the extra complexity of processes with parallel activities inhibits the exploitation of parallelism. It is easier to define a strictly stepwise process. It is easier to monitor the instances of such a process, because each state of such a process instance consists only of one activity. It is even easier to follow a stepwise process, because there is no need for any synchronization mechanism. However, the considerable time savings created by exploiting parallelism justify the extra efforts needed to manage parallelism.

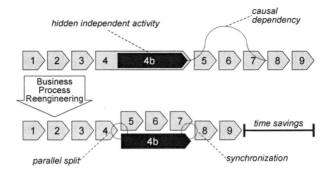

Fig. 2.2. Identifying and extracting a potentially parallel activity.

Nevertheless, the complexity of parallel processes is a hurdle. Consider a successfully running process. First, it is not easy to determine those chunks of work of this process that are not strictly causally dependent. Second, it might be considered a risk to change the process at all. Modern business process management suites offer various kinds of support for parallel activities – a comprehensive overview of the process control mechanisms offered by today's business process management suites is given by [307].

It is always worth looking at the concept of parallelism, not only directly for opportunities of parallelizing activities. For example, imagine a process that is run by one person only. Here, formally there is no difference with respect to throughput in running several process instances sequentially or in parallel. However, in practice there can be differences. For example, the person can start and run a couple of processes A, B and C in parallel, i.e., first finishing the first step of each of the process instances, then finishing the second step of each instance and so on. This can have a the subtle time-saving effect, i.e., the person gains local routine for the performed steps this way – see Fig. 2.3 for an illustration.

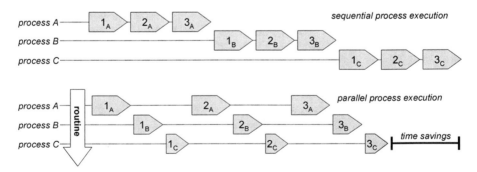

Fig. 2.3. Gaining routine with tasks by running process instances in parallel.

This argument is similar to the one found for the pattern of retaining familiar work items found in [308]. The larger the set of processes that are run that way, the more convincing is the argument. Similarly, the argument is more convincing when long-running processes are considered. However, the counter effect may also be observed for this example, i.e., perhaps the person becomes confused by this parallel approach resulting in additional time needed.

2.2.4 Versions of Business Processes

Parallelization of processes is about identifying chunks of work that are not causally dependent. Versioning of processes is about identifying alternative chunks of work in an existing process and eliminating superfluous activity by distinction of cases.

A business process is a net of activities that work together to achieve a defined goal, i.e., a defined business objective. Once a business objective is defined to be supported, this business objective determines the set of activities that are necessary to achieve this. Sometimes it is possible to distinguish cases dependent from conditions from the business context. Sometimes not all of the activities of a business process are actually needed to achieve the defined goal, but nevertheless all the activities are always executed. A business process that handles all variants of a multi-faceted scenario without decision points can be called a bloated process in which some activities are superfluous in some cases. Then, it makes sense to design a process version for each identified case consisting of activities that are necessary in the respective case and save resources this way.

Figure 2.4 shows an example of such bloated process and its reengineering. Once alternative activities exist you insert decision points. If a decision never relies on information that emerges during process execution it can be drawn to the front of the process now deciding between two versions of the subsequent process. It might be considered a matter of taste whether to consider the resulting process with its initial case analysis as a complex process or rather as a bunch of process versions. For example, in Fig. 2.4 it would be possible to describe the business process with a diagram in which starts with first and second activity, continues with a decision point and then continues with activities of each of the two cases.

In Sect. 4.1 we will distinguish between two different viewpoint on business process, i.e., the viewpoint of business process supervisory, which is the viewpoint of the business process modeler, and the local viewpoint of the worker in a business process. A description of the reengineered business process in Fig. 2.4 that uses an inner decision point instead of an outer decision point might be better to understand from the global viewpoint of business process supervisory, whereas the version of description given in Fig. 2.4 might be better for the local viewpoint. It might be easier to clarify the case as the first activity and to deal with no decision henceforth. Assume that in the case of the business process in Fig. 2.4 it turns out that the first case always can

be handed by a certain person and the second case can be handled always by
another person. This information is not given in the upper diagram in Fig. 2.4
and, without further comment, it would not be given in a diagram that defers
the decision point after the first and second activities – at least not for the
first and second activity. However, this important information is given in the
lower diagram in Fig. 2.4 .

Most importantly, the question of where to insert the decision point is
usually not just a matter of taste. This is so, because the decision point itself
is a real-world entity. The choice about where you insert the decision point into
your business process model has an impact on where the decision is actually
made in processes in the real world. A deeper discussion of such real-world
arguments or variants of it like what we call domain-oriented modeling can
be found, for example, in Chapters 4 and 6.

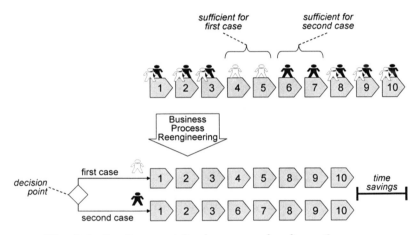

Fig. 2.4. Creating specialized processes for alternative cases.

There are less obvious scenarios than the one just described, in which
there is potential for time savings. Sometimes, it makes sense to ask whether
in certain cases things can be done differently than in the past. Figure 2.5
shows an instance of such a business process and its refactoring. The issue
here is to generate alternatives by analyzing whether existing activities can
be specialized to more efficient ones in certain lean cases.

The creation of versions of business processes in the above sense somehow
leads to more flexibility. The processes are more flexible in that they react
to more cases in a specialized way. However, it is worth mentioning that
this is not the kind of flexibility which is currently discussed in the area
of adaptive workflow systems – see [294, 296], for example. Here flexibility
means adaptivity, i.e., it means that the workflow management technology
allows for adopting business processes to new requirements during run-time.
As we will discuss in Sect. 2.4, there is an ongoing continuous improvement

process (CIP) in the successful enterprise that consists of monitoring business processes and adjusting them to new situations – see also Fig. 2.6. Today's business process management technologies are suitable for managing versions of processes, however, current commercially available products do not offer support for the redefinition and adjustment of processes at run-time, i.e., in the presence of running processes.

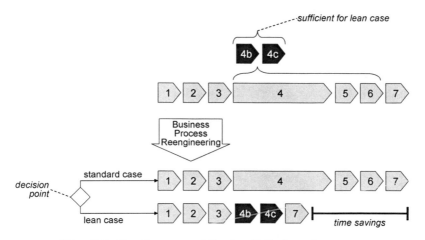

Fig. 2.5. Creating a specialized activity for a lean case.

2.2.5 Reducing Control

Separation of duties is a best practice, in particular, if we have to deal with quality control. For example, in software engineering it is common to define test design and test engineering as separate roles and let people other than the developers fulfill these roles. It is common sense that code reviews and code audits should not be made by the developers of the code themselves.

The theme of reducing control is about something different than quality control. It is about a certain kind of control that stems from a culture of mistrust against employees. So it is about control against abuse of processes – be it accidentally or intentionally. For example, an employee could do a business trip that is actually not necessary or another employee could go for holiday despite the fact there is currently a peak load in one of his or her projects. That is why there are holiday and business trip application forms that are reviewed by management staff. Business process reengineering encourages contrasting the costs of a potential abuse with the costs of control that is necessary to prevent the abuse – all against the background of a fair estimation of the risk of the abuse. Typically, the risk of an abuse is much lower than initially believed.

If some control and checks are about accidental abuse, then, removing the control from managers is hard to distinguish from giving decision making responsibilities to employees that has been discussed in Sect. 2.2.2.

2.3 Business Process Benchmarking

How can business process excellence in the sense of business process reengineering be reached? How is it possible to move towards an optimal performing corporate structure? In Sect. 2.2 we already discussed typical patterns of reengineered business processes. But even with these patterns as background knowledge the question of how to systematically reengineer business processes remains open. Clearly, benchmarking is an approach, i.e., so-called strategic benchmarking [352] or business process benchmarking [53].

Process benchmarking is about conducting an as-is analysis of the existing business processes and then comparing them to similar business processes of other companies that are considered to have outstanding performance – typically market leaders in their domain – and to eventually adopt best practices to optimize one's own business processes. For example, groups of benchmark partners from different domains, i.e., non-competitors, can be formed to conduct process benchmarking. This means process benchmarking is more than process optimization. It eventually targets process optimization, but it is more than measuring, analyzing and improving processes. The crucial point is the comparison with others, i.e., not benchmarking against target performances but benchmarking against performances of others.

2.3.1 Benchmarks in IT Governance

In some domains, there are associations that gather best practices in processes and conduct standardization efforts. The area of IT governance is a good example. Here we have ITIL (IT Infrastructure Library) [56, 267, 189, 305, 210, 54, 55, 268], the ITIL related ISO 20000 [181, 183] and COBIT (Control Objectives for Information and Related Technology) [187, 188]. COBIT is an example of process orientation and process definitions. COBIT defines best practices for IT governance, in doing so it is business-focused. This means it addresses not only the stakeholders that are directly concerned with IT, i.e., the IT executives, IT auditors and users, but also the top management and the owners of the business processes. Furthermore, it is process oriented. This means that the best practices are defined as processes that are organized in a process framework. COBIT defines 34 processes that are grouped into 4 domains, i.e., planning/organization, acquisition/implementation, delivery/support, and monitoring.

As an example, let us have a look at a typical process definition, i.e., define/manage service levels in the process domain of delivery/support. This gives an impression of the level of discussion of COBIT. The process definition consists of four pages of text and tables, divided into a process description, a description of the control objectives, management guidelines and a maturity model – each one page. The process description explains the function and rationale of the definition and management of services levels. The description of control objectives lists concrete actions to take, e.g., the definition of service level agreements (SLA), the definition of operation level agreements (OLA), and the monitoring and reporting of service level agreements. The management guidelines actually connect the process to the other COBIT processes, i.e., it is defined what kind of input the process gets from other processes and what kind of output is delivered to other processes. For example, the 'define/manage service levels' process gets an IT service portfolio from the 'define a strategic IT plan' process in the planning/organization process domain and delivers contract review reports to the 'manage third-party services' process. Furthermore, the management guidelines detail the activities of the control objective description and specify who in the organization is responsible and accountable for them and who should be kept informed about them. The maturity model defines maturity levels in the style of the CMM (Capability Maturity Model) [275, 276, 274], i.e., there are six levels zero to five: initial, repeatable/intuitive, defined, managed/measurable, optimilzed.

2.3.2 Organizational Learning

Benchmarking for best practices is an inter-organizational effort; however, it is also a very promising approach if it is done in-house. Then, such efforts are usually called organizational learning approaches [77, 280, 63]. Actually, learning is crucial for enterprises. Crucial parts know-how, i.e., know-how about processes and best practices in particular, are kept alive by social interaction [88]. Such know-how is communicated from seniors to juniors, often in daily operations and often ad hoc and in a word-of-mouth fashion. That means that learning takes place on demand – in processes and projects whenever problems have to be solved. With organizational learning typically something different is meant – it is about making explicit these learning activities. On the basis of this, learning can be fostered by creating awareness of it importance. Furthermore, organizational learning is about concrete tools and methods that support learning in the enterprise.

A prominent approach to organizational learning is, for example, action learning [297, 298]. In the action learning approach managers, e.g., project managers, and process stakeholders, e.g., engineers, of the same domain meet in sessions in order to find solutions to concrete problems. The session is moderated by a facilitator. Action learning assumes that learning is based on programmed knowledge and targeted questioning. The programmed knowledge facet is about expert knowledge; it is about the systematic understanding of best practices and also about mistakes that should be avoided. Action learning has is roots in efforts of the Mining Association of Great Britain that brought together coal mining experts in order to learn together and to learn from each other. This means action learning techniques are also suitable for inter-organizational learning. However, unlike process benchmarking, which is not necessarily but typically about benchmarking against excellent enterprises in different domains, it is about bringing together knowledge from enterprises in the same domain.

2.4 Business Process Management

Business process reengineering involves business strategy. However, optimizing business processes on the operational level – fine-tuning of concrete workflows in the main processes – is also an important issue. Business process management is about the controlled execution and continuous improvement of business processes. The objects of business process management are the business processes of an enterprise in general, i.e., business process management considers both activities that are supported by information technology or actually executed full-automatically and those that are processed completely manually. The granularity of activities controlled by business process management is not canonically fixed. Fig. 2.6 shows a possible business process management lifecycle model that is similar to the plenty of those used in practice.

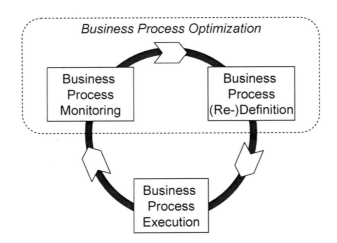

Fig. 2.6. Business process management lifecycle.

The definition of business processes encompasses the description of the goals of the business processes and the definition of service level agreements resp. operation level agreements, in particular, the definition of required performance figures. Furthermore, it encompasses business process modeling, i.e., an elaboration of the interplay of business activities and resources. Then business process execution means that the defined business processes are actually working. It is a matter of taste whether efforts in fine-planning business processes – like the definition of workflows in a workflow management tool or the actual implementation of applications or changes to applications that support business process activities – belong to business process execution or rather to business process definition.

Executed business processes are monitored, i.e., data are gathered about who actually did what, when and why and, ideally, further comments of stakeholders on what was good and what may be improved. Here, business activity monitoring [238, 117, 136, 52, 64, 214] (BAM) comes into play. Business activity monitoring is the real-time extraction, i.e., automatic extraction, of business performance indicators (BPIs) from the enterprise applications. Business activity monitoring is usually understood as a systematic enterprise-wide effort, i.e., it is not about single extractions of information from a few systems but about the massive crosscutting extraction of information from as many enterprise systems as possible. That is why business activity monitoring is also perceived as an enterprise application integration topic.

In a next cycle of the business process management lifecycle the data that were gathered during business process monitoring are analyzed and yield to an improved definition of the business processes. Now, the business process definition becomes a business process redefinition. In our lifecycle model we say that optimization consists of business process monitoring and business process redefinition.

2.4.1 On Business Process Management Lifecycle Models

Lifecycle models – also lifecycles for short – like the one in Fig. 2.6 are used to explain the building blocks of business process management. Business process management products – both technologies and consultant services – often come with their own lifecycle model. Despite the fact that lifecycles, e.g., product lifecycles, usually somehow express sequenced phases, business process management lifecycles cannot be understood as strictly staged models, i.e., temporal models, of what is going on. If at all, they express some causality between the stages in the lifecycle. For example, in Fig. 2.6, business process monitoring is not done after business process execution but during business process execution. Similarly, no business process monitoring can be done without executing business processes.

Different lifecycles consist of different building blocks; in particular the number of building blocks varies greatly. In the lifecycle of Fig. 2.6 we have aggregated several activities like service level agreement definition, business process modeling, workflow definition, process implementation, gathering data, analyzing data and rethinking processes into coarse grained building blocks. In practice, often lifecycles are used that make these fine-granular activities explicit, which sometimes makes it even more difficult to understand the ordering of the activities in the lifecycle as staging – be it temporal or causal. For example, it is very common to have a business process optimization stage in the lifecycle that occurs typically between business process monitoring and business process definition. However, as depicted in Fig. 2.6 business process optimization is rather not an activity in its own but consists of business process monitoring and the redefinition of the processes.

Prominent business process management lifecycles are the DMAIC lifecycle of the process-oriented quality strategy Six Sigma and the PDCA lifecycle. The PDCA lifecycle, also called the Deming wheel [69], Deming cycle or Shewhart cycle is used by established process quality frameworks like CMMi, ISO 9000 [175, 177], COBIT and ITIL. The PDCA lifecycle –see Fig. 2.7 consist of four steps: plan, do, check, act.

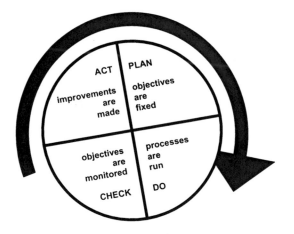

Fig. 2.7. The Deming wheel for quality control.

2.4.2 Six Sigma

Six Sigma [152, 153, 154] – 6σ – is a method for improving process quality by minimizing its variation, i.e., by minimizing the variation of considered target characteristics of the results of the process – see also [319, 320] for the origins of systematic, statistics-based quality control in industrial manufacturing. Six Sigma was developed by Motorola and is considered as a leading process improvement strategy today. A process with little variation is considered more robust. It is better because the outcome of the process is more predictable and the quality of its outcome is more reliable. Six Sigma projects are not restricted to minimizing process variations. The improvement of the quality of the results of a process can also be a target, but then the method to do this also involves understanding impacts on the variation of the exiting processes – observing variations, understanding correlations and minimizing variations is the fundamental approach of Six Sigma. The name Six Sigma stands for six times the standard deviation σ. So, the name Six Sigma indicates the ideal

success of a Six Sigma project: with respect to a considered characteristics —
called CTQ (critical-to-quality characteristics) in Six Sigma – variations of a
result that are not tolerable, i.e., failure outcomes, lie outside the area of six
standard deviations to the left and to the right of the mean value. In the case
of a standard normal variation this means, for example, that only 0.0003 per
cent of the results are still non-tolerable result – so the ideal target of Six
Sigma are zero-failure processes so to speak.

Six Sigma can be used to improve both technical processes, i.e., production processes, and non-technical processes, like planning and management
processes. However, improvement of production processes are very typical examples of Six Sigma projects and this is where Six Sigma originally stems from.
A Six Sigma project follows the so called DMAIC lifecycle consisting of the
following phases: define, measure, analyze, improve, control. During definition
target characteristics are identified and assumptions are made about which
factors might influence the variation of the target characteristics. The target
characteristics and factors must be measurable. During measurement, data
about the defined characteristics and factors are gathered. It is the task of the
analysis to understand which factors actually impact the target characteristics. Standard statistic tools like Minitab are used to conduct the analysis. By
understanding the correlation of characteristics and factors based on statistics Six Sigma can be considered as a sophisticated data mining approach: Six
Sigma not only looks for plain dependencies of stochastic variables but also
has the variations of the variables as input information to its analysis.

Business process management and the Six Sigma approach are hosted by
different communities. It is fair to say that business process management
evolved rather from planning and controlling enterprise resources and Six
Sigma evolved from looking for impact factors on production processes. In
business process management the definition and fulfillment of service-level
agreements is crucial; in the Six Sigma approach the characteristics that are
critical to quality and assumed impact factors of existing processes as well as
their relationship are the object of investigation. The Six Sigma approach to
analyzing processes is very concrete; it looks at the statistical variations. Six
Sigma projects can also be used to improve enterprise resource planning processes and, on the other hand, business process management concepts and, in
particular, business process management technologies can be used to establish
a framework for conducting Six Sigma projects [198]. However, in general the
concrete method of analyzing the correlations of statistical variations is not a
must for the improvement of business processes. One thing is very important
about Six Sigma: its success once more indicates the pivotal role of industrial
manufacturing and the production processes in modern enterprises.

2.5 Business Continuity Management

2.5.1 Threats onto Business Processes

Business continuity is about threats to business processes. It is about those threats that substantially impact the usual operation of business processes in a way that prevents the organization or enterprise from fulfilling its mission with eventually severe impact on costs or revenues. So, the threats dealt within business continuity considerations are severe incidents that typically do not stem from the conditions of the respective business model but rather somehow from the environment the business operates in. Table 3.1 lists some of the typical threats considered in the area of business continuity. Taken as an objective, business continuity aims to maximize the stability of the business against those threats. Therefore, business continuity management [157, 111, 283, 284] is about becoming aware about as many threats as possible and preparing – with commercially reasonable efforts – the business to handle them as well as possible.

Table 2.1 results from a poll conducted by the Chartered Management Institute [360] on disruptions experienced in the UK in the year 2007. It clearly shows that loss of IT heads the list of experienced disruptions. However, the figures also tell that also those risks that are usually considered as non everyday risks like extreme weather conditions or fire clearly occur often enough to be considered for systematic treatment. The table also contains other in-

	experienced	BCP covered	BCP used
Loss of IT	38%	81%	9%
Loss of people	32%	53%	3%
Extreme weather e.g. flood/high winds	28%	58%	5%
Loss of telecommunications	25%	75%	5%
Utility outage e.g. electricity, gas, water, sewage	21%	57%	6%
Loss of key skills	20%	49%	2%
Negative publicity/coverage	19%	36%	2%
Employee health and safety incident	17%	52%	3%
Supply chain disruption	13%	37%	2%
Damage to corporate image/reputation/brand	11%	35%	2%
Pressure group protest	7%	23%	1%
Industrial action	7%	28%	2%
Environmental incident	6%	51%	2%
Customer health/product safety issue/incident	6%	1 %	1%
Fire	6%	68%	2%
Terrorist damage	3%	57%	2%

Table 2.1. Disruptions experienced in UK in 2007 according to a poll conducted by the Chartered Management Institute with a base of 1257 respondents.

teresting figures. It shows that only a part of the respondents of the poll have systematically considered the potential disruptions and eventually addressed them in their business continuity plans. Furthermore, it shows how many respondents were actually able to use an existing business continuity plan. The clear gap between these two latter figures is a key argument for further research and development of tools and techniques in the area of business continuity management.

2.5.2 The British Business Continuity Management Standard

Business continuity management spans the whole cycle of analyzing the business with respect to critical actions, systematically addressing critical actions, designing reactions to unavoidable incidents, and exercising and maintaining those reactions. The British standard BS 25999 [43] is an internationally highly recognized standard in the area of business continuity management. BS 25999 considers business continuity management as a major crosscutting activity, which must be truly embedded in the company in the sense of awareness of it and support for it, in order to be successful.

Figure 2.8 shows the BS 25999 business continuity management lifecycle. A major activity in the understanding of the organization is business impact analysis (BIA). Business impact analysis identifies critical action. It is about determining the impact of failure of critical actions, i.e., eventually it tries to estimate direct and indirect costs of failure of critical actions. Furthermore, it has to be understood which incidents can yield to the disruption of critical actions. A kind of pervasive incident elicitation has to be conducted and then the probability of each single incident occuring has to be estimated.

The stage of determining the business continuity strategy in Fig. 2.8 is about the important fact that the preparation against threats is not only about fixing reactions to possible incidents. It has to be checked whether it is possible to change the existing business processes in a way that makes them

Fig. 2.8. The business continuity management lifecycle according to British standard BS 25999.

more stable against the identified threats from the outset. In some cases it might even be possible to get entirely rid of some of the identified critical actions. Attempts must also be made to diminish the probability of incidents and risks wherever possible at reasonable costs. Also insurances against risks must be considered systematically. Eventually, for those risks for which you have decided to accept, appropriate responses must be defined. All this is sometimes summed up roughly by a 4T model of dealing with risks: treat, tolerate, transfer, or terminate.

Appropriate response to incidents is at the heart of business continuity management. Figure 2.9 shows the incident timeline as presented by BS 25999. The overall target of incident response is to resume to normal operation of the business as soon as possible. As an appropriate response to an incident a defined emergency mode of operation and services must be entered in which the absolutely necessary level of processes to fulfill the enterprise's or organization's mission can be guaranteed. The incident timeline shown in Fig. 2.9 distinguishes between three phases, i.e., incident response, business continuity – here in the narrow sense – and recovery. The target is to have concrete plans for each of the three phases ready to execute. During incident response stakeholders are informed and necessary immediate actions are taken. The business continuity phase is about recovering and executing versions of critical business processes. The recovery phase leads the organization back to normal operation.

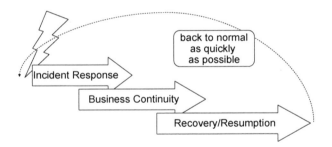

Fig. 2.9. The stages of the incident timeline according to BS 25999.

2.5.3 IT and Business Continuity Management

Business continuity management does not address information technology outage as the only threat. But of course it is an important one, because information technology is a mission critical asset – see Sect. 2.6 – and still the disruption of loss of information technology is the most often experienced one, e.g., according to Table 2.1.

Depending on the branch and the concrete purpose of a computer system, the impact in costs and revenues of information technology outage can be

substantial for an enterprise. It is said that in banking the total outage of
the core systems, i.e., those that deal with transactions on bank accounts, can
yield to the bankruptcy of the bank already after two or three days. Therefore,
for the core systems of a bank high availability technology like mainframe
computers – often spatially replicated – or high availability clusters are used.
Take a medium enterprise from the industrial production domain as another
example. Here, the logistics applications that enable the company to deliver
these products in extended supply chains are mission-critical. The outage of
these applications do not lead to a bankruptcy of the enterprise immediately
as in the aforementioned banking example, however, actually every day or
even every hour of outage can be directly measured in loss of revenue. Not to
speak about the loss of customer satisfaction and trust and therefore indirect
loss of revenue in the long run. For such medium-critical systems a really
high availability solution might be considered overkill, but still a nearly high
available system is desired. For example, midrange computers might yield a
solution, in particular if there are spatially distributed.

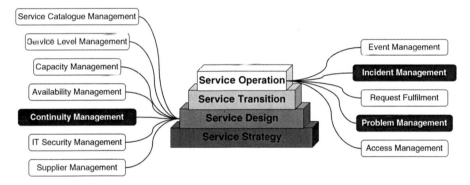

Fig. 2.10. ITIL v3 best practices stack tackling business continuity.

Outage of information technology is a well-perceived threat in business
continuity management. IT continuity management as a systematic approach
to keep IT running exists in parallel to business continuity management efforts
in enterprises. For example, ITIL explains IT service continuity management
as supportive to overall business continuity management in an enterprise [189].
But then, a closer look to IT continuity management shows that mature IT
continuity management efforts contain also the major activities seen in overall business management, like business impact analysis and risk analysis, of
course, with a focus on IT outage. Similarly, in IT service continuity management the same threats as in overall business continuity management are
considered, e.g., extreme weather, utility outage – see Table 2.1. IT outage
is not a threat considered in IT service continuity management, IT outage
is rather the impact of the threats. We believe that ideally teaming together

overall business continuity management and IT service continuity management would mean to remove redundancies in activities and considered threats on the level of IT service continuity management.

Figure 2.10 shows an overview of the ITIL service lifecycle [268] with a focus onto topics related to continuity management. Incident management deals with the malfunction of single services as perceived by users of services. A malfunction can indeed be the interruption of a service but also a reduction of quality of a service, e.g., in terms of usability. Incident management is not about reaction to major failure of an entire IT infrastructure or data center, it is about help with everyday incidents of IT services. Systematic incident management is about routing requests via a help desk, prioritizing request and reacting to them in a proper manner. Incident management is at the heart of IT infrastructure management. Therefore, incident management is typically the first ITIL service operation process in ITIL projects, i.e., the process that organizations introduce first when they start with ITIL. Problem management is a service operation process that has been introduced with ITIL version 3. Problem management is about the systematic collection of causes of incidents and events in the everyday IT infrastructure management. In ITIL a problem is not just a synonym for an incident but a source of a kind of incident. The gathered knowledge can be exploited in the sequel to find ways to prevent incidents from the outset.

Incident management and problem management are processes of the service operation element [54] of ITIL. ITIL sees IT service continuity management as the means to resume to normal operation in the case of major failure of IT infrastructure within predefined times. As a consequence, IT service continuity management is tackled within the service design element [305] of ITIL.

2.6 Information Technology as Mission-Critical Asset

Enterprise applications are mission critical for today's enterprises. Information technology improves strategy, tactics and operations. Due to globalization the markets change more quickly and enterprises must react to emerging technologies more rapidly. Information Technology plays a key role in the transformation of businesses, it is at the heart of changes in enterprises.

In the 1990s there were not only rumors about the new economy [327], also the old economy was roaring. Internet technology – the important driver of the new economy – is here to stay and must be considered strategically also in old economy enterprises [289], because it is not only relevant for new marketing and sales channels but also for in-house systems. But even without this, we have seen huge efforts in outsourcing and spin-offs in the 1990s. Note, that splitting a company needs preparation – this means that there is the need for business process reengineering beforehand and it usually means the creation of a decentralized IT system landscape beforehand. In any case, there was an increasing awareness about information technology as a mission-critical asset of an enterprise. This was the decade when chief information officers (CIO) operated on the strategic level.

Actually, in practice, business processes can hardly be discussed without considering the enterprise IT. The overall architecture of the enterprise IT systems is the issue, i.e., the system landscape. New IT products can be the enabling technology of improved business processes, on the other hand, we have to deal with legacy problems, i.e., existing information technology can slow down business process reengineering efforts.

2.6.1 Flexible and Adaptive Information Technology

Flexibility of business processes has always been and still is regarded as an important success factor for enterprises – see also Fig. 2.12. An appropriate information systeminfrastructure [147] is a key enabler for flexible business processes. Major IT players in the enterprise application domain have been strategically preparing their products for flexible and adaptive structure and functionality. Concrete examples of this strategic orientation include IBM's Capacity on Demand technique (CoD) in the midrange computer and mainframe area and SAP's Netweaver initiative in the commercial off-the-shelf area.

IBM's Capacity on Demand is a combined virtualization capability and licensing model for all e-server platforms, i.e., for i-series, p-series and z-series computers. Basically, the machine is delivered with more computing power than the customer actually needs at the moment of delivery. Some of the processors are idle, but if the customer needs more, for example, in times of peak load, he just uses more processors and pays for the extra computing power. In this way the customer is able to react better to changes in his enterprise's context. Obviously, this model brings the advantage of immediate and calculable scalability to individually owned machines that you otherwise only have when using services of a data center. Actually, the Capacity on Demand capability is advertised as an enabler for On Demand Business.

2.6.2 Enterprise Application Integration

The On Demand Business business metaphor is IBM's answer to the challenges of the new globalized and rapidly changing markets. An 'on demand'-business is able to dynamically react to new emerging demands, opportunities and threats in its internal and external business environment [168]. So On Demand Business is about flexibility of the enterprise. However, On Demand Business is not only a business metaphor it is also a conceptual solution framework [186]. It describes business transformation approaches and, in particular, concrete On Demand Business techniques like the aforementioned Capacity on Demand.

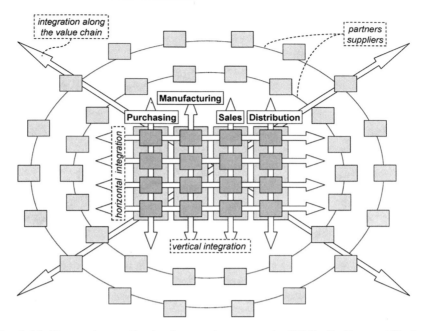

Fig. 2.11. Enterprise application integration as seen by IBM's On Demand Business strategy.

A central theme in the On Demand Business argument is enterprise application integration [147] – three kinds of integration are targeted [168]: vertical integration, horizontal integration and integration along the value chain, see Fig. 2.11. Here, vertical integration means the improvement of the information flow between the silos in one main process resp. line of business, horizontal integration means the improvement of the information flow between main processes, and integration along the value chain actually stands for the improvement of the extended supply chain, i.e., the improvement of the information flow between the enterprise, its direct business partners and suppliers and even beyond with its indirect business partners and suppliers.

Actually, enterprise application integration is said to be the key to the transformation to an 'on demand'-business, i.e., the key to achieve reactiveness and responsiveness. How does enterprise application integration help with the flexibility of an enterprise? Because stakeholders at all level of the enterprise feel that the flexibility of the enterprise is impeded, basically, by lack of information or – to more precisely stated – by the inflexibility of the information flows. As you will see in later chapters, enterprise application architecture [103, 108] is a major issue in business process management addressed by many business process technologies.

In a poll [251, 292] on the challenges posed by business processes, approximately 150 IT executives were asked by Forrester Research which concrete business problems they would classify as important or very important with respect to their current enterprise applications – please have look at Fig. 2.12 for the outcome of this poll. The problem addressed by horizontal integration, i.e., the inadequate support of enterprise applications for cross-functional processes is amongst the top-problems according to the poll visualized in Fig. 2.12. The counterpart of integration along the value chain can be seen in Fig. 2.12, e.g., in the enterprise applications' lack of business process extensibility to external partners and the lack of support for collaboration between employees, business partners and customers.

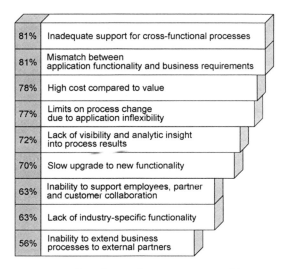

81%	Inadequate support for cross-functional processes
81%	Mismatch between application functionality and business requirements
78%	High cost compared to value
77%	Limits on process change due to application inflexibility
72%	Lack of visibility and analytic insight into process results
70%	Slow upgrade to new functionality
63%	Inability to support employees, partner and customer collaboration
63%	Lack of industry-specific functionality
56%	Inability to extend business processes to external partners

Fig. 2.12. Forrester Research poll on which business problems are important resp. very important.

2.6.3 Total Cost of Ownership

Several objectives must be met to make a successful and stable system: performance, scalability, availability, security, maintainability. In theory, performance has two aspects, i.e., reactiveness and throughput, which are usually mutually dependent. In theory, scalability is about the costs of extending the system, if it is not able to handle the given load any more. A system architecture is scalable, if it is prepared for extension. However, in practice, there is another understanding of scalability. Scalability just stands for the number of clients a system can serve. So, in practice, performance rather stands for the reactiveness of a system – performance and scalability together stand for the load a system can handle properly. With respect to availability it has to be distinguished between planned and unplanned downtimes. Planned downtimes are those that are needed for system administration tasks and known in advance. Usually, it is only the unplanned downtime that is considered by availability considerations. Maintainability addresses costs for the actual system maintenance, i.e., system administration, and also costs for changes to the system. In a broader sense maintainability is also about costs for end-user support services.

If information system products have to be selected, eventually, total cost of ownership (TCO) [201] must be addressed. The total cost of ownership comprises costs for hardware and software, costs of the rollout project and costs for system maintenance and system administration. Therefore the total costs of ownership are always calculated for an assumed lifetime of the considered information system – it is simply not enough to consider the initial purchase costs of an information system. The costs for system operations including costs for system maintenance and system administration are hard to predict and sometimes even hard to determine once the system is running. So, in advance, costs of an information system sometimes can only be estimated rather than calculated. This is even more true if risk management aspects come into play. Then the above definition of total costs of ownership is not completely adequate any more. This problem arises for all of the aforementioned driving forces affecting system stability. For example, with respect to availability you have to estimate the costs of system downtime; or with respect to security you have to estimate the costs of the case that somebody infringes your system. From these estimates you must then derive how much more you are willing to pay for extra availability and extra security.

Formally, e.g., by the Gartner Group, there is a distinction between so-called direct and indirect costs. Direct costs are budgeted expenses, indirect costs are unbudgeted expenses. Unbudgeted expenses are those that are unforeseen or overlooked. They can stem from technological risks or from expenses hidden in overlooked cost units, residing, e.g., in cost centers other then the IT department. In this terminology, typical examples of indirect costs are expenses for end user training and support. Indirect costs can in principle often be made direct costs by estimating them and making them explicit by assigning them to an appropriate cost unit connected to the considered information technology.

Only a holistic treatment of software, middleware, database management systems, hardware, and system administration can balance the several driving forces. In such a holistic treatment of information systems the database technology viewpoint on them has always proven to be a particular mature one in the past – both in practice and in research. The database community helps improving stable system architecture by fostering robust database technology [322, 242, 30, 142, 5].

2.6.4 Total Benefit of Ownership

Care must be taken in analyses that are done to understand whether a certain IT strategy should be taken or a certain IT infrastructure should be created.

Estimations of the total cost of ownership address only the cost side of these even more complicated analyses. Return on investment (ROI) is the widely used term in profit/loss calculations. Formally, it is the ratio of expected profit to needed capital. In practice, return on investment calculations are done on different levels of observation, i.e., financing of a businesses, business units, projects, or technical equipment, e.g., new IT infrastructure. However, with respect to information technology even the viewpoint of return on investment calculations with their focus on measurable cash flow is often to narrow to realistically evaluate the benefits of an optional investment. New opportunities and additional flexibility created by a new IT infrastructure are yet other criteria that often have to be considered. An example of an approach that addresses the real benefits of an IT investment is Forrester Research's Total Economic Impact (TEI) method [245], which considers total costs of ownership, the business value and the options that are created by IT in evaluating it.

As we said in Sect. 2.6.3, indirect costs belong to the total cost of ownership. And actually, in practice stakeholders usually incorporate indirect costs in realistic calculations. The indirect costs that deal with risks of malfunction of information technology, i.e., unplanned down times or security threats can be estimated. However, even if the costs of a single malfunction can be robustly estimated there is another level of indirection, i.e., the problem of estimating the probability of such malfunctions. So, if done correctly there is in general at least a worst case and a best case calculation of total cost of ownership; ideally, the outcome of the total cost of ownership analysis is actually deviation of costs.

The problem of mixing certain costs with probabilistic costs in total costs of ownership is that it opens the door for obfuscation of the certain costs. Therefore, we propose a different viewpoint depicted in Fig. 2.13. Here, the total cost of ownership consists of certain measurable, budgeted costs only. All probabilistic costs – usually indirect costs of uncertain malfunction events but also all other probabilistic costs – are considered separately from the total cost of ownership. The probabilistic costs are considered on the side of the anyhow vague determination of the total benefit of ownership. Some of the benefits of information technology can only be roughly measured or cannot be measured at all. They are often nonetheless important. So it is the case for, e.g., an improved customer relationship on behalf of improved customer processes and also for an improved overall flexibility of the enterprise gained by IT which we have discussed in Sects. 2.6.1 and 2.6.2. Furthermore, the total benefit of ownership is made of assessable profit and cost savings, which are two sides of the same story. Usually, in the area of business process optimization information technology is considered to contribute to cost savings, if information technology is the core asset in a new project or production line its contribution to the profit can be determined. Cost savings and profit together make up a kind of direct, absolute return on investment which is lowered by the probabilistic costs in our model.

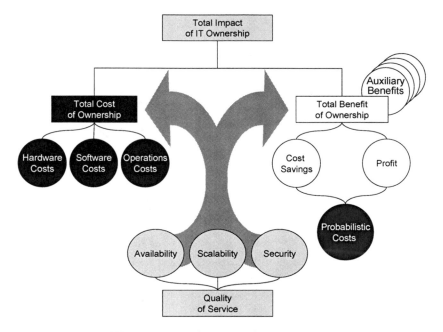

Fig. 2.13. Total impact of IT ownership.

Now, we want to consider the notion of total impact of IT ownership for the areas of business process reengineering and management which can be mutual dependent as discussed in the introductory section of this chapter. Business process reengineering and management lead to better performance and therefore have their impact. Often, the impacts are directly measurable in terms of cost savings or time savings. Often, the impacts are not as easily to determine. Information technology can be used as an enabler of business process reengineering and management. Now, there are two possible views on the total cost of ownership calculation for the supporting IT. The first one sees the decision for the optimizations independently from the decision for a concrete IT support. Then, consequentially the estimated impacts cannot be incorporated into the total cost of ownership calculation. This case usually occurs when a certain kind of optimization is already standard in the sense of strategic benchmarking, i.e., there is no doubt that the enterprise will benefit from the possible changes and the choice of technology boils down to the evaluation of existing products. However, if innovative optimizations that need new comparatively high cost technology have to be evaluated, it is very likely to make sense that the estimated impacts are included into the total cost of ownership calculations.

2.6.5 On Client-Server Computing

It is a commonplace to oppose mainframe-based architectures to client-server architectures in the following way: mainframes are viewed as the still existing legacy systems that are inflexible silos and client-server computing as the modern alternative. First, as a minor comment to this, if an enterprise resource planning system runs on a single host computer, this is usually not a mainframe but a midrange computer [325, 93] or another kind of high-end server. Mainframes are used where extreme system robustness and availability is required. There they have been used are still used, for example, to run the mission-critical core systems of a bank [286]. Midrange computer products are also called servers today and also other high-end servers are used as single host computers for enterprise IT.

IT system architecture is the architecture of software and host computers, i.e., it is about the deployment of software components on host computers and their relationships. This means the client-server paradigm is really not about a mere software architecture only, it is about software distributed over separated server machines. It might be the correct observation that often a legacy silo system on a single host computer is the main reason that a business process reengineering project does not take off; but from this it is not possible to conclude that the reason for this is the deployment of the software on a single host computer. More likely, it is due to the software design of the silo application. Very likely, we have to deal with a programming system that has been written for a single usage scenario on a single machine in such a situation. This means no productizing [45] has occurred when the system was developed, i.e., no investment into the creation of generalized software components has been undertaken. It is the lack of generalized software components that hinders future reuse and makes the system inflexible and hard to adapt to new requirements – it is not the deployment on a single host computer. Obviously, if a programming system is designed for flexibility and adaptivity the deployment on a single host computer is no loss.

Client-server architecture has been often motivated as a cost-saving alternative to silo system architectures. But please pay attention, this cost-saving argument is debatable against the full background of total cost of ownership. With respect to the host architecture aspect the argument of client-server architecture is not true in general. Of course, a bunch of commodity servers can easily provide the same computing power as a given midrange computer for a much lower price. However, if availability and maintainability are major driving forces in a given scenario, the result of a sincere calculation of the total costs of ownership can often tell another story. With respect to the pure software architecture aspect the question that must be answered always is whether the efforts in productizing actually pay off eventually.

Distributed object computing technologies, i.e., CORBA, DCOM and the like, that are identified by their communities themselves with client-server computing, is often used in enterprise application integration, in particular in wrapping legacy systems to make them accessible to current application server technology. For example, the project in [286] that we mention in Sect. 8 uses CORBA technology to wrap banking applications – some of them are important legacy systems based on IMS (Information Management System) transaction monitors and hierarchical databases. In enterprise application integration projects client-server technology is not used to design a system landscape from scratch, on the contrary, it is used to wrap and glue existing applications.

But there are reasons why real client-server architecture, i.e., distributed deployment of software components, is relevant for enterprises. The first issue is ownership. Based on business culture, enterprise units might want to own and run their own IT independently. Second, if the target of splitting a company is the major driving force of corporate reengineering efforts, introducing a decentralized IT exploiting client-server architecture principles might be necessary as a preliminary action.

2.7 Quality Management Systems

In this section we discuss a quality management system model that is reductionist in terms of organizational functions but sophisticated in terms of interfaces between the organizational functions. Established quality management systems [182, 178, 181] are process-oriented. For conformance with concrete quality management systems the definition of processes is crucial. A mature – or let us say viable – quality management system, is a spiral feedback control system, i.e., a feedback control system that itself is subject to controlled change and therefore evolves in conjunction with the business that it aims to improve. Cybernetic management models are very elaborated feedback control systems [21, 22, 23] . Quality management systems are cybernetic. If applied in the intended manner a quality management system becomes so pervasive in an enterprise that it becomes the management model of the enterprise.

A mature quality management system consists of two mutual dependent functions, i.e., a business process steering function and a business process execution function. Usually, quality management systems are presented on the basis of a business process management lifecycle. We have described the notion of business process management lifecycle in Sect. 2.4.1 – see Figs. 2.6 and 2.7. We have already discussed the problem that business problem management lifecycles can hardly be understood as strictly staged models against the practice of business operations in Sect. 2.4.1. Here, in our model we do not use the term lifecycle but the term feedback control system, partly also in order to emphasize that, in general, we should also be prepared for continuous or at least quasi-continuous control with real-time reports and extremely rapid reaction. We have chosen the term business process steering function to have a new term that is not in conflict with the names of phases of one of the existing major business process management lifecycles. Other terms like business process adjustment function or business process supervision function would also be possible. For example, in terms of the PDCA lifecycle the business process steering function consists of checking, acting and planning, whereas the business process execution function corresponds to the doing phase in the PDCA lifecycle.

There are two interfaces between the business process steering function and the business process execution function, i.e., a steering interface and a feedback interface. For each point in time, the steering interface consists of a set S of steering parameters $S_{t,1}, \cdots, S_{t,l_t}$, a set T of additional target agreements $T_{t,1}, \cdots, T_{t,m_t}$ and a set A of additional business improvement activities $A_{t,1}, \cdots, A_{t,n_t}$. The feedback interface consists of a set K of key performance indicators $K_{t,1}, \cdots, K_{t,o_t}$ and a set R of additional performance reports $R_{t,1}, \cdots, R_{t,p_t}$.

The steering parameters S are target agreements between stakeholders of the steering function and stakeholders of the execution function. A steering parameter is a well-defined, measurable figure of a defined business process. The target agreements T are further target agreements that cannot be defined as measurable figures in terms of defined business processes. The business improvement activities are all kinds of activities other than target agreements that are intended to improve the efficiency or effectiveness of the enterprise. The key performance indicators K are measurable figures about defined business processes. The performance reports R are further information about the performance of the enterprise that cannot be defined as measurable figures in terms of defined business processes.

The steering function analyzes the performance of the enterprise. It analyzes the environment of the enterprise. It analyzes and adjusts the strategy [326] of the enterprise. It analyzes the key performance indicators and additional performance reports. It reviews the business processes of the business process execution function. It reviews the functioning of the business process execution function in general. As a result of this, it resets the steering parameters, negotiates further target agreements and instructs further business improvement activities. Furthermore, it continuously improves the steering interface and the feedback interface.

We call a viewpoint that tries to understand as much of the functioning of an enterprise as possible in terms of the parameter sets S, T, K and R a mechanical viewpoint. We call a viewpoint that tries to understand as much of the functioning of the enterprise as possible in terms of the parameter sets S and K a purely mechanically viewpoint. The gap between a mechanical or even purely mechanical viewpoint and the actual functioning of the enterprise should not be neglected in quality management system projects. The parts of the functioning of the enterprise that are not amenable to a mechanical viewpoint may contribute substantially to the targeted results and the success of the enterprise.

3

Research Opportunities in Business Process Technology

Improvements in business process technology are clearly demanded by the strategic need of today's enterprises to become more flexible in the sense of reactiveness to the more and more rapidly changing business environments.

IT systems in an enterprise are seldom designed from scratch, they evolve along new demands over the years, so that system landscapes [156] emerge. So, in practice, the issue of making enterprise IT more flexible is about fostering the flow of information by enterprise application integration efforts – protection of investment is the rationale for this pragmatic approach. In research, we are free to look at the problem with a fresh look – actually from scratch. Now is the time to systematically analyze the needs, driving forces and benefits of business process technology by looking onto the plethora of concrete business process management products and their features from a conceptual viewpoint. In the terminology of current software engineering technology and software processes it is the task to define a component-based platform for business processes that unifies modeling, construction, operations and maintenance of business process software. Such a goal is not only a mental exercise for researchers, also industry is foreseeing such new integrative products that go beyond current business process management suites and the term business process platform has been coined for them.

With respect to business process technology we have identified two potential fields of research, i.e., executable specification and components. We delve into these topics in Sects. 3.2 resp. 3.3. They are the major topics of this book. The topics address the improvement of business process technology independent from specific business functionality. It is also interesting to invest research into the dimension of specific business functionalities – again from an enterprise application integration viewpoint. In particular, we currently still see a gap between IT support for administration and production processes in manufacturing enterprises. It should not be forgotten that excellence in production is a foundation of today's businesses [155].

Enterprises react to technological trends to stay competitive. In the past, more and more concrete applications and systems were introduced to address

D. Draheim, *Business Process Technology: A Unified View on Business Processes, Workflows and Enterprise Applications*, DOI 10.1007/978-3-642-01588-5_3,
© Springer-Verlag Berlin Heidelberg 2010

more and more problems, starting from basic numerical control systems to today's manufacturing execution systems [237, 202], from basic accounting systems to today's enterprise resource planning systems, from basic reporting capabilities to today's analytical processing systems, from basic electronic data interchange to today's logistics management systems. The potential of automation is still huge in modern enterprises. In general, a focus on the mere administration side of businesses is too narrow. There are current initiatives like MESA and ISA-95 that address the integration of business processes and production processes. We delve into this topic in Sect. 3.5. Having the production process in mind can prevent us from making flaws in the design of future business process platforms from the outset.

3.1 Business Process Platforms

For us, the term business process platform does not stand for some kind of improved integration of standard components into business process management suites. For us, the term business process platform has two aspects, i.e., executable specification and component-based architecture. The point is that the creation of a high-level specification mechanism for business processes comes first, i.e., we believe that the existence of such a notion of executable specifications is a precondition for a working component architecture and not vice versa. This viewpoint differs crucially from how commercial product vendors approach the problem of creating a next generation business process platform. The approach we see at the vendor's side follows a certain tradition of enterprise application integration that has ruled the design of business process technology in the past, i.e., the understanding of enterprise application integration as a step-wise improvement of the information flows in an enterprise system landscape with the objective to touch existing systems as little as possible or even not to touch the systems at all instead of radically refactoring, reengineering or even reconstructing the systems. Therefore the promises of component architecture for business process management suites usually do not go beyond the simplification and better support for hooking realizing software parts together, i.e., the provision of a plug-in architecture. However, the languages for the construction of software parts are not the focus of improvement – they are considered as given.

In research, on the contrary, we have the chance to approach things more fundamentally. We can consider languages and mechanisms for the construction of software parts and those for gluing software parts together as a whole. Furthermore, we can view systems from outside, i.e., the viewpoint of system specification from an end-user's viewpoint – we are not restricted to the viewpoint of the given virtual machine defined by a concrete programming language. This means that there is a potential to design a domain-specific language for the specification and construction of business process software – and if the job is done right, specification and construction are actually the same, which is expressed by the notion of executable specification. We believe that only an appropriate notion of compositionality of such an executable specification mechanism yields a truly powerful component architecture for business process software.

By the way, it is strange that we have already seen fourth generation (4GL) languages like RPG (Report Generator) for the midrange computer AS/400 that have been designed for the implementation of business logic and the typical form-based dialogues of enterprise applications but today's advertised new business process management suites all rely on third generation (3GL) languages for the implementation of the software components they hook together. And actually we see migration projects in practice from systems that are implemented in such domain-specific technologies to platforms that are based on a current object-oriented programming language. Superficially, such migration projects are sometimes motivated by the desire to migrate to object-oriented technology. However, the argument only works if you take for granted the superiority of object-oriented technologies over older ones. However, the maturity of domain-specific 4GL languages like the aforementioned RPG should not be underestimated. There are usually more concrete reasons for such migration projects. One reason could be simply the better availability of programmers for a newer non-proprietary programming language. Another could be the insight that the higher costs of a current system in terms of total costs of ownership actually do not pay off, because the non-functional requirements on the system are actually not so high that they justify the costs. Another reason could be the following from many classical legacy problem scenarios: the functionality of the system has to be made available in the setting of a newer technology – most probably web technology – and it has been estimated that re-implementing the system is the cheaper or at least less risky alternative to wrapping and embedding the system.

We said that the analysis of the driving forces of business process management on the problem side and the features of current business process technology on the solution side is necessary preparatory work for the design of next generation business process platforms. We believe that a scientific analysis must not be misled by the promises of any software engineering metaphor. In particular, a mere programming language level discussion can easily miss the point here. A system should be considered as an entirety of software, middleware and hardware – the issue in question is how good these components are orchestrated and in how far their design is streamlined by overall objectives and design rationales. We believe that such considerations are important to reach technology independency eventually. For example, RPG shows its value as part of the holistically designed AS/400 system [325, 93] – today known as i-series, 'System i5' or 'System i' – with its co-designed and co-constructed operating system, database management system and virtual machine system, i.e., OS/400 – today known as i5/OS – DB2 and TIMI (Technology Independent Machine Interface) respectively. The reason for the system's robustness is in this case that the hardware and software components are designed for each other following crosscutting design principles.

3.2 Executable Specification of Business Processes

We have seen steady efforts to make business process specifications executable, both in academia [134] and industry [247, 272]. There are two non-mutual and converging communities that foster this trend, i.e., the business process modeling community, e.g., [265], and the workflow management community [164]. Business processes are an issue in enterprises, e.g., [151, 150], even without executable semantics of processes.

Workflow control has its origins in concrete technologies for computer-supported collaborative work (CSCW) based on document processing like Palo Alto's OfficeTalk [192] in the 1970s or Polymer [232] in the 1980s, on the one hand, and in more general rapid development frameworks based on a worklist paradigm like FlowMark [218], on the other hand. A lot of to-day's commercial business process management suites [247] actually started as workflow management products.

3.2.1 Means of Business Process Automation

In principle, the target of executable business process specification can be approached top-down, by hooking business process modeling tools with executable systems, or bottom-up by enriching workflow engines. However, the gap remains; there is no canonical mapping between the components that are under the control of workflow technology and the entities addressed by business process modeling. The view of business process modeling is rather a global one, i.e., the net of business activities and exchanged information entities. The view of workflow control, on the other hand, is a local one, looking at the human computer interaction and having a concrete worklist paradigm at hand for processing workflows. We believe that the gap between business process modeling and workflow control should be systematically investigated. As a quick gain, it is possible to exploit the results of such investigations as best practices in practical business process projects. In the long run the results can help in the unification of both levels and the design of an advanced business process management suite.

A step in bridging the gap between business process modeling and business process management can be done by an investigation of advanced role-model concepts from a workflow patterns perspective. There has been a rigorous discussion of workflow patterns in the workflow community [1] that helped in the investigation and analytical comparison of existing workflow technology. This workflow pattern discussion has already been broadened [308] by the consideration of workflow resources, i.e., different users. User and user role models are at the heart of the workflow paradigm. Considering users and roles can bring a human-computer interaction viewpoint to the discussion of workflow patterns refining the otherwise global, i.e., observational viewpoint of an overall action flow. The findings of such human-computer interaction focused investigations can be exploited in the definition of an executable specification language for business processes. For example, the definition of the single user session of a submit/response-style system as typed, bipartite state machine can serve as a basis [89]. Here, the human-computer interaction is form-oriented – it consists of an ongoing interchange of report presentations and form submissions. In this setting it is possible to understand the notion of worklist as an interaction pattern in single user session scenarios and to proceed by generalizing the defined semantic apparatus to a form-oriented workflow definition language.

We believe that a future business process platform should allow for the executable specification of workflows and dialogues. In such a platform there will no longer be any artificial distinction between the workflow states and the states of the dialogues that bridge the workflow states. This means, system dialogues and workflows are unified [109]. An immediate major benefit of this platform is that important BPM techniques like business process monitoring and business process simulation are no longer artificially restricted to some coarse-grained workflow states, they become pervasive. Furthermore, the business logic is partitioned naturally into services of appropriate granularity this way. The decision as to which parts of the supported business process is subject to workflow technology and which parts make up the dialogues is orthogonal to the specification of the business process, i.e., a posteriori. The definition can be changed allowing for a yet unseen degree of flexibility in business process specification.

3.2.2 Inter-Organizational Business Process Automation

It is a further challenge to integrate business process platforms with approaches for inter-organizational supply chain management and extended supply chain management [348, 347]. This challenge has a technical and a conceptual, i.e., business relevant, aspect. The technical challenge is about distributed deployment. If the component architecture of a business process platform is done properly support for distributed deployment can be added easily to the platform. As we will argue in the course of the book we consider a component architecture as appropriate for a business process platforms if it allows for the unrestricted decomposition of software at the outermost level of process specifications.

Support for distributed deployment is good also for intra-organizational purposes; anyhow, with the correct exploitation of virtualization technology [65, 137] there is the chance that the differences between software architecture [132] and deployment architecture vanish – in particular, in these days of emerging virtualization technologies for commodity servers like Xen [78] or VmWare [331]. But as we have mentioned, there is also a business related challenge of inter-organizational distribution of business processes and this is the challenge of negotiating responsibilities. It will be interesting to see which kind of information technology can actually support and add value to this issue.

3.2.3 Executable Specification Communities

The synonyms for executable specification range from old ones like automatic programming [279] to today's model-driven architecture [248, 40, 90, 91].

> *"In short, automatic programming always has been an euphemism for programming with a higher-level language than was then available to the programmer. Research in automatic programming is simply research in the implementation of higher-level programming languages."* [279]

Executable specification is about gaining a new level of abstraction in the description of systems that have an operational semantics. Such endeavors are typically domain-specific, i.e., phenomena in the program design that occur often are identified and become new constructs of a new virtual machine. Therefore it is fair to say that domain-specific languages [349, 79] and even generative programming [67, 98, 99, 100, 86] are also in the realm of executable specification. Actually, it is a common misconception about model-driven architecture that this approach gains a higher-level of abstraction for general purpose program system construction. On the contrary, the research community in model-driven architecture is very well aware of the fact that the real work to be done is in defining domain-specific modeling languages that then can be exploited further to generate systems. The model-driven architecture approach is rather about setting the stage for the systematic definition of modeling languages and a kind of standardization of tool support for these definition efforts, i.e., we think it can be understood somehow as a disciplined approach to meta case tools [159, 160, 115, 246, 212, 197].

3.3 Component-Based Development

The notion of software component has been discussed as early as the NATO software engineering conference [256, 51]. Components are about code composition. But people associate more than composition mechanisms with the concept of components. Actually, there are lots of abstraction and composition mechanisms available in programming languages – routines, procedures, modules [277], objects. However, the discussion of components goes beyond the design of composition mechanisms, it also goes beyond the discussion on how to decompose systems [278] for maximal robustness or reuse. However, different communities put different emphasis in their discussion on component technology, so the concept comes with different flavors. There is a sub industry aspect, an infrastructure aspect, and a large system construction aspect.

As we will see in due course these aspects are not mutually exclusive. We need to discuss these three aspects in Sects. 3.3.1 to 3.3.3 in order to gain a better understanding of current and future trends in component-orientation for business process management suites.

The notion of business process platform as currently used and foreseen by industry has component-orientation as a crucial asset. Here, the sub industry of components is dominating, expressing the vision that next generation business process management suites are prepared for gluing together ready-made business logic components. The development of an appropriate component-model for business processes is driven this way. Our approach to component-orientation is more fundamental. Our concept of component is really just composition and composability. The usefulness of composability is beyond doubt. What we are seeking is a notion of composition which makes that the composition of arbitrary business process specification immediately yields a valid new business process specification. It is our conviction that just "yet another plug-in component architecture" that targets easier deployment of business process implementations will not bring the promised new quality of business process technology. Our targeted notion of component-orientation for business processes is indivisibly connected to the design of a next-level specification language for business processes – we consider an appropriate component architecture of business process platforms rather as a by-product of robust design efforts of a high-level specification language and not as an independent asset.

3.3.1 Sub Industry Aspect of Component Technology

One important aspect of component technology is that they are about establishing software sub industries. This is probably the earliest usage of the term component [241]. This means the term component is used for the division of programming efforts at the level of software houses. In [241] input-output conversion, two and three dimensional geometry, text processing, and storage management are given as examples for possible components supplied by specialized software houses to other software houses. With respect to this sub industry aspect frameworks and application programming interfaces (APIs) clearly are components.

Still, the sub industry aspect is often considered as the defining aspect of component technology. However, the perception of the topic has changed. In motivations of component technology research ordinary, i.e., existing application programming interfaces are usually not mentioned but rather domain-specific business logic components. Here the specialization is along industrial sectors or concrete businesses.

3.3.2 Infrastructure Aspect of Component Technology

In practice, concrete component technologies are about adding technical value to a specific technological domain by creating an infrastructure for it – we therefore use the term infrastructure aspect. These technological domains crosscut industrial sectors. Examples of technological domains are the field of visual programming, the field of distributed object computing and the wide field of enterprise computing. Component technologies address one such domain with a combination of foundational software services and tools. One very ubiquitous view of component technology is to see it as an extension of object-oriented programming technology [335].

For the sake of completeness we list the usual examples. SUN's JavaBeans are a component technology for visual programming that must not be confused with Enterprise Java Beans (EJB) that are part of the Java EE (Java Enterprise Edition) standard formerly known as J2EE, which addresses enterprise computing. DCOM (Distributed Component Object Model) is an example of a component technology that addresses distributed object computing. CORBA (Common Object Request Broker Architecture) [264] also supports distributed object computing, however, it is usually not mentioned as a component technology in its own right, only together with CCM (CORBA Component Model) [266] it is perceived as a component technology that addresses enterprise computing and is similar to Java EE. OSGi (Open Services Gateway Initiative) is an example of a Java-based component technology that enables systematic hot deployment of software , i.e., support for dynamic – in particular also remote – deployment and update. It is initiated and exploited by the embedded software community. A prominent usage of OSGi is as the foundation of the integrated development environment Eclipse.

In the domain of enterprise computing, object-oriented application server technologies like Java EE are perceived as component technologies. Here, component technology is seen as an extension of standard object-oriented language platforms with features for persistence – most typically in the form of support for object-relational mapping – distributed programming and transactional processing. For example, in [260] we find this view on component technology as an extension of object-oriented programming with features for concurrency, persistence and distribution – among possibly others. Classical transaction monitors [29, 138, 141] like IBM's CICS (Customer Information Control System) [61] or BEA's Tuxedo (Transactions for Unix, Extended for Distributed Operations) also offer such features and even beyond – they usually tightly integrate support for user interface programming and dialogue control.

An interesting example for a component technology in the domain of enterprise computing is IBM's San Francisco framework [39]. This framework is interesting because it is a rare example of an initiative that actively incorporated the sub industry aspect into its efforts from the beginning. The San Francisco framework is Java-based. The architecture of the framework consist of three layers [38], see Fig. 3.1, i.e., the foundation layer, the common business objects layer (CBO) and the core business processes layer. Independent software vendors can construct their solutions – typically for customers in a vertical domain – by customizing and reusing software entities from each of these three layers. The foundation layer [304] deals with the typical crosscutting problems of the enterprise computing domain, which are, basically, transactions, persistence and security but also others like national language support (NLS). Furthermore, the necessary support for distributed object computing is provided, i.e., an object!request broker (ORB), support for externalization and so on. With respect to distributed object computing the foundation layer was designed after the OMG standards CORBA and COS (CORBA Service) – though no formal adherence to these standards was targeted.

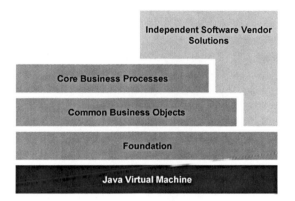

Fig. 3.1. System architecture of IBM's San Francisco framework.

With the common business objects layer the San Francisco framework starts to go beyond the discussed infrastructure aspect of component technology. The software entities provided here contain real business information and logic as default behavior. The software entities in this layer are rather general in the sense that they occur in several vertical domains. Examples for these entities are address, business partner, customer, calendar, time and currency [39, 193]. Actually also some design patterns [62, 130] for reuse in the next layer are implemented in the common business object layer. The next and highest layer of the framework, i.e., the core business processes layer, is about vertical domains. The software entities in this layer have been designed with domain experts from several companies in the particular domains. Examples for vertical domains addressed by this layer are the domain of business financials with support for, e.g., payable accounts, receivable accounts, and general ledger, the domain of order management with support for, e.g., sales and purchase orders, and the domain of warehouse management with support for, e.g., receiving and shipping of materials [193].

3.3.3 Large System Construction Aspect of Component Technology

Considering all the discussions on component technology we followed in the past we think it is fair to say that another important aspect of component-based development is simply that it is about the construction of large systems. It is common sense among developers that programming large system is fundamentally different from programming small systems. The larger a system becomes the more complex it becomes and you need special mechanisms to deal with the complexity. All the abstraction mechanisms in programming languages have the purpose to get complexity under control. The usual abstraction mechanisms found in programming languages are sufficient to build arbitrary layers of abstraction, so, in principle they are sufficient to deal with programs of any size. On the other hand, also small programs in the sense of programming in the large can be large enough for requiring the usage of programming language abstraction mechanisms in order to get into control of their complexity. So, the question arises: why do we need to discuss mechanisms that go beyond the usual programming language abstraction mechanisms? Or to pose the question differently: when is a program large, i.e., large in the sense of programming in the large [70]? One possible answer could be: programs are not large, projects [45] are.

In principle, each software system can be programmed by a single developer; however, often a wanted software system cannot be programmed by a single developer in a set time frame. Now, projects with more than one person differ fundamentally form single-person projects. There is overhead for communication, need for system documentation, need for system integration, and need for project management. Projects with more than one person, i.e., team projects are large. And programs that are developed in large projects are large. By the way, projects with distributed teams, i.e., sub-contractors, are usually even larger – that's why they are called mega projects in [135], a paper on the Boeing 777 software. So, team projects cost extra resources. And programming in the large actually addresses software programmed with more than one person. In the original paper [70] on programming in the large, or to be more precisely, in the paper that coined the term programming in the large, the notion of a module interconnection language (MIL) is introduced that should support developers in programming in the large. Two of the general objectives of the envisioned module interconnection languages explicitly address support for dealing with the overhead of division of labor. It is said that a module interconnection language should serve as a project management tool and as a means of communication between programming team members. Other objectives of the envisioned module interconnection languages are to serve as a tool for designing and concisely documenting large-scale program structures.

In answering our above question on when is a program large we said that one possible answer could be that programs are not large, but projects. We deliberately did not say that the answer is that programs are not large, but projects. Whenever a programmer feels overstrained with dealing with the complexity of a program he would be tempted to call the program a large program. This is a fuzzy characterization because defining when a developer is overstrained is not as easy as defining when a project is large – see above, we said that a project is large if it consists of more than one person. It would be superfluous to seek an answer to that question but the fact is that since the existence of programming languages we have seen a plethora of tools emerging that help programmers to get control of their code, e.g., profilers, shape analysis tools, style checkers, documentation generators, refactoring tools, versioning tools [84] to name a few and, last but not least, integrated development environments.

The major value added by an integrated development environment (IDE) is not that it combines several of the aforementioned tools as features but that it allows the developer to experience the code as a structure of hyperlinked code entities. For example, consider the major motivation of the aspect-oriented programming paradigm, i.e., the problem of maintaining the call positions of a code entity. This problem is also addressed in integrated development environments. Here, you can list the call positions of a method and the integrated development environment supports you in uniformly manipulating these call positions by its in-built refactoring capabilities. As any of these mechanisms that go beyond standard programming language features, also component technologies add value to the task of controlling complexity of large programs. Even if in academia the discussion of component technology is sometimes rather focused onto programming language constructs, in practice, a concrete component technology typically consists of a combination of new programming language features, tools, and software services.

Actually, in [45] yet another characterization of programs becoming large is given. There an artifact named "programming system product" is considered. A program which is implemented by a single person becomes a programming system if it consists of parts implemented by different programmers. In another dimension a program becomes a programming product if it is developed for more than one usage context. Different objectives like adaptivity, reusability and maintainability now become an issue. Brooks coined the term productizing for the transition from a program to a programming product – see Fig. 3.2, which also gives estimates for the extra efforts needed for the transitions in both dimension. With the consideration of productizing the loop is closed to the sub industry aspect of component technology that we have discussed earlier.

3.4 Exploiting Emerging Tools for BCM

We have discussed the importance of business continuity management for enterprises, how it targets the stability of an enterprise's business processes

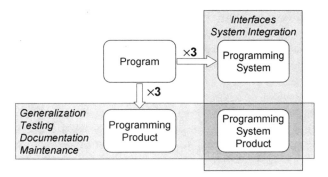

Fig. 3.2. Efforts for division of labour and productizing according to Frederik Brooks [45].

and the basic principles how business continuity can be achieved in Sect. 2.5. In order to support business continuity management there exists a range of proprietary tools, e.g., for writing business continuity plans, assessing risks, analyzing business impacts [32]. These tools usually come as combined structured editors, database repositories and bunches of templates for plans and questionnaires.

Both developing and eventually enforcing business continuity plans with the accompanying activities of risk and impact analysis are usually highly collaborative efforts if done properly. There are elements of knowledge management in these tasks and social aspects must not be neglected. Therefore, it seems natural to use some kind of CSCW tool (computer-supported collaborative work) or groupware [143] to get these things done. The several team collaboration software and social software products [116] that are currently emerging in the realm of the Web 2.0 metaphor form today's generation of CSCW tools.

According to [116] a social software product is expected to provide at least shared workspaces, management of shared documents, discussion forums, user profiles – all this supported by appropriate user and access control management – to count as a team collaboration and social software. Team collaboration software helps exchanging knowledge and joint building of knowledge bases. Therefore wikis [240, 215] and web logs (blogs) naturally fall into this software product category. Other features that fall into the area of team collaboration and social software, i.e., features that can be found in concrete products of this software category are about allocating and tracking tasks, managing projects, integration of calendars, controlling workflows, social tagging and bookmarking, visualization and analysis of social networks, content feeds, people search capabilities, in particular with respect to skill management, decision support for teams like support for prioritizing items, voting and ranking. Support for basic groupware features, i.e., email and team-based calendaring, or tight integration with respective products is expected. Also other traditional but more advanced groupware features like instant messaging and video conferencing belong to the repertoire of team collaboration software.

Against the background of all these just mentioned team-supporting software features team collaboration software seems a natural candidate as a tool in business continuity management. Imagine the process of risk assessment, impact analysis and finally estimation of risk probabilities. The processes for gathering the necessary information and afterwards categorizing and ranking the information items can be greatly supported by the features found in today's team collaboration software products.

Unfortunately, the unconsidered idea to support business continuity management by web-based team collaboration is naive against the background of the especially strict security needs of the considered domain. An important threat considered in business continuity management is always any kind of intrusion leading to several security actions from facility security to all the issues of IT security. For potential intruders the plans that deal with any kind of threats can be of interest. Therefore security requirements of the business continuity management domain are significantly high. People working in this domain and conducting the business continuity management often stem from the security sector or IT security sector. The problem is that people from the security sector are often biased against web-based technology; they often tend to work only with tools they have long experience with. Therefore, it can be challenging to convince stakeholders in the business continuity management process to use a web-based team collaboration platform. The openness of such platforms can be easily considered just too insecure. Of course, there are possibilities to make the usage of a web-based platform secure. The platform itself can be secured with virtual privacy network technology, but more obviously it is possible to fully separate a small intranet from the outside world and make it the basis for the team collaboration platform.

On the other hand, first experience already tells us that the capabilities of team collaboration and social software are really promising for business continuity management. At least we know this from one of our own projects where a simple wiki has been used in order to grasp and communicate the business continuity plan. Here, the wiki has proven particularly practical because it immediately integrates the business continuity plan with other existing documentation of the system architecture in a lightweight manner. A simple plain wiki system has been used. Mature domain-specific team collaboration software would extend the plain wiki software with templates and predefined workflows for business continuity planning and implementation.

3.5 Integration of Business and Production Processes

There is a huge potential for optimization of processes in today's industrial manufacturing. Important targets of improvement are production efficiency and product quality. Optimization is a complex task. A plethora of data that stems from numerical control and monitoring systems must be accessed, correlations in the information must be recognized, and rules that lead to improvement must be identified. Despite concrete standardization efforts existing approaches to this problem are often low-level and proprietary in today's manufacturing projects. The various manufacturing applications in a company must be turned from isolated spots of information into well-thought out integrated data sources [47, 16] that make up an overall solution.

The lowest level considered in automatic manufacturing is the automation level, i.e., the level of machine and device control. However, the automation level is not merely about automated tasks. For example, machine maintenance, transportation control and stock control are important issues at this level. The entities controlled by control computers are machines, cranes, transport belt systems or other transport mechanisms, chemical processors, converters etc. This is the level of computer numerical control (CNC), robot control (ROC), motion control (MC), programmable logic controllers (PLC), cell controllers (CC), data collection systems (DCS) and so on.

The technical integration of production devices is an issue in its own right. This is the domain of fieldbus technology like Modbus, CAN (Controller Area Network), PROFIBUS (Process Field Bus), AS-i (Aktuator Sensor Interface) – to name a few. Fielbusses are network protocols that have their strength usually at OSI level 2 – data link layer. A technology that addresses the issue of vertical integration of production devices immediately at the level of application programming interfaces is OPC ('Openness Productivity Collaboration' formerly known as 'OLE for process control') [269]. The technical integration of production devices is in a sense a horizontal integration. In the discussion of this section we are rather interested in the vertical integration of automation control shop floor control and production planning. However, vertical and horizontal integration are not completely orthogonal issues. In particular, a strictly data-centric horizontal integration approach could greatly ease vertical integration efforts from the outset.

3.5.1 Automatic Shop Floor Control

In a fully automatic plant in today's manufacturing industry there are automatic shop floor control systems or process control systems that control and track the interplay of the machines. This is the level that is often called SCADA (Supervisory Control and Data Acquisition). To give an impression we describe a fictional shop floor control system. Though the example system is fictional its described functionality is very close to a real world system from the area of material refinement. However, we abstract from the concrete domain and from the full complexity of the system, because the terminology and the details of the concrete domain do not add to the understanding of the concepts implemented by the software. In this example there is a fully integrated software control of all processors and transport devices in the plant. In a control center a supervisor sees a screen similar to the one depicted in

Fig. 3.3. Material is shipped into the plant in batches. The batches ship in from another plant in the factory. Each batch has to be processed sequentially by three kinds of converters A, B and C. There are several processors for each kind of processor, because the processing stages take different amount of time. For example, processing the batch by one of the B-processors takes approximately twice as much time as processing the batch by an A-processor. Therefore, there are twice as many B-processors as A-processors, otherwise, the B-processor stage would become a bottleneck.

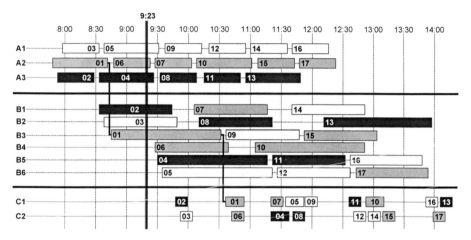

Fig. 3.3. An example manufacturing execution system.

In the graphical user interface in Fig. 3.3 the material flow proceeds from left to the right, from the top to the bottom. Actually, the graphical user interface shows a Gantt diagram of what is going on in the plant. A bar in the diagram stands for the processing of a batch in a certain processor. There are no edges connecting the bars in the diagram. The material flow is given by the numbering of the batches that remains the same throughout the different processing stages. Just to give an example, we have painted the edges for the material flow of batch with the number '01' into the diagram. A fat vertical line on the screen serves as the current-time indicator. The crucial point is that the diagram on the screen is not just about planning, it is really about control. If the current-time indicator passes the right end of a bar element, the corresponding batch is fully automatically removed from the current processor and moved into the next processor according to the schedule in the diagram. Workers in the plant are triggered by events on the production process and not vice versa. Workers can be considered to be embedded into the production process, i.e., they do not control it.

Even the scheduling, i.e., the assignment of processors to batches is done automatically by the system. The optimization target is resource utilization.

However, the supervisor in the control panel has the opportunity to reschedule the batches, i.e., to overwrite the default schedule proposed by the system. Furthermore, he can adjust the processing time per batch and processor. This way, he can react to exceptional events based on his expert knowledge. For example, he knows that a certain batch can only be processed on a certain processor, because this processor has a certain feature that is needed in the concrete case. Or one of the processors needs to pause for a while, for example, for maintenance reasons. Or the supervisor recognizes that a certain batch actually needs more processing time on its current processor than initially assumed. With respect to this it is necessary to know that the supervisor has a second screen on his desk which shows a dashboard with miscellaneous information about the current state of each of the processors.

3.5.2 Manufacturing Execution Systems

At the level of enterprise resource planning systems managers use production planning systems (PPS) for rough planning of the production. Rough planning means that managers use aggregate values for capacities and performance of production resources. Rough planning also means long-term planning, i.e., the time units managers deal with during production planning are rather months, weeks or days at the least. The management needs to give the planned production schedule to the production department as an internal order and needs feedback about the actual production in order to compare production figures with planning figures and to have a hook for high-level quality control and potential production process optimization. It also needs the feedback to improve its production planning process by an adjustment of the aggregate values used during planning.

Without further IT support there is a huge gap between production planning systems and the automation level. It is the task of manufacturing execution systems (MES) [202] to bridge this gap – see Fig. 3.4. Most importantly, with manufacturing execution systems production process planners detail the rough planning they receive from production planning to a level of detail at which shop control becomes possible. The time frames manufacturing execution systems deal with are much smaller than the ones of production planning systems – they are in the range of days, working shifts or even minutes. Full-automatic shop control systems allow for real-time planning, control and monitoring of a plant. Therefore manufacturing execution systems are natural hosts for shop control systems.

To give an impression of what manufacturing execution systems are about we list their functions as defined by the industrial standardization body MESA (Manufacturing Enterprise Solutions Association) [244]:

- Resource allocation and status.
- Operations and detail scheduling.
- Dispatching production units.

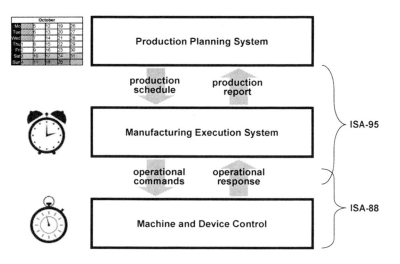

Fig. 3.4. Production planning, execution and control system architecture.

- Document control.
- Data collection acquisition.
- Labor management.
- Quality management.
- Process management.
- Maintenance management.
- Product tracking and genealogy.
- Performance analysis.

A manufacturing execution system supports the systematic fulfillment of the production schedule given by the management and also supports the delivery of the production reports needed by the management. It is that integration aspect between automation level and enterprise resource planning of manufacturing execution systems that is often emphasized. However, from the above list it becomes clear that a manufacturing execution system already adds significant value in the production department even if it were not connected with production planning systems. It supports daily operations with concrete features – maintenance management and quality management are good examples. On the other hand, it becomes also clear that a manufacturing system should be connected to the enterprise resource planning somehow; for example, consider labor management and human resources management.

3.5.3 Current Automation and Business IT Initiatives

We see better and better integration of production systems with enterprise resource planning systems as the current trend in information technology in manufacturing enterprises. It is fair to characterize this issue also as targeted integration of production processes and business processes. Actually, it is a bit odd, because from a conceptual viewpoint production processes are no different from business processes, on the contrary, they are business processes. However, it is common to use the term business process rather for administrative business processes, i.e., such processes that deal with enterprise resource planning, and therefore to distinguish them from the technical production processes.

In the following we use also the term automation and business integration for the integration of production systems with enterprise resource planning systems and even beyond with the integration of business intelligence (BI) systems.

Current initiatives like MESA and ISA (Instrumentation, Systems and Automation Society) address this vertical system integration issue. STEP (Standard of Product Model Data) [180] standardizes the description of both physical and functional aspects of products. ISO 15531 (MANDATE) [184, 66] provides a conceptual data model for manufacturing resources, manufacturing engineering data, and manufacturing control data. Both STEP and ISO 15531 are examples of standards that pursue a data-oriented viewpoint on the manufacturing scenario. As depicted in Fig. 3.4 ISA [314] addresses the standardization of models and terminology of batch processing at the automation level with ISA-88 [170] and the standardization of the information exchange between manufacturing execution and enterprise resource systems with ISA-95 [171, 172], see also [179]. In ISA-95 uses further terminology, in particular it uses 'Manufacturing Operations & Control' for the level of manufacturing execution systems and 'Business Planning & Logistics' for the level of enterprise resource planning.

The current trend of production and business process integration again has the objective to eventually lead to more overall flexibility and reactiveness of the enterprise. The features of a manufacturing execution system add benefit even if they do not lead to a measurable impact on reactiveness of the manufacturing enterprise. A manufacturing execution system can improve performance by speeding up the information flow between management and production and by optimizing the utilization of resources. By its data acquisition and reporting capabilities it can help to improve product quality. Anyhow, a foreseen improved reactiveness of the manufacturing enterprise is a major driving force for better integrated manufacturing execution systems. Major vendors make this argument in their current manufacturing IT initiatives like SAP with adaptive manufacturing [310]. At the technological level SAP's adaptive manufacturing initiative stands for the standardization of interfaces for third-party software vendors to SAP's own enterprise resource planning systems. At the strategic level SAP's adaptive manufacturing argues with an envisioned adaptivity of the manufacturing enterprise.

3.5.4 Industrial Information Integration Backbone

Current initiatives for automation and business integration take the situation of separate automation systems, manufacturing execution systems and enterprise resource planning systems as given and concentrate onto the clarification of the roles and responsibilities of these systems and the interfaces between these systems. This is a classical way of proceeding that we usually see in system integration trends. Certain classes of systems evolve and manifest themselves, then integration is about easing and standardizing the information flows between these systems. It is always worth considering more radical integration that creates a new class of system from scratch that unifies the systems that need to be integrated. In the case of automation and business integration we think it is interesting to think about the design of combined manufacturing execution and enterprise resource planning systems this way accomplishing integration from the outset. In such a system the different functionalities can remain software modules or software layers, however, they are integrated via a shared data model and database for which we coin the term industrial information integration backbone (IIIB) – see Fig. 3.5.

Arguments for Separation of Automation and Business Systems

There are also reasons to stick with the currently architecture of separate systems for manufacturing and enterprise resource planning. These are the usual reasons. One is the protection of investment with respect to exiting systems. Another is a make-or-buy decision in favor of buying available products and integrating them instead of building the whole system from scratch. Both enterprise resource planning systems and manufacturing execution systems are complex. Already for each class of system it must be carefully analyzed in a given scenario whether it is cheaper in the sense of total cost of ownership – see Sect. 2.6.3 – to deploy an existing commercial-off-the-shelf software system or to build an entirely new one. And these systems are so complex that there are specialized vendors for each of them – we already mentioned SAP's adaptive manufacturing approach to integrate manufacturing execution systems by third party vendors. Another reason is the desire to address different levels of quality of service of different applications with appropriate organizational structures along distributed application servers. For example, consider availability. Enterprise resource planning systems might not require high availability in an enterprise, whereas the availability of manufacturing execution systems – at least the availability of shop floor control systems – is easily a mission-critical issue. Similarly, there is often what we call an ownership issue or self-sustainment issue, i.e., the fact that different IT systems are built and maintained along the organizational structure of an enterprise driven by departments that sometimes long for as much independency from other business units as possible.

A further counter argument is simply that the functionalities of a manufacturing execution and enterprise resource planning system is simply too extensive to be delivered by a single vendor. In particular, the argument is that there must be specialization of the systems to meet different needs of different enterprises that stem, e.g., from vertical domains or the concrete sizes of the enterprises. Obviously, in the indicated field there must be doubt that it is possible to build a system that can fulfill the needs of all the diverse manufacturers – the no one-fits-all problem. All this is a sub industry argument. At least it could be the argument that because of the large amount of functionality it is desired to build the optimal solution in a concrete scenario by combining it from different software vendors. With respect to this counter argument it is interesting to see that ORACLE outlined in [309] its general product direction for manufacturing execution systems towards a single combined ERP/MES application. Actually, in April 2007 Oracle released the Oracle Manufacturing Execution System as part of its E-Business Suite, which is an enterprise resource planning system. The solution has been announced as a product for enterprises that operate in environments of low to medium complexity.

Arguments for Integration of Automation and Business Systems

All of the above are counter arguments against the concept of an industrial information integration backbone approach. However, there is a single but very strong argument for the architecture to integrate manufacturing and business IT via the database from the outset and this is flexibility. It is just the principle of data independency, i.e., the principle of centrally designing, operating and maintaining the data independent from the applications that exploit them, that improves flexibility of the total information system.

In general, having a database as a central hub for integration is a proven pattern as is already inherent in the currently widely discussed service-oriented architecture and explicitly seen in enterprise service bus technology. In the original enterprise computing related strand of service-oriented architecture – see Sect. 8.2 for a discussion and Fig. 8.2 in particular – the services in service-oriented architecture form a hub in a hub-and-spoke architecture of applications that this way are integrated and use each other in a flexible manner. It is not essential that the services tier in a service-oriented architecture possesses its own database, i.e., in principle the service tier can be a mere message generator collecting data from the applications it integrates on the fly and distributing them. However, it is a typical technical pattern that the service tier has its own database to persistently buffer data. This is where the service tier begins to become an enterprise service bus which is also discussed in Sect. 8.4. The notion of enterprise service bus is a loose concept for enterprise application integration that combines persistent messaging, in particular, publisher-subscribe functionality, with new features like content-based routing in the realm of web services technology, i.e., enterprise service busses are the web-services related instances of message-oriented middleware. And indeed, established persistent messaging technologies like IBM MQSeries [350] are in their own right examples of technology for integration of applications via a database. However, it is fair to say that the driving force for the exploitation of persistent messaging was not step-wise enterprise application integration but building lightweight but at the same time still robust alternatives to distributed transactions in transaction processing systems that are distributed on a geographical scale.

The counter arguments against the integration backbone discussed earlier are pragmatic reasons that pay tribute to existing system architectures that evolved. The standardization of message flow between applications makes the market for these applications more agile by bringing flexibility into the decision-making of customers in selecting a concrete product, but it does not address the flexibility of the systems themselves fundamentally.

Like any other approach to design a unified automation and business IT product the industrial information integration backbone does not address the aforementioned no one-fits-all problem. However, the integration backbone is an architectural principle. Not all systems are bought because of careful build-or-buy decisions. So, if a system is built, for example, for an enterprise in a special vertical domain, the integration backbone can be a design option. We just say that in such cases the design efforts should not be automatically directed and possibly misled by the existing and emerging industrial integration standards, because those standards arose to improve the message flows between applications in de-facto scenarios of manufacturing enterprises. They should not be taken without review of blueprints for building a system from scratch.

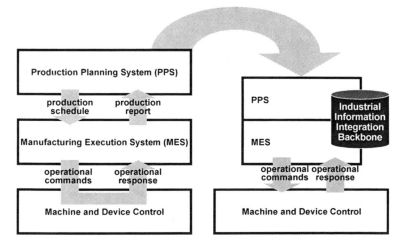

Fig. 3.5. Industrial information integration backbone.

The discussion of whether using a message-based approach or a data-based approach to the integration of manufacturing execution systems and production planning systems is an instance of a general discussion of distributed versus centralized systems. The aggregated driving force of such discussions has to be total cost of ownership – see Sect. 2.6.3. Concrete typical driving forces in such general discussion can be price, performance and reliability [140]. However, it is not clear from the outset which architecture is cost optimal in a concrete situation. For example, the robustness of a distributed system built from low cost components can be better than the robustness of a centralized system built from high cost components [228]. As long as the community lacks a constructive cost model on the basis of standardized software system components, software architecture will remain heuristics-based.

3.6 Integration of Business Processes and Business Intelligence

So far, we have discussed in Sect. 3.5 the integration of manufacturing execution systems and enterprise resource planning systems. A similar architectural discussion arises when looking at the integration of enterprise resource planning and business intelligence. Beyond the already state-of-the art point-of-sales analyses their is an ongoing trend in systematic business activity monitoring (BAM) [117, 236]. The standard architecture enabling analytical processing in today's enterprises has separated online transaction processing (OLTP) and online analytical processing (OLAP) systems. These systems are really separated, i.e., they consist of software that resides on different servers. Between these systems there is yet another system, often also on a separate server, that is responsible for the extraction of data from the transaction system, the transformation of the data into formats that are suitable for analytical processing and the transportation – called load – of the data into the analytical system. This latter man-in-the-middle system is called ETL layer (extraction, transformation, load). Conceptually the point is that there are two kinds of system, i.e., systems that are there for daily operations in the enterprise and systems that are there for analyzing the outcome of these daily operations and – with the current trend of business activity monitoring – also for observing the daily operations themselves. In practice, you can find also systems that combine the three layers onto one server, but these systems are then ad-hoc solutions in small, uncomplex business environments. If the layers are run on a single server in practice this is not about creating an innovative data warehousing architecture like the one we are discussing in the sequel but just about exploiting available business intelligence products on a simple server infrastructure wherever possible for occasional analyses. However, what we are talking about here is systematic analytical processing on a large scale, so ad-hoc architectural alternatives are not of interest here.

In the discussion of data warehousing architecture the term analytical processing fits the intention of these systems, whereas, at a first sight, the term transaction processing may seem to be a bit odd for the systems that support daily operations. It seems odd, because one connects the term transaction with technical concepts like ACID transactions or transaction monitors. Even in this sense, the usage of the word transaction processing system for systems that support daily operations is a good fit, because it is correct that the technical notion of transaction is dominant in these systems. Anyhow, the term transaction processing is quite good, because it can be understood as hinting not to technical concepts but the ephemeral nature of data emerging and disappearing in IT systems that support daily operations – we will have closer look onto this topic in due course.

Again it is compelling – both from a scientific viewpoint but also from an innovative product viewpoint – to think about a radically different system architecture that integrates the systems under consideration from scratch. In such architecture the schemas that form the basis for transactional processing – called transactional schemas for short in the following – and the schemas that form the basis for analytical processing – similarly called analytical schemas – reside in the same integrating database. In such an architecture the analytical schemas are views on the transactional schemas and the definitions of the view update mechanisms correspond to the ETL layer of current data warehousing (DW) architectures. The architectural notion of integrating via the database in this case pays tribute to the increasing hunger for more and more data extraction and shorter and shorter update cycles for the analytical data [44]. The significantly shortening of the extraction and transformation times in concrete data warehousing architectures is one of two aspects of the current active data warehousing (ADW) trend, which is an issue both in industry [149] and academia [257]. The other aspect of active data warehousing is about closing [343] the loop between analytical and transactional systems, i.e., feeding back information from analysis to operations automatically and exploiting analytical data in rules that control business logic and business processes in IT for daily operations. The closed loop aspect of active data warehousing is another argument to consider the integration backbone approach. Together with the foreseen need to exchange information between transactional and analytical systems eventually in real-time it actually leads somehow naturally to this approach.

3.6.1 The Origin of Today's Data Warehousing Architecture

As with most ubiquitous system architectures there are two kinds of reason why data warehousing architectures today look the way they are. The first kind of reasons is about how the systems emerged; the second kind of reasons has to do with concrete pragmatic issues of system operations. Both kinds of reasons are mutually dependent. With respect to the first, i.e., the evolution of today's data warehousing architecture it has to be understood first that there have always been different kinds of let us say functionality groups of enterprise information systems and different kinds of data. Let us approach this by taking a data-centric viewpoint.

Classically, it is usual to distinguish between master data, transaction data and inventory data. Today there is actually one more kind of data, i.e., analytical data and that is the point as we will discuss later. As you will see, the distinction between the classes of data is fuzzy and with time the boarders between them diminishes more and more. The master data of an enterprise are those data that must be available for usage by many applications over a long period of time. They are updated seldom and therefore they are also sometimes called fixed data or basic data. Typical examples of master data are customer data, supplier data, article data or personnel data. Transaction data are permanently new arising data. They are captured during the execution of daily business processes. Examples of transaction data are accounting transactions, reservations, purchase orders, bills, receipts. The life time of transaction data is limited from the outset. However, often you can find them consolidated and aggregated as analytical data in data warehouses. Transaction data are exploited in that they impact the update of inventory data. The inventory data represent the business figures; they originate from the accumulation of transaction data. Like master data, inventory data are stored for a long period of time. Typical examples of inventory data are account balances, business volumes and goods in stock. This means that the notion of inventory data is more comprehensive than inventory data in the narrow sense, i.e., data about goods in stock – it is accumulated data about all the goods and values in the enterprise. In some commercial-off-the-shelf enterprise applications you will find a more coarse-grained distinction between master data and transaction data only – the inventory data are then usually subsumed under master data. However, it is actually the existence of inventory data in transaction processing systems that interests us here, because its consideration is very instructive in the discussion of data warehousing architecture.

The question is why the different kind of data are distinguished by their typical duration. Why not just store all transaction data forever? One answer lies in technical limitations. Storing all transaction data means maintaining a log of the enterprise life stream [101] and this is just too much data to be stored. However, with more and more computing server power available – see the results of the benchmarks by the Transaction Processing Council (TPC), e.g. [345, 346], and Storage Performance Council (SPC) – the argument becomes weaker. For example, for years the retailer Wal-Mart stores data about each shopping cart, i.e., sales figures and data about the products sold within one customer transaction, in its data warehouse [355] — have a first look at Fig. 3.6 – resulting into a data volume of 600 tera bytes in 2006 [14]. Other reasons for not storing all transaction data can be found in the topic of data protection and here, in particular, in a need for adherence to law regulations. Actually, with respect to this issue also the converse is true. Currently, we see a trend towards systematic business transparency – think of Sarbanes-Oxley

Act (SOX) [34] and Basel II. A lot of enterprise are currently challenged with implementing crosscutting data auditing [258, 214] mechanisms that ideally record all data messages exchanged in the enterprise IT for later analysis.

Along the lines of the different kind of data just discussed there have always been different kinds of functionality in enterprise applications. The first one is about gathering data from daily operations and processing them. The reports that are generated in this operations mode are usually lightweight and they serve only to enable daily operations and transactions. The reports are not there for business analysis. The second kind of functionality is about generating complex reports on the basis of inventory data. These reports are needed in controlling and planning. This means that reports for decision support could always be found in enterprise applications. Over the time the potential for systematic multi-dimensional transformation of the transaction data for supporting decision support has been recognized. Also data mining with its algorithms to discover correlations and dependencies between stochastic variables entered the scene. Dedicated decision support systems were built, data marts that deal with chunks of enterprise data to address particular required analyses and also holistic data warehouses.

It is a usual phenomenon that enterprise IT systems grow to system landscapes, because new needed functionality are not introduced as new features of existing applications but introduced as additional software and server systems. So is in the area of analytical data. With the need for a new generation of analytical capabilities new supplementing decision support systems were introduced. The organizational pattern behind this is to never touch a running system. Analytical processing is technically cost intensive, i.e., it longs for significant extra server computing power. In the aforementioned analytical processing example of Wal-Mart a 1000 node massively parallel computer by NCR/Teradata was used in 2006 to deal with the 600 tera byte analytical data. The Wal-Mart example is an extreme example of a high-end data warehousing solution – indeed, it is fair to say that Wal-Mart has been the outrider for data warehousing. However, the example gives an impression of the relative cost-intensiveness of analytical processing. Still it is not possible for small and medium enterprises to buy high-end data warehousing solutions. A new solution must allow for precise determining the risk of burdening an existing IT infrastructure, which is responsible for supporting daily operations with a robust quality of service, with extra load for cost-intensive analytical queries. Therefore, it is the correct architecture to build a separate system for this solution that is allowed to connect the existing system only occasionally and for limited durations, typically in times where the transactional system is known to be rather unused – during the night for example.

3.6.2 Marrying Transactional and Analytical Schemas

Unifying transactional schemas and analytical schemas into a single database server holds the potential for an unseen degree of connection between trans-

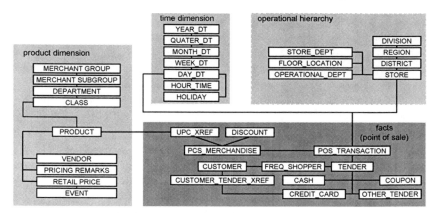

Fig. 3.6. Cut-out of the Wal-Mart data warehouse schema.

actional and analytical processing – with respect to speed, maintainability and possible utilization. This is not about throwing together existing products onto the same server. It is about making transactional and analytical schemas the unified basis for both transactional and analytical applications, again in the sense of data independency. Transactional schemas and analytical schemas are just regions of a whole database schema in such a solution. Programs that transform and transport data between these regions replace current ETL layers and these programs are just further applications that access and manipulate the data in the sense of data independency. Here, in principle, it does not matter whether these transforming programs reside on a separate application server or on the database server itself, however, it is very likely that they will be placed onto the database server exploiting active database features.

Application Separability

The problem with each combined transactional and analytical solution is that it must support what we call separability or application separability. Separability is the possibility to guarantee the robustness or quality of service of one application independent from the influence of other applications in a system of applications. For example, operating system processes are a concrete mechanism that target separability. In multi-tier system architectures separability becomes a subtle issue. The classical tiered data warehousing architecture naturally supports quite strong separability, because the systems are actually separated. The connection between the systems is limited to the times the ETL layer reads from the transactional systems. ETL layer products support the maintenance of this connection by providing means to schedule the extraction. For the separability of the envisioned architecture database management system features are necessary that allow for an advanced prioritization of the database tables and the threads accessing these tables along the lines of a mature access model. Actually, commercial database products offer such advanced features.

As a proof of concept, a first step in the direction of fully integrated transactional and analytical processing could be undertaken by running existing database, ETL layer and data warehousing products in separated capsules of an appropriate virtualization software or of an operating system that natively supports virtualization like i5/OS with its hypervisor. Such an approach yields separability, however, in the beginning there is obviously no advantage in terms of tighter interweaving of transactional and analytical processing. However, once the system is running on the same machine it can be seen as whole and it can be patched in a very targeted way to try out potential speed ups of the extraction and load processes. Technically, such an attempt is only possible if the system is a complete white box to the experimenting developers. So, natural candidates in such an attempt are open-source products for the data warehousing technology, e.g., Mondrian (Pentaho analysis services), for the database technology and, in particular, for the virtualization software, e.g., Xen [78].

Completely Crosscutting Information Backbone

Systems evolve. New systems with new functionality are added while the impact and value of these systems can not be really estimated at the time of their introduction. From time to time it can be fruitful to analyze for a certain kind of enterprise functionality whether the driving forces on the problem side and the existing architectural patterns on the solution side are fully understood. If some stage of maturity is reached it is time to think about systematically designing a unifying architecture from scratch.

In Sect.3.5 we have discussed the integration of manufacturing exececution systems with enterprise resource planning systems via the database, in this section we have discussed the integration of enterprise resource planning systems with analytical processing via the database. This eventually leads to an extension of the industrial integration backbone so that it spawns all the different kinds of applications discussed [114]. We have visualized the resulting architecture once more in Fig. 3.7.

Once such a database backbone is created, in particular, with the unification of transactional and analytical schemas, it would be possible to think about thoroughly applying multidimensional schema design over all levels of data in the functionality stack. Today, it is state-of-the art to exploit multi-dimensional schema design for point-of-sales analysis, see the Wal-Mart database schema in Fig. 3.6. It is possible to ask what has been sold, when, where, why, by whom, to whom, why? The analytical power lies in the opportunities to drill down and roll up the dimensions of this question. With respect to activity monitoring exploiting multidimensional schema design [236] means to pose similar question about who did what, when, why, with which resources, results, performance etc.? Imagine the analytical potential in combining this with the data from the production process, eventually leading to an IT system integration from the top floor to the shop floor.

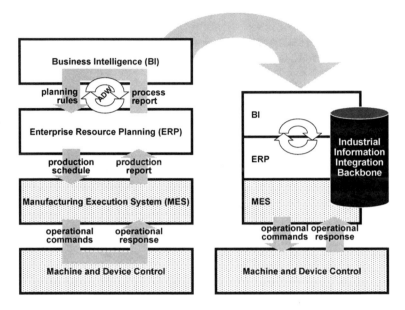

Fig. 3.7. Completely crosscutting information backbone.

Information Backbone Compared to Data Mart Architecture

In Sect. 3.5.4 we conducted a discussion about the arguments for the integration versus arguments for the separation of automation and business systems. This discussion was conducted against the background of enterprise resource planning systems and manufacturing systems. It is instructive to repeat this discussion here with the viewpoint of analytical processing of manufacturing data. The analytical processing systems in Fig. 3.7 form a business intelligence layer that is placed on top of the enterprise resource planning systems layer. Actually, there exists also analytical processing that directly gets its data from the manufacturing systems. Unlike business intelligence such analytical processing is typically not there for supporting strategic planning and decision support but for supervising and improving the production processes. Analyses like those found in six sigma projects – see Sect. 2.4.2 – would be typical. If such systems are also integrated via the information backbone approach this would result into an architecture depicted in Fig. 3.8. We have already mentioned in Sect. 3.5.4 that the information integration backbone architecture is a hub-and-spoke architecture and this aspect is visualized better in Fig. 3.8 than in Fig. 3.7.

Analytical processing in order to improve the quality of a production process means mining production data. It is very typical that the data necessary for a concrete data analysis are stored in a dedicated data mart. This way a landscape of data marts grows with one data mart for each kind of analysis. A practitioner's argument against a centralized database approach that replaces the data mart landscape is a performance argument. It is said that bringing back the analysis data into the production databases would unacceptably slow down this production database. An analysis is made of complex algorithms and queries against a data mart and a complex query that gather data from production databases. If it is possible to do several analyses on some extracted data it is reasonable with respect to performance to separate the extraction efforts from the analyses efforts. With a data mart landscape approach such a separation is enforced by system architecture. But the fact that a concrete system architecture enforces an architectural principle is not a strong argument for this system architecture. It is also possible to rebuild the data mart schemas in a central production database with the same performance benefits – off-loading in the shell so to speak. The data marts are then realized as non-updatable views, i.e., as materialized queries. It is often an option to save computing time by pre-computing results or manifesting part computations as reusable data – think of all the several kinds of indexes for information retrieval, for example.

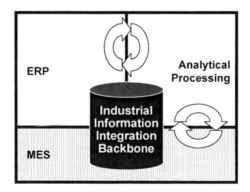

Fig. 3.8. Direct analytical processing for manufacturing data.

Nevertheless, it also has to be said that on the basis of current technology the integration approach really does not have to be the optimal one in terms of total cost of ownership. Bringing back data mart as a schema into the central database can lead to extra costs if the central database only scales up relatively expensive. If the data mart is, for example, relatively small and does not require the same service level agreement, it can easily be that the realization with an extra commodity server is the best price option. Furthermore, there might be provisos against integrating the data marts into the central production database by the production database owners. In a concrete case the dedicated data mart server solution is usually just the standard one in the sense that it effects the overall systems operations and is easier to estimate. Again, these counter-arguments against an information backbone approach must be traded off against its significantly improved conceptual maintainability and flexibility. It remains a research issue here to establish a system of quantifiable driving forces onto the selection of the costs and risks of the optimal information system architecture.

4

Semantics of Business Process Models

This chapter is about business process models, their semantics and their non-formality. It is about business process modeling and its non-formality. The semantics of business process models is an important topic, because there is a gap between business process modeling and executable workflow specification. Basically, there are three overlapping problem areas that lead to this gap:

- Non-formality of business process modeling languages.
- Unawareness of technical business process complexity in business process modeling languages.
- System design orientation of workflow technologies.

The semantics of business process modeling languages are non-formal. The subject that they describe, i.e., business processes with all their aspects is, in general, not amenable for formalization. And even if certain aspects of business process can be formalized, the activity of business process modeling in enterprises is non-formal. The non-formality of business process modeling is justified. Business process modeling is a form of system analysis, it can serve as an 'as is'-analysis or a 'to be'-analysis of the enterprise. System analysts want to invest only as much as effort into their activity as is necessary to fulfill the objective of system analysis. Sometimes, only an understanding of crucial aspects of the business processes is needed at some relatively high level of detail.

Business processes are supported by information technology. However, business processes are different form the IT systems that support them. IT systems have a technical complexity that is often not relevant for an understanding of business processes. Sometimes, technological opportunities and technical details that could be important in the definition of business processes are overlooked, because, in general, the technical level is not important from a business process modeling viewpoint. This means that the unawareness of technical business process complexity in business process modeling languages can be considered as intended, but it can harm. In any case it means that

D. Draheim, *Business Process Technology: A Unified View on Business Processes, Workflows and Enterprise Applications*, DOI 10.1007/978-3-642-01588-5_4,
© Springer-Verlag Berlin Heidelberg 2010

there remains a gap between the business process modeling and IT system specification. This gap becomes more comprehensible if workflow technology is considered. Concrete workflow technology products follow a concrete design metaphor, which is either a concrete groupware approach or a concrete enterprise application integration approach. With respect to formality, the workflow definition languages that are used in workflow definition tools of concrete workflow technologies are different to business process modeling languages in general. Workflow definitions are also a form of business process specifications but through their interpretation by a concrete technology they have a formal semantics, which is an executable semantics.

In this chapter we will look at the ambiguities of business process models that arise in practice in today's business process modeling projects. Sometimes, concrete business process modeling languages and methodologies come along with a formal flavor by giving definitions of their modeling elements that sound very strict, systematic and consistent – formal. However, a closer look at the definitions sometimes shows that they are not as formal as they appear. A formal appearance of a definition is not enough if it lacks a formal basis or context in which the definition can be interpreted. Furthermore, at a closer look you may encounter that useful business process models do not adhere to the defined semantics of the used business process modeling languages. Sometimes it is simply not possible to be consistent with the definition of a concrete modeling element even in small examples. Natural language with all its ambiguities is an appropriate tool to describe business processes. Business process modeling languages are used to support natural language descriptions, not vice versa. Business process modeling languages visualize business processes. Visualizations of complex issues are central in good documentations of systems and so are business process models. However, business process models alone are not sufficient to describe business processes at the needed level.

The chapter wants to develop problem awareness about the non-formality of business process modeling languages. It wants to develop problem awareness about pitfalls of increasing and decreasing the formality of business process modeling languages. It does so by clarifying important example ambiguities of business process modeling language. Therefore, we will look at the specification of goods and information in Sect. 4.2 and the usage events in business process models in Sect. 4.4. Throughout the chapter we encourage to distinguish between a global supervisory viewpoint and local working viewpoint on business processes. Against this background we discuss the several intentions of business process modeling. In order to deepen our understanding about the semantics of business process models we have also to discuss distinctions to the semantics of workflow definition languages. The semantics of workflow definition is also discussed in Sect. 7.1 by a characterization of the interaction of users with workflow management technology and an explanation of the worklist paradigm.

This chapter is about semantics of business process modeling languages. Semantics is about languages. Semantics is about talking about languages. In the chapter you will find lengthy discussions about the meaning of terminology like the discussion of differences between business processes and workflows. Such discussions are of practical importance, because system analysis in general and business process modeling in particular are about communicating about systems; they are about talking about systems. The discussion in this chapter may help in preventing and clarifying common misunderstandings and language pitfalls in business process management projects.

4.1 Global and Local Views on Business Processes

There are different kinds of views on business processes. A basic difference is whether you are involved in the definition of a business process as a business process modeler or business process designer with the need to oversee nets of activities as a whole or in the execution of a business process as a worker where it is in principle sufficient to have knowledge about single activities.

Without further explanation the term business process and the term workflow could be considered as synonyms. A business process is a well-understood interplay of activities that targets a certain business objective. A workflow can be considered as having exactly the same meaning. In practice, the two terms are actually often used synonymously. Sometimes, you might prefer to use the term workflow in situations where you rather want to discuss the interplay of work activities mechanically or schematically without a focus on the workflows' business value. In the workflow technology community as presented by the Workflow Management Coalition (WfMC) [356] there is a clean distinction between business processes and workflows. As just defined, a business process is a net of activities that together achieve a business goal. A workflow is an automation of a business process. We have cited the original definitions of the Workflow Management Coalition in Sect. 9.1.1.

The definition of workflow as given by the Workflow Management Coalition needs some remarks. Firstly, a workflow as considered by the workflow technology community not necessarily an automation of a business process in the true sense of the word. In enterprises you can find software processes and system dialogues in IT systems that support business processes to achieve their goal. These software processes and system dialogues are then also called workflows and actually they are of major interest for us. These workflows do not substitute the business processes that they support, they coexist with the business processes they support. A system dialogue that shows a report to an employee must not be confused with the activity that is executed by the employee. Even fully-automatic processes usually only add value in the sense of accompanying other business processes that involve activities executed by humans. Furthermore, many processes that are considered fully-automatic must be accompanied by activities that are executed by humans, for example, activities of controlling or supervision. There is also the option that a business process is completely substituted by its automation, but this case is not the main case studied by the workflow technology community.

Secondly, the workflow management community has an even more narrow meaning about what a workflow is than one might guess from the definition given by the Workflow Management Coalition, i.e., the implementation of a software process or system dialogue on the basis of a concrete workflow management system as defined by the Workflow Management Coalition, i.e., an interpretation of a workflow definition by an appropriate workflow technology product and its exploitation to control the flow of information or to orchestrate other IT applications.

In this book we try to use the term workflow consistently for software processes and system dialogues that support business processes. Moreover, we usually use it for those workflows that are defined for the interpretation by a workflow management technology. Furthermore, our main focus is human workflow. In the upcoming examples workers are attached to the activities of the workflows. Nevertheless, it can be that an activity with an attached worker runs full-automatically and that the person assigned to it only has an accompanying role rather than an activity-driving role. Anyway, we are mainly interested in the human-computer interaction necessary for the functioning of the workflow. The automatic control of some automatic processes is also important. Here, workflow definition can be seen as a high-level programming paradigm. In principle, if a human is also just considered as an entity transforming items a generalized view on human workflow and automatic workflow is possible immediately. However, for the moment we stay with the notion of human workflow. We explain our usage of the term business process and the term workflow once more in Sect. 9.1.2.

We have said that we try to use the term workflow consistently for software processes and system dialogues that support business processes. Sometimes we deliberately do not so. For example, in Sect. 7.1.1 we talk about a process instantiation menu for a menu that gives the user of a workflow management system the opportunity to start new instances of processes. The name process instantiation menu is natural, because the workflow that is started is there for supporting a business process. Also the usage of the terms process and business process for a workflow are natural in this context. The user of a workflow is not interested too much in the distinction between business processes and workflows. The distinction is rather in the realm of professional jargon or technical terminology. Once more, we want to point out that today's workflow management technologies are sold as so-called business process management suites. And even the Workflow Management Coalition who distinguishes between business processes in general and workflows as their automation uses the term process definition for the workflow definition in their workflow reference model – see Fig. 4.3.

In practice, the distinction between business process and workflow vanishes. For example, former workflow technology products today ship as business process management suites. It is always possible to identify the core functionality of business process management suites that deals with the enactment and control of automated workflow activities as workflow technology. However, the word workflow in itself does not require fully automated activity control.

4.1.1 Business Process Definition

This section is about business process definition. Business process design, business process modeling and business process specification are used as synonyms for business process specification in this book. Business process definition stands for the activity of defining a business process as well as for the artifact that results from this activity. The same is for business process design. In practice, the terms business process definition, design, modeling and specification are also almost synonymous. You might want to use the term business process design if you want to stress the creative aspect of the activity. You might want to use the term business process specification if you want to express that a business process definition is distinguished by an extra degree of formality.

Business process definitions and workflow definitions are both given as nets of activities. Business process definitions and workflow definitions even look the same. For example, the workflow definitions created with a workflow definition tool of a workflow management product look like business process models painted with a business process analysis tool. Business process definitions are the result of the activity of business process definition, i.e., in terms of business process management lifecycles like the ones shown in Figs. 2.6 and 2.7 they stem from the business process definition phase. Workflow definitions are the result of creating them with a workflow definition tool. It is fair to say that workflow definition rather belongs to the implementation of business processes and therefore it could be said that workflow definition rather belongs already to the business process execution phase or 'doing'-phase of business process lifecycles.

Nevertheless, many things that can be said about business process definitions can be applied also to workflow definitions. The aspect of business process supervisory discussed in a general manner in Sect. 4.1.2 is such an aspect, but also certain aspects of decomposition, visualization or simulation. With respect to these general aspects workflows can be considered a specialization of business processes.

Figure 4.1 shows the definition of a business process, i.e., a business process model. It is a visual definition that is oriented towards BPMN (Business Process Modeling Notation) [265]. A business process definition is a blueprint or template for concrete business process instances. In this section we only consider the most basic human resource mechanism, i.e., a single worker can be assigned to an activity. More sophisticated role-based mechanisms that can be found in commercial tools will be discussed in Sect. 7.2. A business process definition can be seen as the static description of business processes, whereas the execution of a business process is coined a business process instance. The workflow management community also uses the terms build time and run time of workflows [164]. We will discuss the relationship between business process definitions and business process instances in more depth in due course.

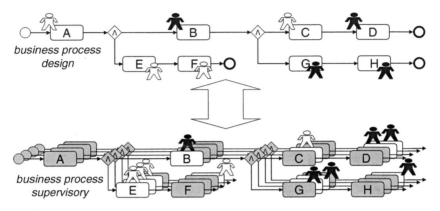

Fig. 4.1. Business process definition and business process supervisory.

Figure 4.1 shows some business process instances below the business process definition. In Fig. 4.1 we use the same notation for the visualization of business process instances as for business process definitions with the only difference that entities, i.e., events, activities, and connectors, are grayed. White color is reserved for those activities that are currently active. In general, there is a manifold of business process instances running. The visualization of the business process instances in Fig. 4.1 represents one point in time of the business process executing system. The current state of a business process executing system can be understood as the set of currently active activity instances. The complete state of a business process executing system consists also of the state of all processed resources.

4.1.2 Business Process Supervisory

Business process instances are subject to business process supervisory. We use the rather artificial term business process supervisory here for the global view on the running business process instances. Operationally, business process supervisory can be thought as consisting of business process control and business process monitoring. But the crucial point here is that the viewpoint of business process supervisory is a global one. There is also another more local viewpoint on the business processes and this is the viewpoint of workers. The global viewpoint of all business process instances is actually interchangeable with the viewpoint of business process design. One is tempted to believe, that, in principle, the business process designer could concentrate on the single business process instance in defining a concrete business process. A business process is just a systematic, i.e., repeatable, means to transform information and goods by activities and with resources so that a business value is created. So, a business process has its interfaces to other business processes in the enterprise, in particular, it is triggered by events stemming from other business processes and therefore the context of a business process must be considered in its design. But despite this interdependency with other business processes, a business process designer could define a business process by only considering a single instance of it. However, this is, at most, only true as long as only functionality of a business process is considered. If business process design is about optimizing the performance of how things are done, a global consideration of all business process instances is necessary in order to fully exploit possible parallelism – see Sect. 2.2.3 on parallelism of business processes.

What interests us here is the point that there are also possible local viewpoints on the business processes, i.e., viewpoints on single business processes and single activities that can forget partly or completely about the context of these entities. Consider a single worker who is responsible for executing activities of a business process. Depending on the concrete business process control that is established, he must be aware to a certain degree of other activities and their sequencing in the business process beyond the activity he is currently executing. Let us assume for a moment an office or plant without any business process automation, in particular, without any IT support for the control of the business processes. Also in this case the business process activities should be coordinated and executed according to the existing business process definitions. Furthermore, as a thought experiment, let us assume that there is no central authority for controlling the correct execution of the business processes. Then, every worker has to be informed about the sequencing of the activities he is responsible for. Furthermore, he also needs to know the workers that are responsible for activities that need to be triggered after activities in his own sub business processes. This is all a worker needs to know to execute his sub business processes. If he has finished an activity he informs the worker of each activity that needs to be triggered. He can do this by calling this person, sending him an email, passing a document, passing goods, tipping on his shoulder or whatsoever. If every worker acts like this all the defined business processes are executed correctly. The business process control works as a distributed game even without a central control authority. Beyond the described knowledge a worker does not to be informed about the sub business processes executed by others. He has a more local view than the business process designer.

Now, if there is a central authority to control the business processes the viewpoint of the single worker can even be more local. At the extreme, the worker does not have to now anything about the dependencies between the single business process activities and he also does not have to know anything about other workers responsible for other activities. The worker is simply notified by the central business process control authority to perform a certain activity and has the duty to report to the authority after he has finished the activity. It is then the responsibility of the business process control authority to trigger all workers according to the business process definition and to route somehow the necessary items – information or goods – between them. Now, the viewpoint of the single worker has become completely local. Of course, with respect to his own activities he will learn about their dependencies by working on them. But he sometimes obviously does not have to do so. An extreme example is the assembly line. Here the worker is highly specialized and may have the responsibility for a single activity only. At the extreme, he does not need to now anything about the functionality of the overall business process and even not the role of his work in it. The assembly line is already an example for automation of the central business process authority.

In practice, you will often find a mixture of automatic, semi-automatic and non-automatic business process control as described above.

Sometimes the appropriate way of organizing work is even not amenable to formalization as a business process being a fixed net of activities with fixed resources attached. Team work for rather complex, creative or even chaotic tasks like prototype construction or crisis management cannot be planned and structured in way it can be done for routine tasks of daily operations. Such important, complex value-adding processes in enterprises are addressed by knowledge management on the conceptual side and by enterprise content management and by certain strands of computer-supported collaborative work on the technological side. Team work is also the domain where we currently see emerging new team collaboration software or social software [116] that somehow aims at exploiting Web 2.0 [271, 207] assets and topics in the intranets of enterprises and organizations. However, let us stay with the business process paradigm and workflow paradigm here.

4.1.3 Business Process Automation

The central business process authority described above in our thought experiment can often be automated. And the workflow product paradigm as described by the Workflow Management Coalition with its workflow enactment service and worklist concept has established a concrete operational semantics for workflow definitions and the automation of workflow control. In this section we explain the interplay of the workflow instances with the workflow enactment service and the worklist in a very concrete and at the same time ad-hoc manner.

Please have a look at Figs. 4.2 and 4.3. Figure 4.2 shows a couple of business process instances in action and a workflow management system that supports these business process instances. Even more, the workflow management system realizes a workflow control for the applications it orchestrates. It therefore takes over – in parts or even completely – the role of business process control of the business process supervisory viewpoint. Figure 4.3 shows the so-called workflow reference model [164] of the Workflow Management

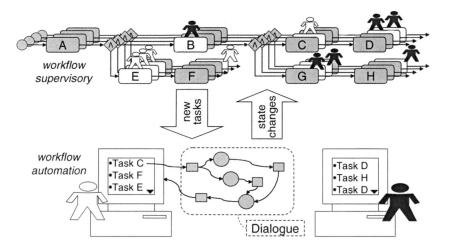

Fig. 4.2. Workflow supervisory and workflow automation.

Coalition. The workflow reference model defines the notion of workflow management system. It explains the interplay of workflow or process definitions, a workflow enactment service, the worklist and controlled applications.

Below the workflow supervisory viewpoint there is another viewpoint called workflow automation in Fig. 4.2. Let us assume that each of the activities is supported by a software application, i.e., in order to execute an activity the worker has to invoke and finish the system dialogue of a concrete application. Such a system dialogue can consist of a single report and form that must be filled out and submitted but it can also be a complex dialogue consisting of several reports, forms and case distinctions the user must step through.

Now, workflow automation means that there is a central workflow enactment service that takes over the role of a central workflow authority. The workflow enactment service keeps track of the workflow system state, i.e., it keeps track of all active activities of all active workflow instances. This workflow system state is called workflow control data in Fig. 4.3. A workflow instance is created if it is triggered by an outside event or another already existing workflow instance. If a workflow instance is created all of its first activities, i.e., the activities that are directly targeted by the start event in the workflow definition become active. If an activity becomes active it is added to the worklist of the responsible worker. For each worker such a worklist is maintained.

Assume that a worker starts a fresh session by logging into the workflow application. Fresh session means here that he has finished all activity supporting applications before closing the last session. The first thing the worker now sees is his worklist screen. For each active activity in his worklist the workflow management system possesses a hook to the application that is needed to work on that activity. So, the user can choose on which activity he would like to work on and can enter the appropriate application via the worklist screen. After the worker has finished the task and exits the system dialogue of the supporting application he is routed back automatically to his worklist screen. At the same time, the state of the workflow execution system is changed. The event of finishing an activity triggers new activities according to the workflow definition and makes them active. Furthermore, the activity the worker has been working on has been deleted from the worklist. Furthermore, new activities that have become active in the mean time are now added to the worklist screen. The described mechanism guarantees the complete and correct proceeding of all workflow instances.

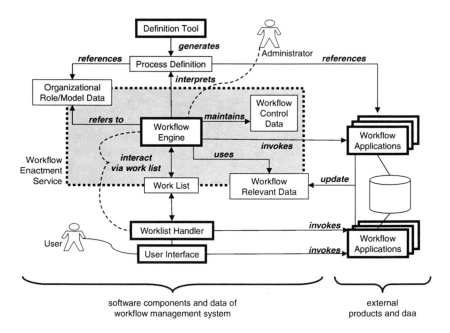

Fig. 4.3. The WfMC workflow reference model.

The worklist concept is crucial for the workflow product paradigm. However, as we will discuss later in Sect. 7.1 it is independent from concrete clients consuming it. Here, in this section we have presented it through a simple worklist screen mechanism that is characterized through the fact that the user either only sees the worklist screen consisting of exactly the application links for the activated activities or otherwise works with the application for exactly one of the active activities. More sophisticated usages of the worklist paradigm are possible. Nevertheless, the described worklist screen mechanism is actually a widespread implementation of the worklist paradigm.

4.1.4 Business Process Supervisory in the Presence of Business Process Automation

In Sect. 4.1.2 we have discussed the viewpoint of business process supervisory as a global one overseeing all business process instances and the global state of the business process executing system. This viewpoint is an important one during the business process design activity, but there is actually the task of business process supervision during the execution of the business processes. We said that business process supervisory consist of business process control and business process monitoring. As we have just discussed the basic business process control can be done automatically, however, there is still need for further business process monitoring.

In general, monitoring can be more than observing, it is usually about tracking and controlling objects. This is also the case with business process monitoring. We have discussed business process monitoring in Sect. 2.4 . Actually, in this discussion, only the observational aspect of monitoring has been mentioned. In the lifecycle of business process management depicted in Fig. 2.6 the role of the business process monitoring stage has been described as gathering data about running processes in order to exploit this data for an improved business process redefinition. However, business process monitoring and workflow monitoring is more than merely gathering information about the business processes and workflows for later purposes, it is about reacting to observed abnormal behavior of business processes. For examples, it could be observed that a certain activity is always handled too slowly by a certain person compared to some figures given in the workflow definition. Then a dedicated business processes supervisor that observes this can react by trying to identify the problem and solve it. As a more extreme example, it can perhaps be observed that some activities are actually dangling, i.e., they have not been started for a long time and have remained idle. A reason can be here that the responsible worker is ill, did not come to work but it has been forgotten to put this information into the workflow management application. Another reason could be that the responsible worker is overloaded with work. In any case the supervisor can reschedule the work items to other workers.

Actually, commercial workflow management technologies offer the means to reschedule work items, typically by authorized administrators but even by the workers themselves. Such rescheduling mechanisms usually require a more sophisticated role-based definition of human resources for tasks, because with our basic human resources mechanism used in this section rescheduling of tasks to workers would result in a redefinition of the workflow.

Dynamic Redefinition of Workflows

The workflow monitoring described is about systematically observing business processes and exploiting the gained information. This is exploited in two ways. On the one hand, it can be used to redefine the workflows; on the other hand, it can be used to make changes to running workflow instances. This means it can be used to improve the workflows at build time and to improve the workflows at run time. The distinction between changes to workflow templates and changes to workflow instances is clean in the sense that changes to single instances affect these instances only but changes to a workflow definition affect all the instances of this workflow – in the future and in principle also at the time of change.

However, the distinction between changes to build time and run time aspects is somehow artificial and depends on a feeling of which kind of changes can be done immediately or quickly. For example, the opportunity to reschedule workers dynamically emerges from loosening a fixed assignment of workers to tasks by a role-based concept which allows for a degree of freedom to reschedule dynamically. This example makes clear that the distinction between build time and run time aspects depends on the concrete design of a given workflow technology. For example, it is possible to design a workflow technology that understands the workflow definition as a template in the usual way but allows hooking alternative activities into a single workflow instance during run-time, a kind of ad-hoc redefinition of workflows so to speak.

A similar issue is addressed by the workflow technology ADEPT in the AristaFlow project [294, 296]. We said before that a change to the workflow definition affects all its instances in the future but also in principle those that are running at the time the workflow definition is changed. The latter can be particularly useful if you have long-running workflows in your system. However, such a feature is a research issue. In general, it is a non-trivial question how to adapt a running workflow instance to a workflow definition that has been changed in a way that makes sense and it is exactly this question that is addressed by the ADEPT platform.

4.1.5 Business Process Instances

Up to know we have used the notion of business process instance intuitively by saying that a business process definition is a template for business process instances. Actually, the notion of business process instance relies on a notion of decomposition of the specification of a business process executing system. The whole specification is cut into pieces which are the single business process definitions. The specification of a business process executing system can be seen as a set of business process definitions. In general one business process definition is limited by a set of start events and a set of end events. So also the definition of the whole business process specification can be seen as a single business process definition and indeed it is possible to explain its dynamics without the notion of business process instance only in terms of active activities as done before in Sect. 4.1.3. In presence of a decomposition mechanism, the specification of a business process executing system as a whole can be called the flat business process model – see Sect. 5.1.2. In Sect. 5.2.2 we will discuss the semantics of cutting a flat diagram into pieces yielding sub business process specifications.

We will delve into the topic of business process decomposition in Sect. 5. For the current explanation it is sufficient to consider a business process specification as a net of activities as usual that is limited by a set of start events and a set of end events. A concrete modeling technique may impose extra conditions with respect to start events or end events. For example, it would be usual to fix that a business process definition must not have multiple start events, or that it must not have multiple end events. If a business process definition has multiple start events or multiple end events it is a bit more difficult to understand it as a functional entity. We already described the concept of business process instance in Sect. 4.1.3 from the viewpoint of business process automation. A business process instance of a business process definition is created whenever an instance of one of the start events of the business process definition occurs. Concrete activities are triggered by this start event and become active. Activities are worked on and new activities become active on behalf of this. Conceptually, a business process instance is the evolvement of such business process state once originated by a start event in the past. At one moment in time, a business process instance is represented by its currently observable business process state. But a business process instance is more, it also has a history. Actually, a business process instance can be identified with its history, i.e., with the history of business process states following each other since an originating start event. The notion of business process instance can be formalized by the notion of an identifying business process identity or token. A new business process instance token is generated once a business process instance is created by a start event and then this token is passed to all subsequently triggered activities. All the active and past activity instances that are tagged with the same business process identifier make up a business process instance. A concept of business process instance can be further hierarchized. As we have said, the notion of business process instance itself relies on a notion of decomposition. Along the lines of a hierarchy of definitions it is also possible to understand the running business process executing system as a hierarchy of business process instances and sub business process instances.

It is instructive to say that a business process instance is a business process run. Figure 4.4 shows a business process definition and a representation of one of its business process instances. We have chosen an ad-hoc notation for the business process instance that is oriented towards the business process definition notation, i.e., activity instances and concrete events are depicted like activities and events in the business process definition with the difference that they are double-lined. Currently active activities, which make up the state of the process instance, are colored white, whereas past activities are grayed. An activity instance points back to the past activity that has triggered it. The diagram in Sect. 4.4 has no formal ambition, its mere purpose is to visualize what the concept of business process instance is about. For example, the neat tree-structure of the business process instance diagram would be lost, if some joins of control flow would occur in the business process definition. Furthermore, it cannot be decided from the diagram whether the C-activity instance occurred before or after the second B-activity instance or even after the second B-activity instance. The latter means that the diagram in Fig. 4.4 is not a complete visualization of the business process instance's history.

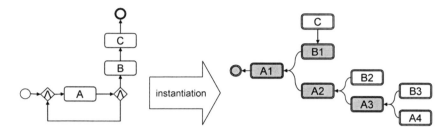

Fig. 4.4. Complex business process state resulting from business process cycle.

However, the example in Fig. 4.4 is good to show that arbitrarily complex business process states can arise, in this case because there is a loop in the business process definition. Furthermore, it is well-suited for the discussion of the semantics of end events. Basically there are two possible semantics, i.e., a preemptive and a non-preemptive one. In the preemptive semantics the process instance is ended, if an end event is reached after the execution of one of the currently active activities. This means that leaving the active C-activity in Fig. 4.4 would preempt the active A- and B-activities. The question is how such preemption is realized with respect to activity instances that are actually executed. If we are talking about workflows of a workflow management system there are two options. One option is to allow the open workflow activities to finish, the other option is to shut them down. In the latter case an appropriate rollback mechanisms must be available that supports the respective execution semantics. With non-preemptive semantics activities can only be ended via end events. A non-preemptive mechanism of end events can also be exploited for establishing an implicit synchronization. The discussion of end event semantics is not restricted to business process definitions and workflow definitions with a single end event, it immediately applies to those with multiple end events in general.

We said that conceptually a business process instance is a business process run. Technically, a business process instance can be identified by the resources attached to it. In workflow technology such resources are an operating system process or thread and global variables. From a conceptual and reductionist viewpoint the aforementioned business process token is also a resource attached to a business process. A business process instance functions as a scoping mechanism for the resources attached to it, i.e., the global state associated with a business process instance is only global with respect to the activity instances that belong to this business process instance and it is not visible to any other activity instance in the business process executing system. If a hierarchical business process instance concept is established, it becomes even clearer that business process instances have a scoping role. Similarly to routines, subroutines and nested routine calls in third generation languages nested business process and workflow definitions can be used to establish hierarchies of scopes.

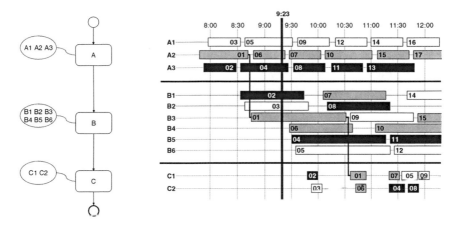

Fig. 4.5. Supervision of production process instances.

Visualization of business process instances plays a role in practice. For example, the tools and diagrams developed for project management like PERT or Gantt diagrams are rather used for planning single instances of business processes, i.e., single projects. You use and can interpret a project plan also for several instances of a project, then it becomes a project instance template and therefore a business process definition. If you use conditions or even loops in your project definition it has to be understood as a template defining a multitude of project instances, even if you plan to conduct the project only once and use conditions only in order to be prepared for different unpredictable cases. In Sect. 3.5.1 we have discussed a software system for automatic shop floor control – see Fig. 3.3. The system visualizes the flow of batches of material through processing stages in a Gantt diagram style. Actually a lot of process instances are visualized in parallel. Each process instance is identified by a unique batch number that is processed during the different stages. In Fig. 4.5 a business process definition is reconstructed from the process instances to the left. Each processing stage becomes a function in the business process definition and the processors are attached to the functions as resources. The attachment of resources is done via a role mechanism. The several processors of each stage form a set and become a role that is attached to the corresponding function. The typical semantics of such a role mechanism fits the situation, it has the meaning that one of the processors takes over the processing of an incoming batch.

4.2 Transformation of Goods and Information

The purpose of business processes is to transform goods and information. With respect to business process definitions two interesting questions arise. How are the transformations of items represented in the business process definition? Is a business process definition actually about specifying transformations of goods and information or is it only about specifying transformations of information? The second question might puzzle you. Why is it a question at all? A lot of information technologies are there for supporting material transforming processes – think of the production planning systems, manufacturing execution systems, and automation software discussed in Sect. 3.5. So a business process definition should obviously allow for the specification of transformation of goods and information. However, as we will see not all modeling language designers have considered the question and some have even explicitly designed languages for the transformation of information only. In any case, working on those questions leads us to a consideration of different possible kinds of semantics of business process definitions. But let us turn to the other question first, i.e., the question of how to represent the transformation of items in a business process. In this discussion, we take for granted the fact that business process specification encompasses both the specification of information and the specification of goods.

4.2.1 Specifying Item Flows

One way of specifying the transformation of items is on the basis of an item flow. This option is obvious, because a lot of business processes in the enterprise that are amenable to process modeling and workflow technology support are actually about passing things around from one place to another where they are processed or transformed. This applies to passing around documents in an office as well as moving around a workpiece in a shop floor. If a visual language is used the flow of items can be specified rather explicitly or rather implicitly. An explicit specification is about annotating the items somehow to the arcs connecting the activities. You can find such an explicit specification, for example, in the data flow diagrams of structured analysis that has been introduced in [300]. Figure. 4.6 is a cutout from an example process chain diagram in [312] that are used in the enterprise modeling tool ARIS, which is the leader in the Gartner magic quadrant of business process analysis tools in 2007 [33, 261]. In such a process chain diagram information objects and auxiliary deliverables – outputs – are placed into the control flow definition.

Basic visual business process diagrams are in the first place about the control flow. If they do not explicitly specify the item flow visually, this can be

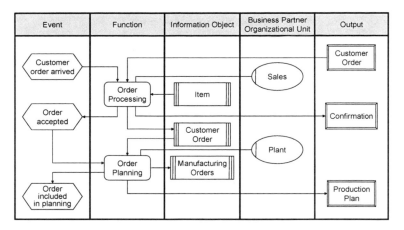

Fig. 4.6. Example ARIS process chain.

for two reasons. Either they serve as a visual view on an overall system specification that defines the item flow somewhere else. Or the defined business process is deliberately specified incompletely. A reason for underspecification can be the need to document a preliminary stage in a documentation process in the sense of documenting 'to be defined'-requirements (TBD) [169]. On the other hand, it can mean that with the functions in the flow diagram some item flow is implicitly specified. Such an implicit specification can be vague if the diagram is used as a strategic process chain, i.e., as a means to document processes on an abstract level that aggregates functionalities and items. For example, if you specify a supply chain to foster strategic discussions about an enterprise, the names of the single stages of the supply chain management are sufficient to implicitly define the goods that are transformed. In such a case a workflow designer may feel that an explicit annotation of items to the connections between stages does not add information but only redundancy. This argument works here, because from a high level viewpoint only an overview of the overall business process is wanted that abstracts away from the detail of the item flow and functions.

Please consider the automatic shop floor control discussed in Sect. 3.5.1 once more – see Figs. 3.3 and 4.5. As we have already discussed in Sect. 4.1.5 the diagram that can be seen on the screen visualizes all process instances running at the plant. The point is that not only past and current processing stages are shown, but also future processing stages. This means the diagram is not only a monitoring view but also a planning and definition view, because it defines the future behavior of the automatic plant. The bars in the diagram have two meanings. On the one hand, a bar stands for a function, i.e., the transformation of a batch of material. In particular, this aspect of the bar is emphasized by the fact that a bar's length visualizes the duration of the processing of the batch of material in a certain stage. On the other hand, a bar also stands for the batch of material itself flowing through concrete processors in the different processing stages. The identification of both the material and the function that transforms this material via the same visual element can easily be done in this example, because in the flows there are no splits. If you have a closer look at Fig. 3.3 you will see that with respect to the same batch of material – identified by the same number in several processing stages – there is always only a strictly sequential order of processing. Each processor has only one kind of product, transforms the product as a whole and eventually produces a single product that then is transported to the next processor. In general, processes are more complex and you need some means to specify how several sub products result from several other sub products.

4.2.2 Global State Transformations

Often, the activities of a business process not only to transform inputs into outputs, often; they also manipulate a global state as a side-effect. Typically we speak here of a global state that is made of information objects but not goods – goods are really shipped around. The business logic and business rules invoked on behalf of activities in a business process manipulate data in central databases. With respect to information, the two concepts of data flow and global state manipulation are mutually interchangeable. If you have a data flow implementing system, i.e., a message passing system, with global state we mean here an extra state that complements the data exchanged between the functional entities. Otherwise, i.e., if the exchanged data are considered as part of a global state, which is an appropriate basis to define semantics of message-passing systems, the above statement that data flow and global state manipulation can be simulated by each other becomes trivial. Anyhow, in theory data passing and global state manipulation are interchangeable. Assume a system of functions with a mechanism for communicating messages and a database. You can get rid of the message-passing mechanism by exploiting the database for interchanging the messages. A sending function tags and stores a message and calls a function without passing the message as a parameter. Then, the called function retrieves the message. The information attached to the message by the calling function must be accurate enough, for example, by encompassing a time-stamp. On the other hand, you can get rid of the database by exchanging the global state with each message and communicating former global state changes to every function. The latter is obviously impractical. But also the first proposed simulation is impractical because in concrete system architectures [28, 141] a dedicated message-passing mechanism might be necessary to reach a cleaner design in terms of separation of concerns or might be necessary because of requirements on the deployment structure of software components.

However, the thought experiment of mutual simulation of message-passing leads us to another message and data design approach. If you design an enterprise application from scratch, it is possible to avoid extra state beyond the messages exchanged between the client and the system. All you need to do is to store each message together with information of the context where it arose, i.e., to store the complete history of exchanged messages. If you do so, you have all the information you need in future system interaction, because all the information maintained by a system also stems from interaction with the system or have been computed from information that stems from interaction with the system. We have discussed this system metaphor in [89] and have coined the term user message system model or simply message system model for short.

The decision to avoid from an information model other than the message model may appear cumbersome to everybody with experience in information system modeling and construction. One major characteristics of the principle of data independency is that the data of the database is designed in a more sustainable way than the data representation needed in one of the several applications accessing the database. Also, there is the argument that a good design of the data in the central database mitigates between the different formats of the information found in the several accessing applications. The sustainability of the application independent data and the sustainability of its data design are perceived as core enterprise assets of a central database. The first point, i.e., the sustainability of independent data themselves does not distinguish a pure message system model from a full-fledged information system model – all information that stems from system interaction is stored persistently in the message system model. However, there is no application mitigating effect in storing data in the message system model. Two applications that, for example, both gather customer data, in general store these data in different formats and furthermore, there is no prevention against redundancies in the growing data repository this way. All applications in a purely message-based system must implement complex retrieval functions against the complete global message log. In doing so they have to deal with many different data formats and data redundancies.

Nevertheless, the message-based system model is not impractical. It is a typed approach to structured document flows. Significant amounts of office work can be reasonably supported by a software system that just enables the defined exchange and flow of electronic documents. Note that this is the reason for the success of certain kind of groupware products like IBM's Lotus Notes Domino Workflow [224, 259] or Microsoft Exchange Workflow Designer that exactly offer support for such document flow. This is where the message system model steps in and tries to yield a theoretical foundation. With respect to those systems that can not be easily realized as document-passing systems the message based system model can also be exploited. The sustainability of the data model of the central database is usually explained by a real-world modeling argument. Real-world modeling arguments are appealing, because they appear natural, however, beyond evidence that the orientation against real-world entities leads to particularly robust data models, real-world arguments do not explain why the central data model adds value. Here, the message based system model offers a pragmatic justification of information modeling along the lines of the above discussion, which brought counter arguments against a purely message based model. Information modeling leads to a trade-off between the data representations in the several applications of an enterprise reducing redundancies, inconsistencies and complexity in central enterprise databases. These are the issues addressed by data quality and data migration projects.

4.2.3 Things and Data in Structured Analysis

Structured analysis [301, 74, 300, 302, 75] is a modeling language and technique for system analysis in the field of data processing. Structured analysis has been widely used in practice, for example, in its first form of SofTech's SADT (Structured Analysis and Design Technique) but also as IDEF-0 (Integrated Definition Methods) [254] and Modern Structured Analysis [361]. In a widely used tutorial on structured analysis [68] a special position is taken on the specification of data and items. Structured analysis as presented in [68] is based on leveled data flow diagrams that are accompanied by a data dictionary. The data dictionary specifies both the data that are stored in information storage and data that are exchanged by processing elements – the so-called functions. The tutorial [68] insists on the reading of such flow diagram as mere data flow diagrams only. If an arc connecting two functions is labeled with the name of a work piece this specifies only that some data about the work piece flows from one processing unit to another. In [300] structured analysis is introduced explicitly as a method for the domain of data processing. However, in [300] structured analysis is introduced as a language for describing things and happenings transforming those things. Data and activities are the means to describe things and happenings in this approach.

In [300] data and activities are the objects that we deal with in our minds and refer to things and happenings, which is explained in [300] with help of a kind of language theoretical discourse. Actually, things are tightly identified with data and happenings with activities, so that the discussion usually distinguishes between things/data versus happenings/activities. Further objects are identified with either the domain of things/data and happenings/activities – nouns are identified with data, verbs are identified with activities; forms are identified with data, filling out forms makes up the corresponding activities. With respect to forms processing there is even a finer distinction between blank forms and completed forms. A blank form is input to an activity that fills out a form and a completed form is an output of such an activity. Form-based systems [139, 89] are particular ubiquitous and important for the domain of enterprise computing.

4.2.4 Specifying Physical Processes and Data Processing

The answer to the question of whether business process definition is about specifying only the flow of information or also about the flow of goods depends on various factors. It depends on the concrete business process technology, the role that a business process definition plays in such technology and therefore the semantics of the business process definition language in such technology.

In an enterprise, both goods and information are transformed. Often the transformation of a workpiece is accompanied by a transformation of data about this workpiece. Eventually, products and services are delivered. Products are tangible results of a process, whereas services are not. There is a difference between the transformation or delivery of a tangible entity and the transformation of information. If you specify a business process in an enterprise, in general there is the need to model both the transformation of goods and information. In particular, in manufacturing enterprises a model of the mere information side is not sufficient. A business process is modeled as a net of processors connected by item flows. Assume that an input of a processor in such business process definition is labeled with the name of an entity. If you are strict about the semantics of such specification it is not clear from the outset, whether the specification of the processor is about processing tangible entities or information. That is why, for example, the event-driven process chain apparatus, i.e., the ARIS house of business engineering [311, 313, 222], explicitly distinguishes between a data view and an output view.

The only difference between the specification of goods and the specification of data lies in the exploitation of these specifications. For example, a data model can be used as a requirements document to implement a database and the specification of goods can be used as part of a plant construction plan. Actually, the semantics of a specification language can be completely determined by the way it is exploited. Several exploitations are possible for a specification and this is not only true for the distinction between specification of data and goods but for each specification in its own right. In a concrete project all concerned stakeholders should agree upon an understanding of how a specification is exploited.

You can describe physical processes with data flow diagrams. You then use data models to describe properties of exchanged work items. You describe those properties of the work items that are relevant to understand and specify the process, in particular, that are needed in the specification of the data flow's functions. Business processes in an enterprise consist of physical processes and information processes. So in a system description you have a mix of physical process descriptions and information process description. You can use the same kind of language to describe the properties of work items and the information stored and exchanged in a computer system. This is not a problem, as long as you make clear the purpose of each part of a specification document, i.e., whether it is about information that should be processed by information technology, whether it is about a work piece that has to be worked on or whether it is about a product or service that has to be delivered. In the following we want to have a clear notion of data processing or information processing. With each work there is usually connected some processing of information, be it supported by information technology or not. For example, if a worker is working on a work piece he may physically grasp the dimensions of the work piece and make some decisions based on this information. However, when we talk about data processing here we mean that the data is stored in a computer system and manipulated by software.

A process modeling languages can explicitly distinguish between information objects and other deliverables like products and services [221]. When using a modeling language for documentation purposes only and the used modeling language does not explicitly distinguish between information objects and others it is nevertheless possible to distinguish between them. Extra comments can be used that are attached to the modeling elements or a naming convention can be introduced. As is always the case with modeling element in modeling notations, it makes little sense to say that it is possible or not possible to model something in a given modeling language. You can always model everything even without a modeling language, e.g., by using paper and pencil to develop your modeling language on the fly. If you only use a modeling language for documentation purposes only, you can always make the necessary extensions in an ad-hoc way to properly express properties of the modeled systems. Modeling languages are not distinguished so much by the number of their modeling elements but by the amount of standardization of usage and semantics of the modeling elements they introduce. Things are different for executable languages, i.e., languages that are used in an execution platform to specify automatic processes or automatic process support. Here, every modeling element has an observable semantics.

4.2.5 On Real World Modeling

The specification of goods in business process models in Sect. 4.2 must not be confused with the notion of real world modeling. If a good is modeled in a business process model as a good it actually stands for this good and not merely for information about this good. Real world modeling is about information modeling, which seems to be a contradiction in itself on a first sight. But it is not, real world modeling must be understood as a metaphor for a certain information modeling discipline. Real world modeling understands itself as information modeling paradigm or data modeling paradigm. A discussion of real world modeling can shed some light on the role of modeling in projects in general and also the role of business process modeling in enterprises in particular. In business process modeling it is sometimes important to express a real world entity like a real estate, e.g., a concrete shop, store, construction belt or group of workers. As another common example, the activities in business process models may reference real activities that happen in the real world. Often, activities in a business process model stand for an IT system dialogue or fully-automatic software process, however, often, activities stand for an observable, doable activity in the real world. An activity in the real world is not as tangible as a real estate, because it is dynamic, but it may be a process that transforms tangible, real-world objects. The activities in a business process model do not stand for information about these real-world activities, they stand for the real real-world activities themselves.

A discussion of real world modeling or the common understanding of real world modeling is also important for the discussion of business domain orientation in Sects. 5.1.4, 6.2.5 and 6.4.

Real world modeling is defined as capturing facts about real-world entities. In the discussion of modeling in general and concrete modeling methodologies in particular we often come across such a real-word argument somehow advertising a concrete modeling technique or approach. The real-world argument "per se" is the above statement that a model captures facts about real-world entities. For example, this real-world argument is used to give a guideline in modeling, in motivating modeling with a certain modeling approach or to argue that a certain modeling language is particularly well-suited for modeling.

As a modeling guideline the above real-world argument is quite void from the pragmatic viewpoint of software system modeling. Should the argument be exploited to distinguish between real-world entities and information about real-world entities? In an office you have a means to store and pass around information even without information technology support. In renewing this office work you model the information on paper and not the properties of paper. So, in modeling an information system everything is a candidate for modeling, also information is a real-world object in the practice of modeling.

One can attempt to reduce the information available in the above example of an 'as is'-analysis of a paper-based office to tangible objects of the real world – even if the information is obtained indirectly by some computations of direct properties of tangible objects of the real world. The argument would be that already in the existing office there exists some level of non-real world objects, i.e., information that corresponds to otherwise real world objects and that this situation just has a footprint on modeling. But how about systems that have to deal with tangible objects and information of tangible objects in parallel? If a modeling approach insist on modeling real-world objects, both the tangible objects and information about them must be treated equally as real-world objects if such a system is modeled. So, the real-world argument does not provide guidance in modeling, because we claim that it actually has no discriminating power – everything is a real-world object and there is no risk of modeling something different than real-world objects.

The entity-relationship language [57] is a semantic data modeling approach [2, 165] that exploits a real-world argument pragmatically. Certain semantic relationships that often occur in systems like the 'is a'-relationship or 'has a'-relationship are made concrete notational elements of the language. Object-oriented analysis [321] is another approach that often emphasizes the real-world argument. Actually, object orientation started as a programming language paradigm for simulation. The original project title of the programming language Simula [262, 333, 200] was Monte-Carlo compiler. As an explanation of a simulation approach the real-world argument actually makes sense. The problem is that the real-world argument has been kept in the motivation for object-orientation as a general-purpose programming metaphor. Here, the program system sometimes is still seen as a simulation of otherwise real-world processes even if the system is actually embedded into business processes and is supports them in continuous human-computer interactions. If a program system is used in such a way which is not for mere simulation purposes structural frictions occur unless it is clearly distinguished between the real-world, models, simulations, systems, system executions and system interactions.

Correspondence theory, i.e., the investigation of the correspondence between a statement about real-world facts and the reality of real-world facts, has interested philosophers for a long time [290, 6]. The relationships of mind, language and phenomena is the subject of investigation of language philosophy, e.g., [359, 318] – be it ordinary language philosophy or ideal language philosophy. However, in order to motivate, explain and use a system specification language it is not necessary to delve into language philosophical issues. We do not need to understand the processes in our mind to make practical use of a formal language. Even for natural language we do not need language philosophy for its practical usage. And due to its very nature as a means of communicating not only definitions, instructions, descriptions and the like but also ideas, feelings, hopes, questions and so on, natural language is incredible more complex and incredible less amenable to the formalization of its semantics. If we want to establish a language for system specification all we need to do is to define how its specifications are exploited. The meaning of a specification language, i.e., the definition of the exploitation of its specifications can be negotiated and it can be taught. Again, it is not necessary to investigate the processes in our minds that are concerned with such negotiations, teaching and learning in order to use a system specification language.

4.3 Exploiting a Business Process Definition

We basically see three different kinds of exploitation of a business process definition or, to say it differently, three different kinds of motivation for specifying business processes. These different kinds of uses for business process definitions are as system documentation, for system simulation, and as a basis for automatic execution. In concrete projects, these three aspects do not have to be mutual exclusive.

4.3.1 Business Process Definitions as Documentation

A business process definition can simply be documentation of a system. Here we need to distinguish between 'as is'-analyses or 'to be'-analyses of processes. If a business process definition describes an existing system as the result of an 'as is'-analysis it can be exploited for the improvement of processes. It can be used as the basis for discussion of stakeholders in the improvement efforts in order to gain a common understanding of what is going on in the existing system.

As a result of a 'to be'-analysis the business process definition is a requirements document for the system that has to be build. To a certain degree it can also be seen as a blueprint for the system that has to be build. If a business process definition is a specification of merely information processing, there is in principle a high degree of freedom in realizing the system by concrete software components as long as the overall transformation is fulfilled. But the semantics of a business process definition is not only the overall transformation that results from it. The activities in a business process definition are usually more than mere abstract entities. Even if they are about information processing, concrete entities are attached to them as resources, i.e., workers as human resources or organizational units.

So, a business process definition is not a specification of a system that realizes the specification's functionality as a black box, it really is rather a blueprint of the system that has to be realized and is therefore also a high-level system architecture specification.

4.3.2 Business Process Definitions in Simulation

Business process definitions can be exploited in system simulation. Here the future system with all its described entities, be it tangible objects or information objects and there interplay are virtually realized by a computer program. The behavior of the future system can then be observed by executing the simulation program, in particular, it can be tested whether desired future key performance indicators will likely be met. The simulation we have just described is a concrete approach of simulation. It is about really playing a simulation game with the models of real-word entities, i.e., a Monte-Carlo simulation like approach. However, this approach can be seen as simulation in the narrower sense.

In general, simulation can be seen as the field of predicting properties of the behavior of a modeled system with numerical methods and algorithms. If properties can be calculated this is better then trying them out by a Monte-Carlo style simulation – calculating system properties relates to running system simulations as proving program properties relates to testing program properties. Statistics is needed in order to reach models that are rich enough for simulation purposes. Typical theories that can be exploited are stochastic processes, in particular Markov chains and their application to process algebra [42], queuing theory [121] or combined theories like stochastic Petri nets [148].

4.3.3 Business Process Definitions as High-Level Programs

A business process definition can have an executable semantics. We have decided to use the term workflow definition for these executable business process specifications. Workflow definition tools are crucial components of concrete workflow technology products. The definition of a workflow in such a product is interpreted by a workflow enactment service. According to the definition tasks are scheduled, documents are routed, business logic is invoked. In such technologies workflow definitions are computer programs. They are part of an encompassing program system. Workflow definition can also have an executable semantics with respect to execution of physical processes. Please consider the control desk screen of the automatic shop floor system in Fig. 4.5 once more. The figure shows process instances and a process definition that has been recovered from the process instances. The visualization of process instances is part of the user interface, whereas the process definition is not; it has been introduced in the figure for conceptual purposes. Via the visualization of the process instances the operator can really control the processes in a drag-and-drop style human computer interaction. Shifting a bar that represents the future processing of a batch from one processor to another really means that this batch will be moved to that processor. If the current time indicator comes to an end of a bar this has the operational semantics of moving the batch around in the plant to the next processor. This means that the visualized process instance planning has an executable semantics.

It is possible to say that also the business process definition in Fig. 4.5 has an executable semantics that it inherits from the executable semantics of the process instance definitions. But in practice you would hardly agree that this specification has an executable semantics, because it is not available to the operator in the same way the process instance definitions are. Assume that the supervisory control and data acquisition system that is conceptually discussed in Fig. 4.5 is a quite heavyweight one with transportation belts connecting large processing machines and processors. In the case of such heavyweight plant control it typically would make no real sense to have also a process definition capability in the control system, because an executable semantics of it is hard to imagine. What should be the meaning of restructuring the processing stages in a process definition? The transportation belts cannot be automatically reconstructed. The processing stages and their interplay are planned and realized for a long-time period.

A requirement for a specification language be regarded as an executable specification language is that it has a completely defined operational semantics. However, in practice a specification language would not be called executable unless all rules of the operational semantics are realized fully automatic.

4.4 Events in Business Process Modeling

In business process modeling languages there are modeling elements for events. Roughly, it can be distinguished between start events, end events, and intermediate events. Start and end events provide a means to decompose an

otherwise flat business process model into a set of defined business processes
that can trigger each other via start events. Intermediate events can be considered as labels of transitions. They can be used to signalize the finalization
of an activity. A typical usage of intermediate events is as wait states before
join connections. Another typical usage of intermediate events is as conditions in conditional branching constructs. Concrete business process modeling languages use events as a hook to informally enrich the semantics of the
language. For example, in BPMN [265] complex operational phenomena like
messaging, timing, error and exception handling, and compensation [131] are
simply turned into a visual presentation by an event.

In common language, events are usually considered as happenings that
occur. Events can have a time duration. Events are observable. Events change
observable properties of the environment. There are events that are considered to have no time duration. They occur at a point in time. Definitions
like the following can also be found in definitions of concrete business process
modeling languages [312, 265]: an event has no time duration, it is an observable, immediate change of the state of a system. However, in the practice
of business process modeling intermediate events are also part of the states
of business process instances. In the true sense of the word, the events in a
process model are the transitions between functions and intermediate events
only. Actually, the intermediate events used in commodity business process
modeling languages are a kind of void activities. In general, events in common
business process modeling actually have a start and an end, i.e., they have a
duration.

4.4.1 Strictly Interchanging Functions and Events

Have a look at Fig. 4.7. It shows two versions of a business process model
for handling an incoming customer registration. The left-hand version (i) uses
a notation that uses interchanging functions and events. A description style
like the left-hand version is common for practical business process modeling
projects, for example, event-driven process chains (EPCs) [312] heavily rely on
this modeling style. The right-hand side version (ii) shows a Petri net [281, 295]
description of the same process. Petri nets are place/transition nets [72]. If
the capacity of each place of a Petri net is restricted to one the Petri net is
called a condition/event net, i.e., the Petri net's places are called conditions
and the Petri net's transitions are called events. In the Petri net the events
take over the role of the connectors in the common business process model at
the left-hand side. The events of the common business process model become
ordinary places in the Petri net. Using events in the style shown in Fig. 4.7 (i)
usually is often perceived as leading to a high redundancy of nodes. Actually,
the events often only repeat the label text of the preceding function in past
tense. In Fig. 4.7 (ii) the places that correspond to the events in Fig. 4.7
(i) can be removed without loss with respect to accuracy in describing the
intended business process.

Actually, business process modeling languages do not necessarily foster a function and event interleaving style of modeling as event-driven process chains do. It can be argued that the event that a function finishes is an event worth considering from the viewpoint of business activity monitoring. Similarly, it is worth considering the time period from the end of one function and the start of the next function, which is actually represented by the events in the considered function and event interleaving modeling style. Nevertheless, these events are canonically given, they simply exist for each function, so there is no need to model them over and over again. If a business process model is used as a specification for the entities that are subject to business process monitoring, the explicit modeling of intermediate places between functions can be justified. However, it would be motivated only if there is also the possibility to omit some intermediate states, so that the decision of whether an intermediate state should be monitored or not is a decision to be made when specifying business process monitoring.

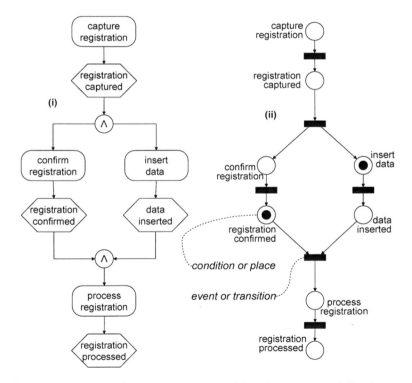

Fig. 4.7. Events in business process modeling languages and Petri nets.

4.4.2 Using Events for Expressing Decisions

Intermediate events are also used for the specification of conditions in conditional branching structures of business process models. Figure 4.8 shows three alternative ways of expressing conditional branching structures in visual process specifications. The first option is to use a modeling element that is labeled with a condition. The outgoing branches are labeled with 'yes' or 'no' indicating whether the condition holds or is broken. This style of specifying binary decisions is often used in ad-hoc specifications of decision procedures and high-level algorithms. It has been in widespread use in the flowchart notation [73, 173].

The second option is to use a modeling element that indicates a decision point and to label the outgoing branches with conditions. Such a construct can be used not only for binary decisions but scales up to decisions between arbitrary many alternatives. For example, the BPMN notation [265] uses this style of expressing decisions. Without further notational semantics the alternative conditions must be complete and unique, i.e., in each state one and only one of the alternative conditions should hold. Otherwise, the construct can cause parallelism or deadlock. Alternatively, a visual notation can fix an evaluation order for the conditions of the alternative branches, e.g., from top to bottom or from left to right. As another option, a visual notation can provide a means to specify the evaluation order. With both solutions, the al-

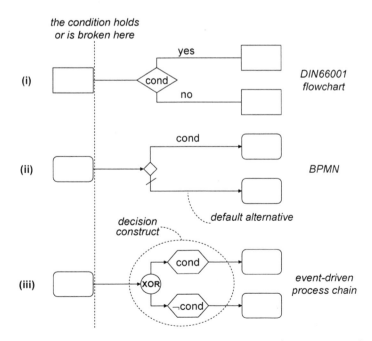

Fig. 4.8. Alternatives to express decision points in visual process specifications.

ternatives do not have to be unique any more. Similarly, with respect to the need of completeness of the alternative conditions, a visual notation can allow for the specification of a default alternative that is taken whenever none of the specified conditions hold.

A third option shown in Fig. 4.8 is to use a modeling element indicating a decision point and to introduce events to express the conditions of the several outgoing branches. This notation is used by event-driven process chains [312]. Actually, this way of specifying a conditional branching structures simply turns the condition labels used in the second described option in Fig. 4.8 into events. So, there is no real difference between the second and third option in Fig. 4.8. The modeling element used to indicate the decision point in Fig. 4.8 is an 'exclusive or'-connector, an XOR connector for short. The XOR connector and conditions at the several outgoing branches together form a decision construct. This is the same for the second described option and for the third described option. An interpretation of the XOR-connector and the following events other than one single construct is not intended. Other semantics easily lead to confusion.

The XOR-connector is usually defined as describing a branching point in a business process with the meaning that always exactly one of the outgoing branches is always taken. Assume that we take this definition as a complete specification of the semantics of the XOR-connector. Then, the semantics of the XOR-connector would be the semantics of a non-deterministic operator. Assume, that the first, i.e., upper, branch has been non-deterministically chosen after the timeline has passed the XOR-connector in Fig. 4.8. Assume further that the condition actually does not hold as an outcome of the preceding action. Now the question arises as to what the meaning of the event and the meaning of the condition in the event actually is. The meaning could be that the process has simply arrived in an undefined state. Another opinion could be that the process has arrived in a somehow dangling state that waits for the condition to become true. Then, the business process specification must allow for the interpretation of an event as a wait state for a condition to become true. But this would really be a non standard interpretation of a business process specification. Even if such a wait state semantics is taken the question remains whether the condition can actually ever become true. Otherwise the wait state would be a kind of livelock.

4.5 Semantics of Events

In this section we discuss the semantics of events in their on right, i.e., as parts of a business process as commonly used in today's business process modeling languages and projects. Events are often used as separators to decompose a large diagram into pieces, or, to say it differently, as interfaces or gateways to business processes. Section 5.2.2 deals with those aspects of events that are connected to their usage as start events and end events of sub business process models or business process model abstractions, whereas this section deals with the basic aspects of events and their semantics.

In the common understanding an event is a happening, it is usually not only some observable property at some point in time, but an observable change of a property of the environment. Actually, in the usual understanding of the word an event is an observable change of a property of the observed environment and not the result of this change. In general it does not stand for some persistence of the property which results from the change.

4.5.1 Persistent and Ephemeral Event Effects

In common business process modeling there is usually a tacit understanding of the fact that the effect of an event is persistent. However, on closer examination this is a subtle issue. Consider the example in Fig. 4.7 once more. The event indicating that registration data has been inserted not only has the semantics of a happening. First, the happening cannot simply occur, it is the outcome, i.e., the result of the preceding data insertion action. Furthermore, the event also stands for a persisting fact, i.e., the reader of the business process model has no reason to doubt that the data stays inserted until the next action is performed, which is the process registration in this case. This means if the data have been inserted before the registration has been confirmed, there is a tacit understanding that the insertion of the data will not be withdrawn until the registration confirmation has been finished and the process registration has been started. In this example, this discussion may seem over-sophisticated: why should the insertion of data be withdrawn in the modeled process while the registration confirmation is still underway and actually, what should it mean that the insertion of data is withdrawn?

But the concept of data insertion withdrawal is not artificial. For example, in a real-world business process there could be the concept of expiration of inserted data, i.e., in the case that the data insertion function which led to the inserted data event is too long ago before the further registration processing could be entered. And indeed, the question of how to model this business constraint in a straightforward way with standard modeling elements arises. Of course, it is possible to extend the specification apparatus by an appropriate notion of time and appropriate modeling elements. For example, timed Petri nets, e.g., [17, 18, 148], could serve as a basis for such confinement of the business process modeling language. Another option is to use some wild-card connector and describe its semantics on the fly with a comment as is shown in Fig. 4.9.

4.5.2 A Detour on Ordinary Language Specification

The specification option in Fig. 4.9 is an instance of a general theme. Often, a precise description in ordinary language is a good option as a means of specification. A description in ordinary language is as precise as its different

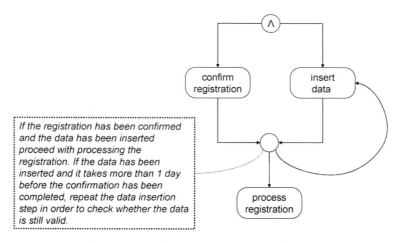

Fig. 4.9. Modeling an expiring condition.

understandings in a group of stakeholders. The larger and the more hetero-geneous the group of stakeholders that has been chosen as a test bed for the accuracy of a specification the better. In this simple sense of non-ambiguity, ordinary language description can be very precise indeed.

If ordinary language is used as a specification language there is always the risk that a specification is misunderstood. Concrete specifications give rise to ambiguity. One can attempt to overcome this problem by introducing a formal specification language. A formal specification language fixes the semantics of specifications in a formal, usually mathematical model. Then, in some sense there is no ambiguity left in the meaning of a specification. A drawback of formal specification is that people usually feel a substantial overhead in learn-ing the formal specification language and also in specifying phenomena with the more formal language. But there is also another severe problem. The real target in making a specification language more precise is to clarify the mean-ing of the specifications with respect to real-world phenomena. Introducing a token game in some mathematical notation as the meaning of specifications may help to mitigate the gap between the language and the phenomena they describe, however, it does not remove the gap. If a formal language is used, it is still necessary to define the mapping between the entities in its mathe-matical semantics and the actually described entities and behaviors. The more complex the environment of the described phenomena is, e.g., in terms of side-conditions and exceptions, the harder it is to fix this mapping. Sometimes the environment in its entirety is not pragmatically amenable to mapping onto the mathematical semantics – it simply does not seem to be amenable to a formalization.

Sometimes a specification in ordinary language that can be understood very well by common sense can become a nightmare if one tries to formalize it, because of the need for formalizing more and more concepts implicit in the ordinary language specification. The more the target environment can be characterized in terms of a manageable set of well-understood rules, the easier it is to establish a formal specification language for it.

4.5.3 Managing Ephemeral Event Effects

Let us have a look at some more example phenomena that may be harder to grasp formally than informally in an every day project. It starts with another instance of the issue that effects of events are usually considered persistent in every day business process modeling. We want to give a real-word example from the healthcare domain. Look at the stub process specification in Fig. 4.10 that defines the start of an operation in a hospital.

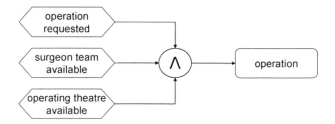

Fig. 4.10. Specification of starting an operation process in a hospital.

If an operation has become necessary, it can be started as early as the surgeon team is available and the operating theatre is available. The business process model in Fig. 4.10 seems to depict this specification correctly. However, questions arise. Assume that an operation is requested, but neither the surgeon team nor the operating theatre is available. Now, a surgeon team becomes available, but the operating theatre is still in use, be it because there is still another operation underway or be it because the operating theatre is currently being cleaned. Now, after some time, the operating theatre becomes available again. Now, assume that in the mean time the operation team is not available any more. For example because some of the needed surgeon team members is needed in another urgent process, or the surgeon team became blocked as a whole, e.g., because it started an important team meeting. Should the operation be done or not? Obviously not – it cannot be done because the operation team is not available. The described situation is rather as modeled in Fig. 4.11 with a Petri net. In this Petri net one of the events or – to say it more precisely – one of the conditions described by the events can be withdrawn.

The discussion shows how events in business process models are usually used, i.e., as descriptions of conditions that hold, i.e., conditions that are non-ephemeral. This also explains why the labels of events in business process models are rather names of state conditions than names of state changes.

Note that this is also true for our example in Fig. 4.10.The label of the event is saying that the surgeon team is available which rather hints to a state description and not the dynamics of a . Otherwise the label should express that the surgeon teams becomes available. If the focus would be rather on the state changes than on the resulting state conditions the chosen labels in Fig. 4.10 are actually flawed from a linguistic viewpoint. Now, as a result it would be possible to elaborate some style guide with respect to naming of business process modeling elements, e.g., fixing that a verb should be used in the labels of events. But it is not our intention here to be normative, we just want to give an impression of possible pitfalls in the usage of business process modeling languages that we encounter over and over again in projects.

If there is a commitment that the effect of an event in a business process specification is persistent the above question simply does not arise. But the example also makes clear that then an event imposes a business constraint onto the modeled processes and their environment. In our case the business, i.e., the hospital, must guarantee that once the appropriate surgeon team has become available, this surgeon team stays available or at least henceforth some other appropriate surgeon team is available.

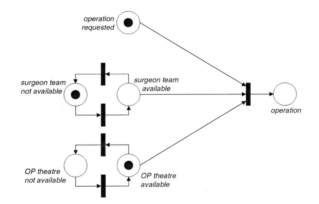

Fig. 4.11. A Petri net specification of starting an operation process.

But what if the modeler actually wants to describe a situation in which the surgeon team may become unavailable after it has been available and also the operating theatre may become unavailable again after it has been available. First, the modeler is actually tempted to model it in the way shown in Fig. 4.10. If the model in Fig. 4.10 is seen as a visualization of spoken language without any strict policy of what is precisely expressed by events the model can actually be read as the above specification in common language. It then inherits the ambiguity of natural language specification. The point is that the natural language specification is not really ambiguous but rather loose in a certain sense. It clearly states that the operation can only be done if both a surgeon team and an operating theatre are available. It simply does not specify whether a surgeon team that has become available should stay available or whether it must immediately be substituted by another one. In that sense the business process model in Fig. 4.10 with the standard understanding of persistent event effects might simply be an over-specification of what is intended.

Let us assume that the intention is to model disappearing event effects in our operation example. Figure 4.12 shows an attempt to model the situation better. In Fig. 4.12 the availability of the surgeon team and the availability of the operating theatre is modeled as one compound event. The compound event explicitly expresses the fact that both parts of the events must be observed simultaneously and in some sense this overcomes the ambiguity of the process model in Fig. 4.10, which we described above. The compound event gains its perceived improved preciseness from the usage of ordinary language to describe it. Interpreted as one compound event in ordinary language most people would disagree that it allows for the case described above, i.e., that the effect of one of the part events disappears before the other part events occurs.

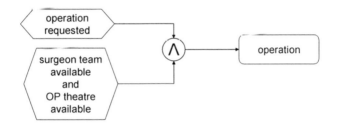

Fig. 4.12. Alternative specification of starting an operation process.

Visualizing a given sentence in ordinary language by using graphical elements for some of the words in the sentence does not improve the accuracy of the sentence in its own right. However, such a graphical presentation of a sentence appears more formal to many people and therefore also appears more accurate. Current business process modeling languages are not mere visualizations of natural language in so far as they try to impose some defined semantics for the modeling elements, in particular for the connectors, they offer for modeling. Nevertheless, business process models inherit from the ambiguity of natural language for two reasons. First, business process models are always a mixture between defined modeling elements and usage of natural language, i.e., the functions and events are given names and descriptions in ordinary language and attempts to fix the semantics of the modeling elements of a modeling language do not help to improve these namings and descriptions. The above comparison of the business process model in Figs. 4.12 versus 4.10 is an example for this. Second, despite some written definition of the meaning of modeling elements, people often just use modeling elements intuitively and actually just in the sense of a visualization of words in ordinary language. Another problem with the accuracy of business process models is that the definitions of the semantics of modeling elements bear the risk of ambiguity, in particular, if they are not mathematically founded. Sometimes, the ambiguity of business process language specifications is obscured by the formal presentation of its semantics. Furthermore, in any case there remains a gap between the defined semantics of the various modeling elements and the behavior and properties of the modeled real-world entities and their environment, which can only be mitigated by a strictly understood and maintained mapping between the model and the modeled.

Attempts to Grasp Ephemeral Event Effects

Let us approach the disappearing event effects in our operation process example more systematically. Figure 4.13 shows a simpler version of the process that does not consider the availability of the surgeon team but only the availability of the operating theatre. The situation is less complex but already shows the issue discussed above. Assume that the operating theatre becomes available before the operation is requested and becomes non-available for some reason before an operation is actually requested.

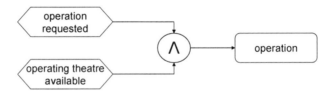

Fig. 4.13. Specification of an even simpler start of an operation process.

Figure 4.14 shows a Petri net model of the situation in Fig. 4.13. In the model we introduced a process other then the performance of an operation as the reason for the operating theatre becoming unavailable, i.e., operating theatre maintenance process. It is simply a concurrency problem with potentially dangling operation and maintenance processes competing for the operating theatre as a resource. There is no need to explicitly model the unavailability of the operating theatre as done in Fig. 4.11. The operating theatre is not available if the corresponding place in the Petri net is not marked. Operations are triggered by a process that requests the operation. The end of this process is represented by a place indicating that the operation has been requested. Similarly, there is a place indicating the request for maintenance of the operating theatre.

The question is now how to transfer the Petri net model in Fig 4.14 into a model in some ordinary business process modeling language. Figure 4.15

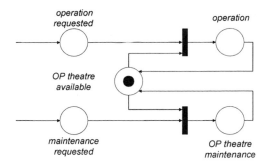

Fig. 4.14. A Petri net specification of the operation process.

shows a first attempt. In Fig. 4.15 the events, i.e., the transition bars, of the Petri net have simply been turned into 'and'-connectors and the Petri net place representing the availability of the operating theatre has been turned into an event. The first of these two straightforward conversions is doable but the latter is problematic. It is problematic, because the start of the mainte- nance of the operating theatre makes the operating theatre unavailable. In the Petri net this side-effect of the maintenance of the operating theatre is appropriately modeled, because the start of the maintenance consumes the token from the place that indicates the availability of the operating theatre. However, in the case of a usual business process modeling language it is not clear that the starting of an activity has an effect on the properties of the environment described in the event preceding the activity. Therefore, unless otherwise clarified in an extra comment, nothing prevents an operation and a maintenance of the operating theatre from occurring in parallel in the busi- ness process model given in Fig. 4.15. In that sense, the attempt in Fig. 4.15 is an incomplete specification of the situation.

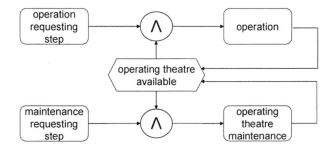

Fig. 4.15. Attempt to model processes competing for a resource.

4.6 Synchronization in Business Process Models

Business process modeling languages provide means to fork parallel processes and synchronize parallel processes. Parallelism in business process systems already comes into play alone by the fact that several instances of a process can be launched from the environment of the business process system. However, we are interested in such parallelism that is caused from inside the execution of a business process instance. In business process modeling languages concrete modeling elements are used for this purpose called, e.g., 'and'-connector, parallel gateway in BPMN [265] or logical 'and'-relationship in EPCs [312]. An and-connector with multiple fan-out is used to fork processes, which are sub process instances from the viewpoint of the currently executing business process instance. An 'and'-connector with multiple fan-in is used to join two process instances. We have used a pair of an 'and'-connector with multiple fan-out and an 'and'-connector multiple fan-in already in diagram (i) in Fig. 4.7. Initially, the meaning of the 'and'-connectors in diagram (i) in Fig. 4.7 follows intuition, however, we have also given a concrete formal semantics of the business process model in diagram (i) by the Petri net in diagram (ii) in Fig. 4.7. All this said, the semantics of synchronization in usual business process modeling languages remains vague. This vagueness of semantics of synchronization is the main issue of this section.

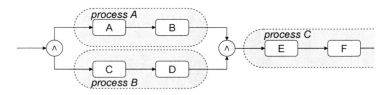

Fig. 4.16. End synchronization of two business processes.

Synchronization in business process models is usually understood as a form of end synchronization. In Fig. 4.16 the initial 'and'-connector forks two process instances A and B. The processes A and B can be considered sub processes of the overall business process. The process instance that finishes first has to wait for the other process instance to finish. When both process instances A and B has finished, the overall business process can proceed with starting the next activity E, i.e., with starting the next sub process named C in Fig. 4.16. This is how the effect ot the second 'and'-connector in Fig. 4.16 is usually understood.

Other interpretations of an 'and'-connector with multiple fan-in would also be possible. For example, the second 'and'-connector could also start two copies of the sub process C after both of the process instances A and B has been finished. This could be understood as an independent proceeding of both process instances A and B, each with its own copies of the activities following the synchronization point. However, the interpretation of an 'and'-connector as an end synchronization and therefore join point of processes that merges several processes into a single new one is the usual interpretation. In terms of Petri nets, it is possible to model both kinds of semantics. In general, the places of place/transition Petri nets [72] can hold an arbitrary number of tokens and it can be specified how much tokens are withdrawn from each place preceding a transition and how many tokens are put onto each place following a transition whenever the transition fires. This means, if the business model in Fig. 4.16 is given a place/transition Petri net semantics, the first, usual interpretation withdraws one token from activity B, one token from activity D and places one token onto activity E, whereas the second interpretation withdraws one token from activity B, one token from activity D and places two tokens onto activity E. Now, the semantics of synchronization starts to become subtle. What if there are more than one instance of the process A and more than one instance of the process B are running in parallel, because of some external triggers not shown in Fig. 4.16? When should an instance of process C should be started exactly? We will discuss questions like this in more depth in due course along another example business process model shown in Fig. 4.18.

You can also express a form of synchronization other than end synchronization with the usual semantics of 'and'-connectors. For example, Fig. 4.17 shows a synchronization of two processes against a synchronization point. The synchronization point is realized as a combination of an 'and'-connector with multiple fan-in and an 'and'-connector with multiple fan-out. For example, if process A has been finished its activity B it is resumed until process B has finished its activity D. Then, both process A and B can be considered as proceeding each with its next activity.

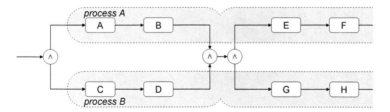

Fig. 4.17. Synchronization of two business processes at a synchronization point.

Figure 4.18 shows yet another simple example of parallelism in business process modeling. Once more, let us have a look at how the semantics of an 'and'-connector with multiple fan-in can be defined. A usual attempt to specify the semantics of the synchronizing 'and'-connector, i.e., the 'and'-connector annotated with the label δ, is to say the following. Whenever the activity C and the activity E has been finished, the activity F is started. A first question arises with respect to this definition. Why do we say "the" in "the activity has been finished". The instances of the activities are not unique, there may be several copies of them, for example, due to the cycle in the business process model in Fig. 4.18. A next attempt would be the following. Whenever an instance of activity C and an instance of activity E has been finished, an instance of activity F is started. Actually, both the first attempt and the second attempt are usual explanations of the meaning of synchronizing 'and'-connectors. For example, the synchronizing 'and'-connector in Fig. 4.7 is explained for EPCs by [312] in the following way. When events 'registration confirmed' and 'data inserted' occur, the function 'process registration' is launched – the vagueness of the notions of event and the occurrence of event is not and issue here; we have discussed this question already in Sect. 4.5. The problem with definitions like the one above is that they are, in a certain sense, incomplete specifications of synchronization as we will discuss now.

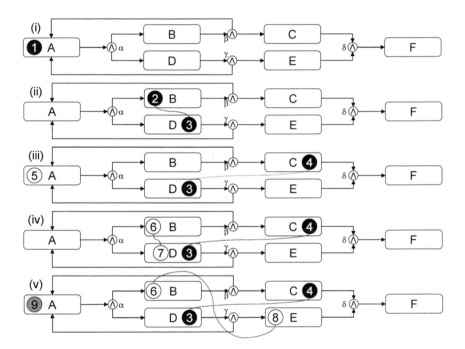

Fig. 4.18. Business process synchronization in presence of cycles.

Figure 4.18 shows a business process model and example of how an instance of the business process model can evolve over time. Diagram (i) shows that the business process has been started with an instance of activity A named '1'. Diagram (ii) shows that activity instance '1' has been finished and activity instances '2' and '3' has been launched in parallel. Diagram (iii) shows that activity instance '2' has been finished and activity instances '4' and '5' has been launched in parallel. Diagram (iv) shows that activity instance '5' has been finished and activity instances '6' and '7' has been launched in parallel.

Diagram (v) shows that activity instance '7' has been finished and activity instances '8' and '9' has been launched in parallel.

Let us assume now, that, as a next step, both the activities '4' and '8' finish, but not yet any of the other activities. Now, the question is whether an instance of the activity F should be started or not. With the definition give above it should be started, because, following the definition, the activity F should be launched whenever an instance of activity C and an instance of activity E has been finished. The question is, whether this effect is the synchronization effect that the modeler wanted to express with the δ-labeled connector. The point is that the sub process instance that has been launched in diagram (iii) has somehow overtaken the activity '3', i.e., the activity instance '7' has been finished before the activity instance '3' and has overtaken it in that sense. By just looking at the token game you might feel that it is more correct that activity instance '4' should be synchronized against activity instance '3'. We have sketched this by drawing dashed lines between those activity instances that seem to be somehow logically connected.

Without knowledge of the concrete business logic it is not possible to decide whether activity instance '4' should synchronize against activity instance '8' or whether it should wait further until activity instance '3' finishes, a further instance of activity E is triggered and also eventually finished. One possible semantics of synchronization would be that an instance of activity C may only synchronize against an instance of activity E if the latest instance of activity A in the history of the business process that occurs before the instance of activity C is also the latest instance of activity A that occurs before the instance of activity E. With this extra constraint, the activity F could not be launched as a result of the completion of the activities C and E in diagram (v) in Fig, 4.18. Figure 4.19 shows the history of the business process instance being in the state of diagram (v) in Fig. 4.18. Activity instance '1' is the latest instance of activity A that appears before activity instance '4', whereas activity instance '5' is the latest instance of activity A that appears before activity instance '8'. Therefore, if the above constraint should not be violated, activity instance '4' cannot be synchronized against activity instance '8'.

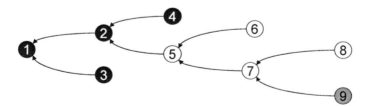

Fig. 4.19. History of the business process instance in Fig. 4.18.

If constraints about synchronization like the one above should be expressible, the underlying formalism should be rich enough to express business process histories, identities of activity instances and the like. For example, with colored Petri nets (CPN) [191] such a framework is provided. In Figs. 4.18 and 4.19 we have switched to another color of tokens whenever a new sub process is created by the instantiation of an initial activity A. We have done this for the purpose of better visualization – several instances of same activity can already be distinguished by the different numbers given to the tokens that represent them.

Another useful means of synchronization for business process scenarios like the one in Fig. 4.18 might be a form of total synchronization that allows the proceeding beyond an 'and'-connector only in cases where all possible instances of activities that are predecessor of the synchronization point has been materialized and finished. This is a quite complex constraint that in general can only be evaluated by the inspection of the whole current business process system state. For the example business process in Fig. 4.18 such a constraint would yield a deadlock, therefore, the business process model in Fig. 4.18 must be modified slightly before the constraint makes sense for it. Figure 4.20 shows such a modification. In Fig. 4.20 a case distinction has been inserted after the activity A. Figure 4.20 shows a state of the business process some steps beyond the state represented analogously for the business process in diagram (v) in Fig. 4.18. The activity instances '3' and '6' has been finished and caused the start of the new activity instances '10' and '11'. The activity instance '9' has also been finished. For what comes it is crucial that the decision point ϵ has evaluated to false after the completion of the activity instance '9' so that no further instances of the activities B and D are created.

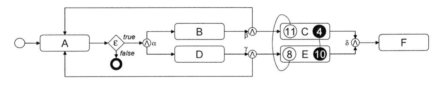

Fig. 4.20. Modified version of the business process model in Fig. 4.18.

For the sake of convenience, without loss of generality, let us assume that no further instance of activity A is created. Then, after completion of all the activity instances '4', '8', '10' and '11' the next instance of activity F can be launched in accordance with the total synchronization constraint as given above. We do not formalize this total synchronization constraint further here, however, it should be clear what is intended with it. Informally speaking, the activity F should not be executed before all of the instances of the activities C and E that have been launched and might be launched as a result of the recursive enactment of sub processes has been finished their work properly. This is a synchronization pattern that actually can be found in business process systems in practice.

Concrete synchronization in business processes easily become complex. The direct, strict application of the rather informal semantics of 'and'-connectors which launches instances of successor activities whenever instances of all predecessor activities has been finished might often not be the one you want to express in a concrete business process modeling scenario. For example, in presence of recursion it is not yet clear any more which concrete activity instances to synchronize against each other. In order to avoid this complexity of recursion, some workflow technology products simply have forbidden loops in their workflow definition language. But this is not a solution. If your business processes follow some natural recursion, you want to model them and you also want to support this recursion with your workflow technology. However, recursion is not the only reason for why synchronization in business processes can become arbitrary complex. Concrete synchronization might also depend on enterprise resource data in general, on complex state of the business process system – have a look at the modeling of the expiring condition in Fig. 4.9 as a simple example – or even data from the enterprise's environment.

Even if you would identify a lot of recurring patterns of synchronization and turn them into modeling elements, there would still be need to express arbitrary synchronizations in terms of the state of a business process and its history. This means that we believe that there is the need for a general synchronizing modeling element – like the unfilled circle in Fig. 4.9 – with multiple fan-in and a means to specify an arbitrary synchronization effect. In Sect. 9.2.10 we further report on synchronization issues in the more concrete setting of executable business process specification.

5

Decomposing Business Processes

Business process specifications easily become large. They easily become so large that it is not possible any more to manage them as a whole. This problem has an effect on, e.g., requirement elicitation, communication, realization and maintenance. Therefore hierarchies of business process models emerge, with modeling elements appearing at higher levels of the hierarchies having more abstract meanings than those at lower levels. In this chapter we discuss the parallel decomposition of control flow and data specification.

5.1 Motivation for Decomposing System Descriptions

Building hierarchies does not imply a particular modeling or documentation process. In particular, hierarchies can be built top-down or bottom-up. Stakeholders in methodology are often biased in favor of a top-down proceeding. Methodology stakeholders in the sense of this discussion are people that have an impact on the definition of the modeling guideline in a concrete project. A methodology stakeholder might have a concrete quality assurance role or job in an organization. A methodology stakeholder might also be an external consultant, or specialist. Methodology stakeholders are often influenced by methodologists, i.e., methodology book authors of methodology coaches or the like. The preference to promote top-down proceedings might stem from the systematic flavor, which a clean top-down approach implies. If a system can be specified and realized strictly top-down the system building project appears to be a mature engineering project. However, in practice you see a lot of bottom-up steps in specification. In projects you usually have a mixture of top-down and bottom-up steps that equalize insights and improvements at different levels of the hierarchy in an iteratively manner until a stable version of the documentation is reached.

Actually, using the term decomposition for the process and the result of building hierarchies of system descriptions can inherently mean a top-down

D. Draheim, *Business Process Technology: A Unified View on Business Processes, Workflows and Enterprise Applications*, DOI 10.1007/978-3-642-01588-5_5,
© Springer-Verlag Berlin Heidelberg 2010

step as well as a bottom-up step. Let us have a look at the bottom-up direction first. An existing system description can be decomposed into part systems that then can be named and used as primitives at a higher level of system description. Decomposition is then the first action in building a new higher level in the hierarchy. On the other hand, a single entity in an existing system description can be detailed by decomposing it into several new entities. If the decomposed entity is not replaced by the resulting new entities but a new lower-level hierarchy is introduced for those entities, then decomposition stands for a top-down step. An entity in a system specification is a subsystem. A subsystem is also a system. So, in the latter case we also dealt with the decomposition of a system. The difference lies in whether we decompose a system in a white-box manner or a black-box manner. White-box decomposition already sees subsystems and arranges them to system parts that can then all become subsystems at a higher level, a black-box decomposition details a system specification resulting in a description based on new subsystems that can then become a specification at a lower level.

Black-box decomposition means that you detail out the elements of a given diagram. Building a model hierarchy bottom-up with white-box decomposition involves two repeated steps, i.e., decomposition and abstraction, which is illustrated in Fig. 5.1. In the decomposition step the diagram is divided into parts. The abstraction step involves naming of the parts that stem from the decomposition and the definition of there interplay. The definition of the interplay of the abstractions can be retrieved from the diagram that has been decomposed. Building a hierarchy bottom-up appears very natural in practice. Modelers start to build a model at the finest level of granularity which is necessary to describe appropriately the phenomena under consideration. They model for a while and then there encounter that the model has become so large that it is hard to understand, maintain and to develop further. At this point, they decompose the system into smaller parts that can be understood easier, build an abstraction and compose these abstractions at a higher level of the hierarchy and try to understand the system easier at this higher level of abstraction.

5.1.1 Getting Complexity under Control

In the field of system description, building hierarchies is about getting complexity under control. Abstraction is often mentioned as the key principle in building hierarchies. Often, abstraction is explained as the omission of details. As we have already discussed in [89], the omission of details can very well be observed in abstractions, but in good abstractions, it is often not the crucial point – at least not in the naive sense of omitting details of concrete entities at the abstract level. For example, there is one widely acknowledged means of abstraction that is about parameterization teamed together with information hiding, i.e., building a parameterized higher-level entity that stands for a family of lower-level entities. For example, in mathematical logics the λ-

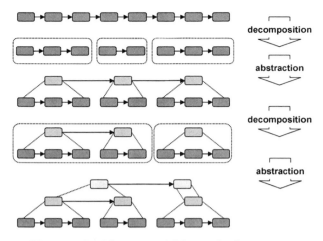

Fig. 5.1. Building a model hierarchy bottom-up.

abstraction [59] introduced by Alonzo Church to investigate the intentional aspect of set-theoretical functions is such a kind of abstraction, but so is modularization [277] as introduced by David Lorge Parnas in software engineering. In powerful cases, abstraction is often about a kind of targeted translation of properties of a system into items of an otherwise, perhaps independently elaborated, theory. For example, by mathematical modeling of the properties of an airplane mathematical reasoning about the flight characteristics of the airplane becomes possible. As a consequence of the mathematical modeling of the airplane, details are omitted. Only those properties are modeled that have an impact on the flight characteristics. However, in this case the omission of details is just an obvious by-product and not the crucial point.

In the field of business process modeling and workflow specification the omission of details is actually the central topic in building hierarchies. But not merely in the direct sense that on the more abstract level details of the more concrete level are omitted. Also the converse is true. Abstraction can also mean that some details are teared from a concrete system description level resulting in a less information loaded version of the system description. The information is shifted to a higher level of system description. This is done by partitioning the concrete system into subsystems with respect to an interesting property type. The subsystems are named and appear as entities at a new level of system description. The information about the properties is then found at the more abstract level of system description, at the level of concrete system descriptions it can be deleted, this way reducing the complexity at the concrete level. Sometimes, along these lines building a hierarchy can even be perceived as adding extra information on behalf of the abstraction instead of shifting the information. This is so, because the process of building a hierarchy can be driven by the analysis of the system with respect to a new property to investigate. Examples for such properties that may drive the building of a hierarchy may belong to the organizational structure of the enterprise that is supported by the described business processes or a sales structure imposed onto such business processes that are sold as services or software services.

5.1.2 Atomic Activities

The crucial primitives of a business process model are the activities. Assume that a business process is modeled without hierarchy. This means, assume in particular that it is not modeled as a high-level business process in a top-down modeling approach. Then the modeler has to fix a level of detail for each of the activities in his business model. In principle, an arbitrary level of detail for the single activities is possible, though there seems to be some tight natural bounds like the single clicks on a computer screen, the single key strokes on a keyboard or similar basic hand movements. An arbitrary level of detail is possible for the activities. However, for a particular project, a level of detail should be fixed by a style guide, at least for the most concrete system descriptions in the hierarchy, but at best for all the levels in the hierarchy. For example, with form-oriented analysis [89, 82, 83, 95, 94, 96, 97, 105, 106, 92, 87, 107] we have proposed a style guide for the level of system dialogue specification. Here, the formcharts have only two kinds of entities that are wired, i.e., the reports that are shown to the user at the computer screen and the server actions that appear as interaction capabilities for the user in the realm of a report.

The activities in a business process model that are not further decomposed into another business process description, i.e., the activities at the leaves of a business process description hierarchy, can be called atomic activities. If the information distributed over all the nodes in a business process hierarchy is gathered together into a large diagram, the resulting diagram can be called a flat diagram. Consider a hierarchical business process description that is complete, in the sense that no leave stands for a description that has to be detailed by further decomposition of activities at lower levels. In such complete system description the atomic actions are the ones that are usually easy to understand in their own right. Their operational semantics is described somewhere else, but by this additional documentation it should be possible to understand the whole specification. The meaning of the more abstract activities at the higher levels in a business process hierarchy is usually harder to grasp. Often, there is no real operational semantics available any more for those activities, which sometimes rather represent organizational functions, i.e., organizational parts than activities in the true sense of the word. It just lacks a unifying operational semantics framework for those functions that have a complex internal behavior with a mixture of stakeholders or roles for the several activities it is made of and a mixture of automatically supported and otherwise manual tasks.

For example, if several basic activities that are executed by the same person in a strict sequence one after each other are composed to a new entity at a higher level and if each of these activities has a neat operational semantics the resulting composed entity is likely to have also some kind of comprehensible operational semantics. On the other hand, if some unrelated activities from different persons or even from unrelated processes, i.e., processes that are started by different events, are mingled together into an abstract entity at a higher level the risk is greater that the semantics of this abstract entity is hard to understand.

Many hierarchies can have the same meaning in terms of the interplay of the atomic activities that they eventually specify. Explained from the bottom-up viewpoint of an initially given flat diagram without any hierarchy, it is clear that many process hierarchies preserving its semantics can be built on top of it. As we will discuss in Sect. 5.6.2, different driving forces with respect to the analysis of new system facets yield different hierarchies. Precisely in cases where the hierarchy does not provide extra information beyond the basic semantics of the flat diagram the choice of hierarchy is arbitrary. There is no evident or compelling general guideline for how to structure and decompose a given flat process specification, although, there are some decompositions that appear much more natural than others – Sect. 6 tries to shed some light onto this issue.

5.1.3 Leveled Data-Flow Diagrams

In general business process models are dataflow diagrams. They do not merely specify the control flow between activities but also what data is produced by an activity and sent to another for subsequent consumption. The specification of the data that flow from one activity to another can be directly attached to the respective transition between the activities. Triggered by Douglas T. Ross, leveled data-flow diagrams have been widely used in practice in the structured analysis family of methods [301, 74, 300, 302, 75, 68] like SADT (Structured Analysis and Design Technique of the company SofTech, IDEF-0 (Integrated Definition Methods) [254] and Modern Structured Analysis [361]. Here, we want to reconsider the approach of decomposing control flow and data flow in synch that has been followed by practitioners for two decades against the background of business process specification and workflow defini-tion. The goal is to have a workflow definition as an executable flat business process specification and to build a hierarchy on top of it to deal with its complexity.

We start the discussion of parallel decomposition of control and data with explicit data flow diagrams. We distinguish between explicit data flow dia-grams and implicit data flow diagrams. Explicit data flow diagrams are stan-dard. They attach descriptions or labels of data items to the transitions of a control flow diagram. Implicit data flow diagrams are more reductionist. In implicit data flow diagrams a data type is connected to each activity in the di-agram. A transition to an activity implicitly stands for the flow of data items of the type that is connected to the activity that is targeted by the considered transition. The major diagrams that has been introduced in form-oriented analysis [89], i.e., the formchart for dialogue specification and the even more basic data type interchange model (DTIM) diagram, are such implicit data flow diagrams. We believe that it is worth considering using implicit data flow diagrams for business process modeling, for example, because we believe that they are easier to grasp and more amenable to formal treatment. We discuss decomposition here on the basis of the usual explicit data flow diagrams for the reason of convenience. It should be possible to transport most of the arguments from the current discussion to implicit data flow diagrams without problems.

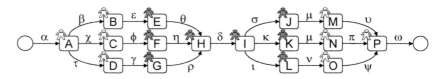

Fig. 5.2. A business process model with data flow and role specifications.

Figure 5.2 shows an example of a business process model with annotated data flow. The data items that flow along transitions are labeled with small Greek letters. The data is specified somewhere else, e.g., in a data dictionary, entity-relationship model, UML class diagram, relational database schema or the like. Furthermore, roles are attached to the activities in the model in Fig. 5.2.

Example Decomposition with Single Entry and Exit Points

Figure 5.3 shows a decomposition of the flat diagram in Fig. 5.2. The flat diagram is cut into two pieces that become stand-alone process definitions, each with its an own start and end state. Start states are also called entries, entry points, start events, initial states etc. End states are also called exits, exit points, end events etc. We choose the term interface points as the generalization of entry points and exit points.

Both the start states and the end states are depicted by unfilled circles in Fig. 5.3. The decomposition results in a process hierarchy with two levels. The two levels are separated from each other by a dotted line. On the higher level the pieces that the diagram in Fig. 5.2 has been cut into have become activities. An activity at the higher level is started as usual when it is triggered by an ingoing activity. It then activates the start node of the business process specification it stands for. An activity at the higher level refers to a business process specification it stands for at the lower level. This relationship is given by a dashed line in Fig. 5.3. The roles assigned to the basic activities of a business process specification at the lower level are merged together and assigned to the corresponding composed activity at the higher level.

The initial transition and the final transition from Fig. 5.2 and the transition at the cut point can be found at the higher level of the process hierarchy in Fig. 5.3 together with the respective data flow annotations. Actually, the original data flow α-transition from the start state to the A-transition in Fig. 5.2 is now represented in Fig. 5.3 by two transitions, i.e., an α-transition from the start state to the high-level state AH plus an α-transition from the start state to the basic A-state in the lower-level diagram. Similarly, the δ-transition, i.e., the cut point, is represented by three δ-transitions in the business process hierarchy – one in the higher process level and two in lower level. And so on for the ω-transition.

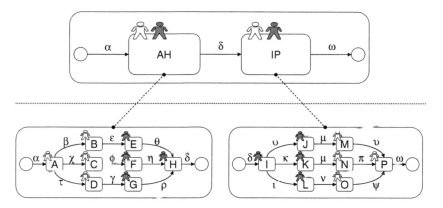

Fig. 5.3. Example for decomposition with unique start and exit points.

On the Notation of Business Process Abstraction

We have used a dashed line in Fig. 5.3 to assign a business process specification to its abstraction on a higher level. Other means of specification of this relationship are possible. A common one is specification by naming, i.e., a name is attached to a business process specification that results as a piece from the decomposition of a larger diagram. Then the name refers to that business process in other business process specifications. In Fig. 5.3 it is somehow done in the reverse direction. The name of the business process is introduced at the higher level specification where it is reduced and is transferred by the dashed line.

The discussion of the notation for business process abstraction is yet another example for a general theme that we want to foster, i.e., concrete notation is not the point, content or abstract syntax is the key. Drawing conventions are not about the content of a business process specification. A mature tool will work internally with a meta model of business processes and will allow the developer to interact with different styles of concrete syntax and concrete visualizations.

5.1.4 Process Hierarchies versus Process Abstraction

So far, in Sect. 5.1 we have talked about decomposition as if it is only about forming strict hierarchies. In general, abstraction mechanisms are independent from the possible decomposition structures they are used for and the strict hierarchy is only one such possible decomposition structure. For example, in the explanation of the abstraction specification of Fig. 5.3 we have said that a dashed line in Fig. 5.3 stands for the assignment of a business process specification to its abstraction on a higher level. Actually, for the small example in Fig. 5.3 it holds that all business process specifications are used as abstract entities only at a higher level in the process hierarchy. A strict process hierarchy is a decomposition structure where the single decompositions form a directed acyclic graph. This means that in strict process hierarchies an activity of a diagram at an inner node can be a basic activity, i.e., an activity which is not further decomposed into others, or an explorable activity, i.e., an activity that stands for another business process specification at a lower level.

Strictly Stepped Hierarchies

Some methodology stakeholders impose an even more strict condition for hierarchies that forbids decompositions spanning more than one level. This means that – with a given strict order of the levels – an entity must only refer to entities on the next lower level as its decomposition. Such strictly stepped decomposition structure may be regarded as having a particular neat and tidy structure, however, actually it is just about an issue of presentation. By introducing wrappers for entities at higher levels in the hierarchy there is a straightforward workaround to transform each strict process hierarchy in the above sense of a directed acyclic graph into a strictly stepped hierarchy. An example of such a transformation is depicted in Fig. 5.4.

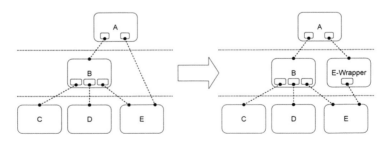

Fig. 5.4. Transforming a decomposition that spans more than one level.

We have said that a strict process hierarchy is a decomposition structure where the single decompositions form a directed acyclic graph. We assume that the levels of a strict hierarchy are implicitly given, i.e., that they are the result of building a hierarchy by decomposing a system. Levels are the result of a usage structure. In general, there is more than one usage path, i.e., directed path, to reach a component in a strict hierarchy from a given other component, because a hierarchy is not a tree but a directed acyclic graph. The level of a component in a hierarchy can be defined as the length of the longest usage path from a component at the highest level down to the component. In Fig. 5.4 the sub business process E resides on the lowest level, because it is used in the definition of the business process B at the next higher level. If the business process E would be used by the definition of process A only, it would belong to the next higher level.

Some modelers might want to have an explicit concept of levels in a hierarchy and a explicit means to define such levels. Figure 5.5 is meant as an illustration of a hierarchy with explicitly given levels. The dashed lines in Fig. 5.4 has turned into solid lines in Fig. 5.5. The solid lines in Fig. 5.5 should be considered modeling elements of a modeling language with the purpose to define levels of a hierarchy explicitly. The possibility to define levels explicitly can be exploited to create levels of conceptual abstraction. The left diagram in Fig. 5.4 is not a strictly stepped hierarchy. From the viewpoint of implicitly defined levels, also the left diagram in Fig. 5.5 is a strictly stepped hierarchy. From the viewpoint of implicitly defined levels, the processes B and E together form the second level in the hierarchy. Only with an explicit interpretation of the given levels the left diagram in Fig. 5.5 is not strictly stepped any more. It can be made a strictly stepped hierarchy, just by moving it to the next higher level, as indicated by the right diagram in Fig. 5.5. The problem here is that the modeler does not want to move the process to the next higher level, because the explicitly defined level express some conceptual level of abstraction and the considered process belongs to the considered level in the sense of these conceptual levels of abstraction. In this case, a workaround based on the introduction of a wrapper process can be applied similarly to the example given in Fig. 5.4.

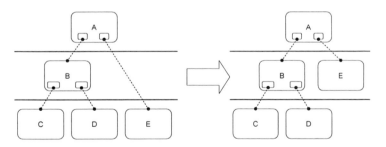

Fig. 5.5. Transforming an explicitly given hierarchy.

Recursion in Business Process Decompositions

Figure 5.6 shows an example where an activity, i.e., the CD-activity at the higher level refers to a business process specification at the lower level and this business process specification is based on an activity, i.e., the AB-activity that refers back to the business process specification at the higher level. Actually, without knowledge of the start event of the overall specification, which is determined by the way the specification emerged from a top-down or a bottom-up modeling process, it is objectively not fair anymore to say that one of the two levels separated by the dotted horizontal line is the lower one and one is the higher one. If the layout of the drawing in Figure 5.6 is neglected, the figure shows a completely symmetric situation, in particular, both of the two business process specification are completely equal with respect to the fact that they both exploit one abstraction of a business process specification from another as an activity. By the layout of the drawing we have fixed that the business process specification CD is the higher-level one and that the specification AB is the lower-level one.

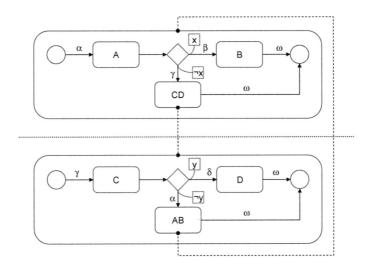

Fig. 5.6. Recursion via levels.

In Fig. 5.6 we have used a gateway for case distinction. For example in the upper business process AB we have used a gateway for testing the x-condition and routing to either the B-activity or to the CD-process. The outgoing edges of the gateway carry different type of data, i.e., the edge leading to the B-activity carries data of type β and the edge leading to the CD-process carry data of type γ. A case distinction gateway with its one ingoing and its two outgoing edges can actually be considered standing for two edges as is shown in Fig. 5.7. Diagram (ii) in Fig. 5.7 uses the conditions from the gateway in

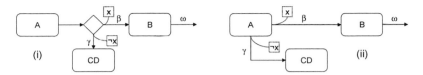

Fig. 5.7. The usage of case distinctions in data flow diagrams.

diagram (i) as what we call flow condition, enabling conditions or activation condition in form-oriented analysis and Sect. 9. Questions arise with respect to the semantics of both conditions that are used by case distinction gateways and those conditions that are directly annotated to edges of data flow diagrams like the ones in diagram (ii) in Fig. 5.7. When are the conditions evaluated? Does the evaluation still belong to the activity they are located to or not? For conditions attached to gateways: is the production of data based on the evaluation of the conditions? Answers to these questions should be elaborated if a diagram is used for modeling; and they must be elaborated if a diagram should be used as a description for the automatic execution of a business process. However, for an understanding of the following discussion it is not necessary to elaborate answers to these questions.

Figure 5.8 shows an example business process instance executed for the business process model in Fig. 5.6. We use the same ad-hoc notation for business process instances in Fig. 5.8 that we have already used in Fig. 4.4, i.e., elements of a business process instance look like elements of a business process model up to the fact that they are double lined and that they point back to the preceding element in the business process instance, because, as we have discussed in Sect. 4.1.5, we somehow want to express the history aspect of a business process instance with its visualization. The example business process instance in Fig. 5.8 starts with an upper AB-process in Fig. 5.6 which starts a lower CD-process which then recursively starts another AB-process which then again starts a final CD-process. The process instance of such recursive process definition can be considered as nested. In the current example, the innermost, i.e., the most recently started, process terminates after a D-activity

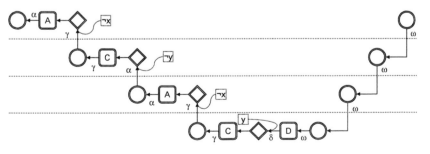

Fig. 5.8. An instance of the business process model in Fig. 5.6.

has been executed and terminates the whole nested process instance on behalf of this. This means that no further activities of the outer process instances are executed. This is so, because the business process model in Fig. 5.6 is end-recursive.

Each strictly hierarchical business process specification can be flattened into a single large diagram. This is so because a strictly hierarchical business process specification does not introduce any recursive control flow due to its acyclic structure. Even no cycles at the same level between abstractions are possible according to the above definition of strict hierarchy. Therefore, the flattening merely involves starting at the top-level diagram and recursively replacing each activity by the business process specification it stands for at a lower level. Also, some non-strict hierarchical process specifications can be flattened. Figure 5.9 shows a flattened version of the specification in Fig. 5.6. The dashed lines that specify the relation between activities and abstracted business processes in Fig. 5.6 together introduce a control flow cycle. This control flow cycle can be found in Fig. 5.9. The business process instance in Fig. 5.8 is also an instance of the business process model in Fig. 5.9, because the three ω-transitions in Fig. 5.8 can be considered a single ω-transition. The ω-transition is painted threefold in Fig. 5.8 in order to visualize that we consider the business process as nested with respect to the business process specification in Fig. 5.6.

Figure 5.9 once more shows the symmetry of the situation. We have established that the specification AB in Fig. 5.6 is the higher-level one only by the layout of the painting. If we chose to make the specification CD the higher-level one instead, all we have to do in Fig. 5.9 is to make the start event target the C-activity instead of the A-activity.

It is easy to transform the process hierarchy in Fig. 5.6 into the diagram in Fig. 5.9, because both of the process definitions in Fig. 5.6 are end-recursive. Things would change if, for example, the ω-transition from the CD-activity to the end point of the higher-level diagram in Fig. 5.6 is changed to target the B-activity. Then, it would not be possible any more to transform the resulting specification into a flat diagram that expresses the same behavior in terms of the used modeling elements and basic activities. This means that allowing for

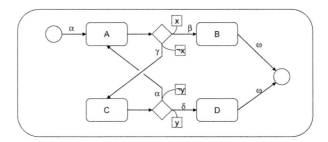

Fig. 5.9. Flattening the recursive business process specifcation in Fig. 5.6.

arbitrary abstractions – or to say it more precisely – allowing for arbitrary cycles in abstracting structures adds to the expressive power of modeling.

Expressive Power of Recursion for Business Domain-Oriented Modeling

Unlike the distinction between strictly hierarchical modeling and strictly stepped hierarchical modeling as presented in Fig. 5.4, the difference between strictly hierarchical modeling and arbitrary usage of abstraction and therefore the usage of recursion is not merely a presentation issue. In terms of the same set of basic activities there are some behaviors that are expressible only with arbitrary abstraction or extra manipulations on the global data space in order to encode some information that can be exploited in appropriate constraints on the control flow.

You can express a repeated behavior of a business process with a cycle in a business process model without abstraction mechanism, i.e., with what we call an activity cycle. You can also express repeated behavior by recursive calls of business processes to abstractions of business processes, i.e., by what we call cycles in the usage of business process abstraction, abstraction cycles or business process cycles for short. However, we think that there are some behaviors that should be expressed better with a business process cycle instead of an activity cycle. There are some behaviors that need extra mechanisms to be described without abstraction mechanism, which violates the principle of domain orientation in business process modeling that we have described in Sect. 6.2.5 and 6.4.

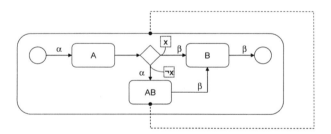

Fig. 5.10. Self-recursive business process model that is not end-recursive.

Figure 5.10 shows a very simple business process cycle. Actually it is an example of a self-recursive business process definition, i.e., the business process model invokes itself as AB-activity or AB-sub-process. The process definition in Fig. 5.10 is not end-recursive. This means that after the execution of an AB-sub-process there is still some work to do – the B-activity – in the business process that invoked the AB-sub-process. Fig. 5.11 shows an business process instance started for the business process model in Fig. 5.10. The sub business process AB is entered over and over again until the recursion exit condition x evaluates to true. The effect of the invocation of an AB-sub-process is the execution of an A-activity, which we assume to be a basic activity. For each nested invocation of an AB-activity an B-activity has to be executed after the completion of the invoked AB-activity.

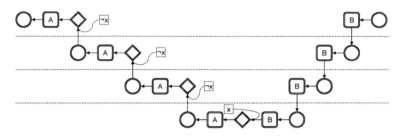

Fig. 5.11. An instance of the business process model in Fig. 5.10.

Figure 5.12 shows an attempt to express the behavior defined by the business process model in Fig. 5.10 with a flat business process specification, i.e., without the usage of abstraction and recursive call. The business process model uses a cycle or loop to express the repeated execution of the A-activity. The recursion exit condition x from Fig. 5.10 becomes the loop exit condition x in Fig. 5.12. The business process model in Fig. 5.12 must ensure that the correct number of B-activities is executed after the loop exit condition x has been evaluated to true. For this reason, an extra mechanism is introduced that counts the number of times an A-activity is executed. The mechanism consists out of three extra activities for setting the counter to zero, increasing the counter and decreasing the counter at appropriate places in the business process model. The execution of the correct number of B-activities is also modeled with a loop that exploits the aforementioned counter in its exit condition.

How could we argue that the business process model in Fig. 5.10 is pragmatically better than the one in Fig. 5.12? Firstly, let us assume that the activities in Fig. 5.10 somehow express real-world activities, i.e., meaningful activities in the real world that have to be orchestrated by the business process. The business process model Fig. 5.12 introduces new activities. What does this introduction mean? Should these activities of counting be actually introduced in the real world? For example, should a worker track the number of executions on a piece of paper? With respect to this, Fig. 5.10 is easier to understand. It simply says, that after recursive execution of an AB-activity a somehow dangling B-activity is executed. It is left open in Fig. 5.10, how the execution of the B-activity is eventually ensured. But this is no difference of this scenario to other invocations of activities that occur after the invocation of an immediate activity, be it a invocation of a sub process or the invocation of a basic activity. The point is that the mechanism that ensures the correct order of execution is not fixed by the business process model. On the contrary, it is assumed that the order defined by the business process model is followed. However, the business process model in Fig. 5.12 explicitly defines a mechanism for the correct order of execution of some of its entities.

Secondly, we believe that the business process model in Fig. 5.10 expresses a conceptual connection of those instances of B-activities with those instances of A-activities that are invoked in the context of the same sub-process instance. The reader of the business process model in Fig. 5.10 is motivated to understand that the A-activity of an AB-process is conceptually related to the B-activity that occurs after the inner recursive invocation of a next AB-process. If this is that what the modeler actually wanted to express than the business process model in Fig. 5.10 again should be preferred over the business process model in Fig. 5.12, because we think that in Fig. 5.12 it is not immediately motivated to understand that the first A-activity is conceptually related to the last B-activity, the second A-activity is conceptually related to the second last B-activity and so forth.

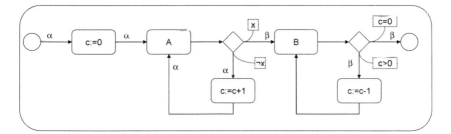

Fig. 5.12. Flattening the recursive business process specification in Fig. 5.10.

Presentation Issues of Recursion in Business Process Hierarchies

If you establish a recursive call in a business process hierarchy, leveling becomes void in a certain sense to a certain degree. We have said that strict hierarchies are directed acyclic graph and have defined the level of a component as the longest usage path to this component moving down from the root to the component. A level in a hierarchy consists of all those components that are equal with respect to their longest usage paths from the root. Up to now, only by the containment in an explicitly defined strictly leveled hierarchy you could construct a notion of higher versus lower levels for a decomposition cycle. We have already seen an example in Figs. 5.6 and Fig. 5.9. There, it would be possible to choose any of the two business process specifications as the higher-level one depending of whether the start state of the process specification AB or the start state of the specification CD is chosen as the overall start state. Even without explicit definition of levels it would be possible to define an alternative, meaningful notion of level and some kind of weakened notion of strict hierarchy that is compatible with the usage of abstraction cycles. The approach is to define that all components of an abstraction cycle belong to the same level.

Refinement Hierarchies

In practical projects strict hierarchies are promoted by methodology stakeholders due to the tidy and neat appearance of diagrams. If you hierarchically organize an already existing complete business process specification bottom-up this will perhaps end in a strict hierarchy quite naturally. You just grasp chunks of the diagram entities as features and make them abstractions. You then describe the interplay of them on a perceived higher level of abstraction. You proceed this way building several levels of abstraction.

Also, top-down approaches and in particular the concept of refinement on the process side are typically connected to strict hierarchies on the artifact side – as if strict hierarchies naturally result from repeated refinements. But such connection is not really justified. If you start with the description of the system at a high level and proceed by detailing activities you might easily come across the situation at one level that you want to recursively call a business process that you have already defined earlier at a higher level. The point is that a certain strict interpretation of the notion of refinement actually leads to strict hierarchies. You might want to argue that – in the true sense of the word – it is only allowed to refine an entity in terms of new entities, i.e., entities that have to be created newly on behalf of a refinement step. Actually, such strict understanding of the notion of refinement would rule out some directed acyclic graph structures as non valid, i.e., those structures that are not trees.

5.2 Unique versus Multiple Entry and Exit Points

A crucial point in the flexibility and expressiveness of business process specifications with respect to hierarchical structure is the question of whether a business process can have only unique or multiple entries and exits.

5.2.1 Exploiting Multiple Entry and Exit Points

In Fig. 5.3 we have used only process specifications with a unique start and a unique exit point in the concrete decomposition and hierarchy of the diagram Fig. 5.2. The problem is that the chosen cut point, i.e., the δ-transition, is actually the only option to decompose the flat diagram in Fig. 5.2 as long as we do not allow for auxiliary modeling concepts like the usage of multiple interface points or multiple paintings of a modeling element. The problem is that the chosen partition in Fig. 5.3 might not be the desired or most natural one. Decomposing in order to get complexity under control is usually not just about arbitrary partitioning of a diagram with the target that the specification that one has to deal with becomes smaller and therefore better to handle. It is good if the parts that result from the decomposition express a feature or notion of the real world. This means that the decomposition is usually driven by some kind of conceptual cohesion of the entities.

The diagram in Fig. 5.2 visualizes a good example for a potential driving force in the decomposition of a business process specification, i.e., the orientation towards roles. The diagram in Fig. 5.2 has three natural regions with respect to the two roles. A first one consisting of the activities A through D, which all have the white role assigned to them, a second middle region with the activities E through L, which all have the gray role assigned to them, and a last region consisting of the remaining activities M through P, which again all have a white role assigned to them. A modeler might want to turn exactly these regions into part specifications and eventually into process abstractions. With the restriction to unique interface points he can not do this simply. Fig. 5.13 shows the solution with the usage of multiple interface points.

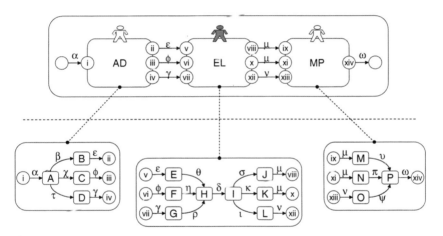

Fig. 5.13. Example for decomposition with multiple start and exit points.

If the restriction to unique interface points is dropped, an identification of interface points must be introduced in order to distinguish them. In Fig. 5.13 all the interface points are uniquely labeled. The transitions of a higher-level diagram are necessary to specify the interplay of activities from the lower specification level across process specification boundaries. Via the uniquely identifiable interface points it is possible to wire transitions from one specification with transitions of another one. We delve into the semantics of multiple interface events, i.e., into the semantics of business process specifications havin multiple interface points in Sect. 5.2.2.

The labeling chosen in Fig. 5.13 is a bit more accurate than actually necessary, because the labels must be unique only with respect to the process specification they belong to and their kind, i.e., entry or exit point. An identification via the annotated data flow is not always possible, because the data flow might also be ambiguous as can be seen for the μ-transitions in the example of Fig. 5.13. Without the interface point labels 'viii' through 'xi' it would not be possible to tell from Fig. 5.13 whether the J-activity or the K-activity are connected to the M-activity or N-activity.

With respect to the roles the decomposition represented in Fig. 5.13 has the valuable effect that the role annotations can be dropped from the activities at the lower level specifications. This is so, because the lower-level specifications are homogenous with respect to the roles. The annotation of a role to a specification abstraction at the higher level of the diagram is sufficient, because such a role specification is valid for all the activities of the corresponding specification. This is the difference to the decomposition solution presented in Fig. 5.3. Here the role annotation at the higher level specification is less informative.

For example, if you are playing the role of a project manager and you want to divide work on the basis of the process description in Fig. 5.13 you assign work in terms of the higher-level activities and you are done. The two persons that you have assigned the activities to can then figure out what to do by delving into the more detailed process description of their assigned activities at the lower level. Each person can do this without coordination with the other person, because the person's tasks are clearly separated from each other by the decomposition structure. The same is not true for the specification in Fig. 5.3. As a project manager you now assign all of the tasks to both of the persons. The persons together delve into the details of all activities. The problem is that each of the person can now see details of the process that he is not actually concerned with, which is a violation of the information hiding principle.

5.2.2 On the Semantics of Multiple Start and End Events

This section extends and complements the discussion on the semantics of events in Sect. 4.5. The semantics of multiple interface points is not easy. Synchronization phenomena have an impact on possible semantics.

A crucial problem is the semantics of start states and in terms of the enactment of process instances. For a business process with multiple start states, which is an activity at a higher level in a hierarchy, e.g., the process and activity EL in Fig. 5.13, it is, basically, possible to fix two kinds of semantics with respect to multiple start events:

- Closed semantics, extensional-like semantics. A process instance is created whenever a start event is triggered. The start of a process instance disables any further triggers to start events in the realm of the execution of the current process instance. This semantics is a self-explaining, i.e., self-contained from the viewpoint of the single business process.

- Open semantics, intensional-like semantics. After the start of a process instance all start events remain enabled, they are gateways to the dynamically evolving context of the process instance. The behavior of a process instance cannot be understood without the context it lives in.

The definitions of open and closed semantics of business process specifications are tight with respect to how events have to be understood during the execution of a business process instance. The further parts of the definition and the arguments based on them are weaker, in particular, for the closed semantics. The behavior of a business process with what we call closed semantics is actually not really self-contained, i.e., it is not really self-explaining, because the semantics of a business process has to be understood always in the context of the system's state, for example, in the context of the data of an information system. This means, in particular, that an open semantics with further events beyond the ones directly modeled in the business process can be simulated within a business process specification with closed semantics. Exactly for this reason we have also used extensional-like instead of merely extensional for the closed semantics and intensional-like instead of intensional for the open semantics. The terminology of extensional versus intensional stems from logics, where the meanings of statements of an extensional apparatus are not influenced by the usage of statements, whereas, the statement of an intensional apparatus can, in general, only be understood as parts of their usage.

Building Hierarchies with Closed Semantics

Each start event can be triggered independently from the outside. If we fix an extensional semantics this means, that once a business process instance is created, all of the start events are disabled for the lifetime of the process instance. This also means that the start of a process instance preempts all regions that are reachable via start events other than the initially triggered. For example, if the activity EL in Fig. 5.3 is started via the interface point (vi) it is sure that the activities E and G will not be executed during the lifetime of the started business process instance and, furthermore, the activity F is executed exactly one time during the lifetime of the business process instance, because also the interface point (vi) is disabled henceforth.

If the business process specifications of a modeling language or methodology are given a closed semantics in the above sense, this means that not all decompositions and abstractions are possible any more. This means that there may be hierarchies built on top of a given flat diagram that do not conserve the semantics of this flat diagram. As an example, please have a look at the flat business process specification in Fig. 5.2 and the concrete decomposition and abstraction of this business process model in Fig. 5.13. With a closed semantics of business process specifications the hierarchy in Fig. 5.13 is a valid one only under certain assumptions. In Fig. 5.2 there is still ambiguity with respect to concrete control flow. In Fig. 5.14 we have given three alternatives of further control flow specification for a sub diagram in Fig. 5.2.

In diagram (i) in Fig. 5.14 the next activity after execution of the A-activity is uniquely determined by a case distinction gateway. In diagram (ii) a parallel gateway forks both a B-, C and D-activity after completion of the A-activity. The strands of execution forked by the parallel gateway in diagram (ii) are not synchronized before the execution of the H-activity. This means that each strand of execution starts its own copy of the H-activity which is indicated by the joining 'or'-gateway. This is not so for the business process given by diagram (iii) in Fig. 5.14. Here, a synchronizing 'and'-gateway is used instead of the non-synchronizing 'or'-statements. This means that the three strands of execution initiated after the execution of the A-activity are re-joined by the 'and'-gateway and a single instance of the H-activity is started. We have used some common notation for the case distinction, the parallel fork and the synchronization in Fig. 5.14. However, the notation is not the point. For example, in Sect. 9.2.2 we do without gateways to express the same aspects of control flow. The point is the meaning of the different control flows of the business processes based on the diagrams (i) through (iii) and therefore we have used some commonly accepted notation for them. For example, we take for granted that the case distinction gateway used in Fig. 5.14 actually has the semantics of uniquely evaluating the given conditions and the given fall through branch.

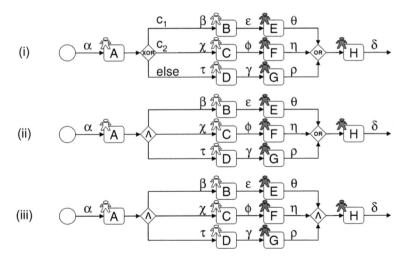

Fig. 5.14. Alternative control flows for a sub business process from Fig. 5.2.

The hierarchy in Fig. 5.13 is based on a cut through the ϵ-, ϕ-, and γ-edges in Fig. 5.2. This cut is a valid cut if the business process in Fig. 5.2 behaves like (i) Fig. 5.14 with respect to the sub diagram specified in Fig. 5.14. Let us assume that the business process behaves like (i) in Fig. 5.14. If an *EL*-activity is started it is guaranteed that no further events (v), (vi) or (vii) that are relevant for the behavior of the process instance will occur henceforth, because the case distinction was unique after the *A*-activity. Therefore, it is possible to disable the entry points immediately after the start of the process instance. In the overall system further events (v) through (vii) can occur in parallel to the current execution of the started *EL*-activity. These events can stem from further processes that have been initially started by the very entry point (i) of the business process specifications. However, these further events (v) through (vii) are not relevant to the currently considered *EL*-activity. On the contrary, each of these events is meant to create a fresh instance of the *EL*-activity which again can have a closed semantics.

Now, let us assume that the business process in Fig. 5.2 behaves like (iii) in Fig. 5.14, i.e., parallel executions are forked and synchronized later. Then the cut through the ϵ-, ϕ-, and γ-edges in Figs. 5.2 and Fig. 5.13 is not valid any more for a closed semantics. If a *EL*-activity has been created, the input interface points cannot be considered disabled any more, because they are relevant to the behavior of the started sub-process instance.

Now, let us assume that the business process in Fig. 5.2 behaves like (ii) in Fig. 5.14, i.e., parallel executions are forked but not synchronized before the execution of the *H*-activity. The answer to the question whether the cut through the ϵ-, ϕ-, and γ-edge is valid or not depends. The rest of the diagram has to be analyzed to answer the question, because it is possible that the initiated strands of execution need synchronization later, i.e., after the execution of the *H*-activity. If the rest of the diagram, i.e., the part started by the *I*-activity and ended with the *P*-activity also behaves like one of the patterns (i) or (ii) in Fig. 5.14 it is a valid cut, otherwise it is not. This means, that, in general, parallel forks do not harm as long as the started process instances are not synchronized.

With an analysis of the whole diagram and its decomposition following the lines of the above discussion it can be decided whether a given hierarchy with closed semantics is valid with respect to a given flat diagram.

Building Hierarchies with Open Semantics

If a business process specification with multiple start events has open semantics this means, that a business process accepts further events via its interface point after it has been started. The concrete behavior of a business process with open semantics can only be understood by looking at and analyzing the whole flat diagram. If you want to understand the behavior of an activity at a higher level of a model hierarchy, in general – or let's say better – in the worst case, you have to recursively unfold all activities of the given level via all lower level down to the lowest level and reconstruct the flat diagram from these unfolded diagrams first. Then, you can analyze the resulting diagram and can understand the behavior of the considered abstract entity as its footprint sub diagram in the whole flat diagram.

Relevance of the Chosen Business Process Semantics

The chosen business process semantics impacts the decompositionality of business processes. However, the chosen business process semantics may also have further advantages and disadvantages.

With an open semantics the modeler has an unrestricted flexibility in building hierarchies. The abstractions made are merely viewports onto a diagram at a lower level of the hierarchy. With a closed semantics only those hierarchies can be built that do not contradict the behavior of the underlying flat diagram. A business process with a closed semantics is a capsule. Once, it is started, its behavior is not influenced by events from the context. In that sense its behavior is easier to understand than the behavior of a business process with open semantics. With a closed semantics you can define and execute a meaningful simulation of the system at each level of the hierarchy, i.e., a simulation in terms of the activities and transition from the given level.

Business processes with only one start event are special cases of business processes with multiple start events. Business process specifications that have only a single unique start event do not automatically have a closed semantics. Once a process with a single start event is start, in general, a further event may drop in through the entry point. However, if you have a modeling language with unique start events in practice, you usually assume a closed semantics for it.

5.2.3 On Reasons for the Restriction to Unique Interface Points

You might ask why one should restrict oneself to the usage of unique entries and exits for business process specification at all and why it is worth looking at this restriction. A straightforward answer is the semantic difficulties of multiple interface points.

Actually, in concrete projects in practice we often see explicit guidelines that restrict entries and exits to being unique for a business process specification. Even without explicit guidelines there is often a tacit understanding of business process modeling that entries and exits, or at least entries should be unique. For example, the concrete UML tutorial [190] states that a UML activity diagram may have only one start state. As an example for an academic publication, the paper [119], which aims at formalization of UML activity diagrams, gives a definition for activity diagrams that allows for a single start state and a single end state only. Section 9.3.2 of the specification of the Business Process Modeling Notation (BPMN) [265] warns the reader that a process specification with multiple start events may be harder to understand. The specification also strongly recommends the reader to use multiple start events only sparingly and advises him that he should be aware of the potential difficulties of other modelers in understanding the intent of a diagram with multiple start events.

So what are the reasons for the deprecation of multiple start states? One obvious reason may be that modelers want to avoid the extra effort to fix further notation and semantics for dealing with multiple entries and exits of a business process specification, in particular, with respect to the interplay between several business process specifications in a hierarchy. Actually, as we have seen in Sect. 5.2.2, significant effort is needed to fix extra notation and semantics for multiple start states; and in practice this effort remains a hurdle.

Another reason might be that business process specification and in particular also their visual presentations, i.e., the business process diagrams, might appear more structured to many modelers and therefore have a more systematic appeal. This argument has two facets, i.e., a local one and a global one. The local one is about the single business process specification with its start and exit point. The global one is about the interconnection of several business process specifications at a higher level in the specification hierarchy. From the local viewpoint a business process specification with one entry and one exit point is immediately understandable as a functional transformation. The data that is given to the process instance at the time of its creation is eventually transformed into data that leaves the process instance via the single exit point. If a process has multiple entry states and multiple exit states it is slightly more difficult to understand it as a functional transform. In case of a single entry point the input type of the functional transformation can be immediately understood as the type of the data item that is annotated to the incoming transition of the process specification. The same applies for the output type in case of a single exit point.

5.2.4 Notational Issues of Unique Interface Points

In Fig. 5.3 we have used the same notation for the start state and the end state. Some modeling notations introduce extra notation in order to distinguish the entry from the exit point. Such a visual distinction is merely syntactical sugar. Anyhow, after different symbols has been introduced, a guideline must be imposed that demands that a start state has no ingoing transitions and a exit point has no outgoing transitions. Exactly these constraints can be taken as definitions in case we do not use extra notations for the start and end event. The start event is the one that has no incoming transitions and the end event is the one that has no outgoing transitions. As important constraints there remains the rule that none of the interface points should have incoming and outgoing transitions at the same time. Actually, no special symbol for interface points is necessary, in particular in the case when it is assumed that all process definitions have exactly one entry point and exactly one exit point. Equally well the symbols for the start event and end event can be dropped completely resulting in some dangling transitions. This causes no harm. In general, this discussion once more leads to the observation that a modeling concept, i.e., the uniqueness of interface points in this case, must in general not be confused with a similar visualization concept.

Some modeling guidelines allow for the drawing of multiple start states. Then they introduce a notion of invocation of a process instance according to the process definition. Then, they give the semantics to the various start states as each being marked with a token upon creation of a business process instance. Such a notation and semantics does not add expressiveness compared to a language that allows only to draw a unique start state. As with all modeling elements it is just the question whether the multiple symbols introduce a conceptually new modeling element or the several symbols refer to the same conceptual modeling element. In the above description of a possible semantics of several start states the choice was made for the reference to the conceptually same entity. Because the several start events are not distinguished further they can be interpreted as representing a single start event that has as outgoing transitions the set union of all those transitions that leave one of the start state's symbols.

Semantically, it is not too important to discuss whether the several symbols represent a single conceptual start state or each one a different start state. The crucial point is that they share an important meaning, i.e., that they are all triggered whenever a business process instance is created. Actually, the several drawings of a start state can be exploited for more sophisticated semantics. Some properties that are shared by all outgoing transitions of a start state can be hosted as annotations to the start state. An example of such a transition property could be the delay after the initial trigger. In the case that some such properties of transitions clutter a diagram the usage of multiple states in the described way could help. In general, the motivation for using several start states for visualizing an undistinguishable start event are layout based, e.g., to avoid crossing transitions or transitions that appear too long. Such reasons are not in the realms of specification accuracy, they are merely about the pragmatics of communicating the contents of a business process specification.

5.2.5 Decomposition by Business Goal Orientation

In Fig. 5.13 we have seen a decomposition of the business process in Fig. 5.2 that allows for multiple start and end states of the abstractions that result from the decomposition. The usage of multiple start and end states reveals more flexibility for decomposing to the developers. In the example in Fig. 5.13 this extra flexibility was exploited for a role orientation in decomposing the system.

A role is a feature. Orientation towards roles is an instance of what we have called feature-orientation [89] in the decomposition of a system. Formally a feature is an arbitrary subset of a system specification. In particular if you are modeling in the hierarchy in a bottom-up fashion, orientation towards features is a common pattern. Here, in business process modeling, we do not have to stick to the feature terminology and do not have to discuss and justify it, because we have the notion of business process at hand. Conceptually, a business process is a net of activities that together achieve a business goal – please also have a look at the definition of business process [356] as given by the Workflow Management Coalition that we have cited in Sect. 9.1.1. So in the sense of feature orientation, business goals are features.

If your business process diagram has become too large and there is need to decompose it into parts in order to get complexity under control it is a natural pattern to be oriented towards business goals. Orientation towards business goals can give guidance in the decomposition of a business process diagram. The activities of the overall large business process are there for together achieving an overall business goal. The question is whether it is possible to naturally identify and define sub goals of this overall business goal. Then, the diagram can be divided into those sub business processes that are necessary to achieve each of the sub goals.

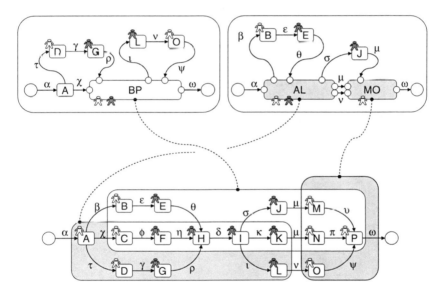

Fig. 5.15. Decomposing a business process according to business goals.

Figure 5.15 shows a division of the business process model given in Fig. 5.2 into parts – or let's say – business sub goals or features. The resulting parts can be exploited in building a next level of a hierarchy. This creation of a next level is not unique. Furthermore, there is the problem that you cannot exploit all parts from a set of overlapping parts. The strict orientation towards business goals allows for full flexibility of identifying meaningful sub parts of a business process. The problem of such freedom in finding sub parts is that the found sub parts may overlap. And so it is in the example in Fig. 5.15. There are three sub-processes in Fig. 5.16, i.e., *BP*, *AL* and *MO*. *BP* overlaps both *AL* and *MO*, whereas *AL* and *MO* do not overlap each other. Two possible alternatives of next levels built on the basis of the three identified sub-processes are shown in Fig. 5.16. The left one exploits the sub-process *BP* and the right one exploits the sub-processes *AL* and *MO*. In both of the alternatives we have used not only abstractions of sub-processes from the lower level at the higher level but also some of the activities of the lower level. This is possible and just means that the hierarchy in Fig. 5.16 is not strictly stepped – we have described the concept of a strictly stepped hierarchy in Sect. 5.1.4.

The two alternative higher level business process diagrams in Fig. 5.15 are possible with an open semantics of business process specifications that we have described in Sect. 5.2.2.

In general, it is not possible to exploit the process *BP* in Fig. 5.15 together with one of its overlapping sub-processes *AL* or *MO* without further explanation. For example, let us assume that the business process shows a parallel control flow after the completion of the *A*-activity, i.e., that we have to deal with a situation as given by diagram (iii) in Fig. 5.14. Then, if both sub-process *BP* and sub-process *AL* together occur in a diagram at a higher level you have a problem in modeling. You somehow need to model a parallel trigger of *BP* and *AL* and without further care and comment this would mean that too many instances of those activities that belong to the overlapping region of *BP* and *AL* are created.

Figure 5.16 shows a yet simpler business process model with two identified sub-processes. The two sub-processes overlap, however, it is possible to combine them in a joint business process specification at a higher level of a hierarchy without confusion. The flat diagram in Fig. 5.16 is, basically, the diagram (i) in Fig. 5.14. There are three possible strands of the business pro-

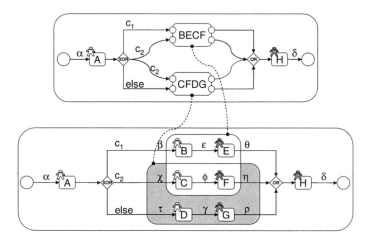

Fig. 5.16. Overlapping business goals that are compatible in a hierarchy.

cess that are uniquely selected after the completion of the A-activity. One of the strands occurs in both of the sub-processes, however, this poses no problem for the usage of the two sub-processes in the upper diagram in Fig. 5.16, because the strands are uniquely selected.

5.2.6 Duplication of Modeling Elements and its Semantics

Figure 5.17 shows an example of a business process model in which some of the modeling elements, i.e., the H-activity and the I-activity, are painted more than just once. Such duplication of modeling elements should be supported by modeling tools. For example, it should be possible to have a means of copying a modeling element by reference so that the relationship between the two copies is maintained by the tool henceforth. For example, a renaming of one of the copies should lead to a renaming of all other copies and a deletion of a modeling element for which copies exist should not be executed without caution by the tool and question which of the other copies should be removed also. It has to be said that semantically there is only one unique conceptual modeling element, and that all the copies or duplicate paintings of a modeling element refer to this conceptual modeling element.

The single paintings of a conceptual modeling element may differ from the conceptual modeling element and the real conceptual modeling element may be given only by the aggregate information given by all of its paintings. For example, the conceptual modeling element H in Fig. 5.17 has three ingoing transitions labeled θ, η and ρ and one outgoing transitions labeled δ. Each of the paintings of the H-activity has the δ-transition as the outgoing transitions but none of the paintings has all of the ingoing transitions. Similarly, each painting of the I-activity shows only one out of three possible outgoing transitions σ, κ or ι of the conceptual I-activity. The fact that the several paintings of a modeling element together form a conceptually modeling element and the importance of appropriate tool support for this fact is expressed by dashed borders in Fig. 5.17.

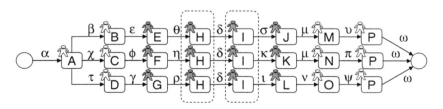

Fig. 5.17. An alternative business process specification with duplicated activities yielding more options for decomposition.

It is possible to fix alternative semantics for the multiple paintings of conceptual modeling elements. The first one is a direct, plain semantics and the second one is what we call a state history modeling semantics. In the direct semantics a painting of a conceptual modeling element simply expresses the behavior and capabilities of the conceptual modeling element. For example, with a direct semantics, the uppermost occurrence of the I-activity in Fig. 5.17 would mean that an actor has not only the possibility to progress with J-activity via the transition σ but also to progress with the K-activity via the κ-transition or the L-activity via the ι-transition. Such semantics can be immediately given but has the risk that duplicate paintings of modeling elements lead to obfuscation of the business process model, because in understanding an activity you always should also have a look at all the other copies of the activities in the diagram.

A state history modeling semantics is another means to interpret several paintings of a modeling element. We have given such state history modeling semantics to formcharts in form-oriented analysis [101, 89]. In such semantics the painting expresses the capabilities of a process dependent from its history. Actually, the resulting meaning is quite natural. We do not elaborate the semantics formally hear, but explain it through an example. With a state history modeling semantics, the uppermost occurrence of the I-activity in Fig. 5.17 has a narrower semantics as the one described before. The meaning of the painting is that an actor has only one possibility to progress, i.e., with the J-activity via the transition σ. This means that in the business process the path via which the instance of an activity has been reached determines which opportunities are available next.

With a direct semantics the business process model in Figs. 5.2 and 5.17 are equivalent, i.e., they describe the same business process. With a direct semantics the business process model in Fig. 5.17 can be considered simply as a bloated painting of the business process in Fig. 5.2. With a state history modeling semantics this is not longer true. With a state history modeling semantics Fig. 5.17 expresses more information about the control flow than the business process model in Fig. 5.2. The information about the control flow expressed by Fig. 5.17 can also be expressed with appropriate comments to or auxiliary constraints imposed onto the business process model in Fig. 5.2, but as long as this is not done the business process model in Fig. 5.17 is more expressive.

If a closed semantics of business process is required, the diagram in Fig. 5.17 interpreted with a state history modeling semantics allows for more options for semantics-preserving decomposition and abstraction than the diagram interpreted with a direct semantics or the diagram given in Fig. 5.2. Figure 5.18 shows a decomposition of the diagram in Fig. 5.17 that gives an impression of the flexibility for decomposition of the diagram.

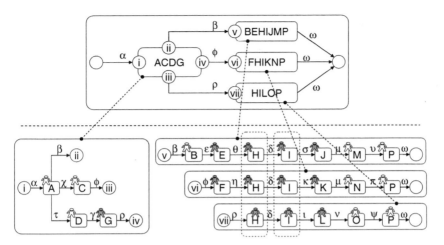

Fig. 5.18. An example business goal oriented decomposition.

5.3 Parallel Abstraction of Activities and Transferred Data

In the hierarchies built so far there is an asymmetry in the abstraction of activities and transitions. For example, in Fig. 5.13 there are more abstract or unfolding activities $ABCD$, EL and MP at the upper level of the hierarchy that stand for more concrete or unfolded business processes at the lower level. The transitions at the upper level remain the same at the higher level as the transitions at the lower level. This means that respect to the transitions and the data transferred between the activities the granularity or level of abstraction remains the same throughout all levels of the hierarchy when moving upwards from the lowest to the highest level in the hierarchy. Such asymmetry in the decomposition of nodes and edges is not practical and will lead to diagrams at the higher levels that are cluttered with transitions that stem from the lowest level.

The ratio of activities and transitions is naturally given in the flat diagram at the lowest level, however, the higher we move upwards the levels in the hierarchy the more this ratio can become unbalanced. And it is not only a question of the number of activities compared to the number of transitions. It is also a question of the conceptual abstraction level. The conceptual abstraction level of activities might not fit any more to the conceptual abstraction level of entities exchanged by the activities. However, it is possible to identify examples of asymmetry in the conceptual detail level of activities and exchanged data in a system specification that make sense. For example, a simple order that is used at the lowest level of the hierarchy of a complex system model hierarchy may be the appropriate trigger of a complex ordering process also at the most abstract level of the system model. The same might be true for simple activities processing complex items or data. It might be possible that a very basic activity for which it makes no sense to decompose and detail it further, for example a simple remove or copy transaction, processes a complex information that is assembled from several data that stem from several other complex activities.

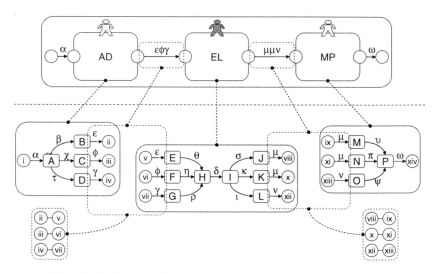

Fig. 5.19. Parallel decomposition of activities and transitions.

The parallel decomposition of nodes and edges, of activities and transitions, of control flow and data flow has been subject of investigation of structured analysis [301, 74, 300, 302, 75, 68]. In Figure 5.19 we show an attempt to express the parallel decomposition of activities and transitions of a business process model. As usual, the activities in the upper, more abstract diagram stand for sub-processes in the flat diagram. The transitions in the upper diagram now stand for sets of transitions in the lower level of the hierarchy. As usual dashed lines assign processes from the lower level to activities at the higher level. Each process has a solid line as a border. Similarly, we now use dashed lines to assign sets of transitions from the lower level to aggregate transitions at the higher level. The sets of transitions that are assigned to a transition at the higher level are visually aggregated with a dashed border.

The sub-processes in the flat diagram can be considered as the result of dividing the flat diagram into parts. Usually a division of this hierarchy building step cuts the transitions of the business process model in two pieces so that all the resulting sub business process diagrams keep all their ingoing edges an outgoing edges from the flat diagram. In Fig. 5.13 the flat diagram from which the sub-processes stem is not available. The information, how the single sub-processes at the lower level are connected with each other is given by the transitions at the higher level. For this purpose the interface points of the sub-processes have unique identifiers. In order to understand the connection of the sub-processes in Fig. 5.13 the lower level is not sufficient, i.e., the flat diagram can only be reconstructed by looking at the whole hierarchical diagram. The point is that Fig. 5.13 is almost a special case for which it is almost possible to derive the flat diagram only from the diagram at the lowest level, because the labeling of the transitions is almost unique. However, the μ-transitions form the counter example, i.e., the two μ-transitions are not uniquely labeled. It is not possible to tell from the diagrams at the lower levels in Fig. 5.13 alone whether the J is connected via its outgoing μ-transition to the M-activity or to the N-activity in the diagram to the right of it.

In modeling tools you can experience a model hierarchy by clicking on unfolding modeling elements at one of the higher levels. As a result of clicking on an unfolding modeling element the unfolded model is shown to the user. Furthermore, a tool should offer the opportunity to print out the flat diagram which can be reconstructed form the hierarchy. Furthermore, with a modeling tool it should be possible to reach a process that is connected to another one via interface points exactly by navigating via these interface points. This means that we do not have to delve too much into notational questions or even detailed questions of uniquely defined concrete syntax here. What counts for us is the content, i.e., the abstract syntax of models. However, it is also important to have a look at concepts of model presentation, like the above discussion of means to experience a hierarchy with a tool. In that sense we also delve into detail question of concrete syntax from time to time, but only with the purpose to clarify aspects of abstract syntax and model representation. So it is, for example, with the explanation of the interconnection of sub-processes in terms of the problems of the concrete visual ad-hoc syntax chosen in Fig. 5.13 and 5.19.

All this said, we want to point out that also in 5.19 it is not possible to reconstruct the flat diagram, i.e., all connections between the sub business process models, from the lower-level diagrams alone. Even worse, the information of interconnection is not yet available any more at the higher level. The necessary information with its unique labeling of interface points at the upper level in Fig. 5.13 has disappeared by the introduction of aggregate transitions in Fig. 5.19. The interconnection information must be maintained somewhere else, which is indicated by auxiliary interface point mappings attached to the sets of transitions at the lower level.

A Detour on Completely Equal Decomposition of Nodes and Edges of a Graph

We think that it is of minor importance but worth to mention that the approach of parallel abstraction of activities and transitions as presented in Fig. 5.19 is not yet a fully symmetric one. Activities at a higher level stand for complete business processes at a lower level, which consist of two kinds of entities, i.e., nodes and edges. However, transitions of a higher level stand for sets of transitions at a lower level. This means aggregate transitions consist of only one kind of entities, i.e., edges. This is so, because the diagrams are cut into pieces by cutting transitions. Such an approach makes sense, because the business processes stand for behavior which consists of activities exchanging good and information, whereas transitions stand only for the transferred goods and information and this should be so at all levels of the hierarchy. Therefore, a rest of asymmetry in decomposing activities and transitions remains.

In order to illustrate what was just said, we want to sketch a completely symmetric approach of decomposing graphs and edges now. This sketch is meant merely as a thought experiment, i.e., it is not meant to be exploited in a modeling method. It is possible to decompose a graph so that both nodes and edges stand for full-fledged graphs recursively consisting out of nodes and edges again. Two rules must be obeyed. Nodes must unfold to graphs that have only nodes as outermost objects. Edges must unfold to graphs that have only edges as outermost objects. We do not formalize the notion of outermost object of a graph here. It should be intuitively clear – please a look at the example in Fig. 5.20. In order to enable a precise, mathematical definition of the above rules, a definition of graphs of the kind $(N, E, s : E \hookrightarrow N, t : E \hookrightarrow N)$ with nodes N, edges E, sources s and targets s is needed in which the functions s and t must be defined as partial functions, which is not standard, but necessary in order to model outermost edges of a graph.

Figure 5.20 shows an instance of the proposed approach of completely equal decomposition of nodes and edges. It is a very simple example of a graph that is merely a path, however, it suffices to illustrate the basic principle. An entity at a higher level can stand for a graph at a lower level that is arbitrary complex – or arbitrary simple – as long as the above rules are respected. For example, an entity can also stand for a graph that consists of a single entity only. So it is for the α-edge, the ω-edge and the H-activity in Fig. 5.19.

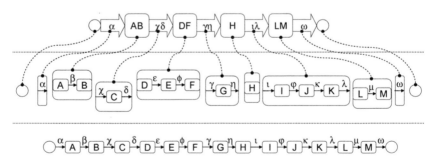

Fig. 5.20. Completely symmetric decomposition of nodes and edges in a graph.

Typed Transitions

The transitions a data flow diagram carry data. In Sect. 4.2 we discuss the transformation of goods versus the transformation of data and means to model both of these phenomena. Here, we assume that the labels attached to the transitions of a leveled data flow diagram stand for data. Data can be described by a type system. The usual type systems from programming languages and modeling languages are, basically, mechanisms to specify sum-of-product data types. A sum data type is the – usually disjoint – union of other data types, it consists of the union of data items of other data types. A product data type consists of tuples of data item of other data types. For example, in object-oriented programming languages and modeling languages like the UML [263], classes are used to specify product data types. Sum data types are introduced by generalization. Sum-like data types are also introduced by associations between classes that have a variable cardinality, e.g., a one-or-zero cardinality '0..1' or a one-to-many cardinality '1..*'. In other programming language type systems product types can be built with records and sum types can be built with variant records. In structured analysis as given by [68] a sum type of two types is specified by $A|B$ and the product type of two types A and B is defined as $A + B$. The mathematical notation for sum data types is usually $A \uplus B$ and the mathematical notation for product data types is usually $A \times B$.

It is possible to describe the data transferred in a data flow diagram not only with a name but also with a type of one of the common type specification languages. For example, the labels of the transitions in the data flow diagrams that we have seen so far in that section can be considered as names of types that are specified further somewhere else. For example, the types of the data transferred in structured analysis are usually described in a data dictionary. The specification of a type describes the constructing of complex data items and can stem, for example, from data modeling, entity-relationship modeling or object-oriented modeling. Given a flat data flow diagram, i.e., a data flow diagram without any leveling, it is easy to understand the data type specification attached to a transitions. In a leveled data flow diagram the question arises, which data type has to be given to an aggregate transition at higher level of the hierarchy.

Figure 5.21 shows yet another example for parallel decomposition of activities and transitions that is even simpler than the example given in Fig. 5.19. If the gateway ϕ in Fig. 5.21 uniquely selects one strand of execution, it is fair to say that the data type $\delta\epsilon$ is the sum data type of the types δ and ϵ. Whenever an interface event of an activity is triggered, a data item of the data type that corresponds to the triggering transition is transferred. This is so for both business process models with closed and open semantics as described in Sect. 5.2.2, for business processes with open semantics it is so for both starting events and further, intermediate events. Therefore, if the ϕ-gateway is a case distinction, the start of an DE-activity in the higher diagram stands

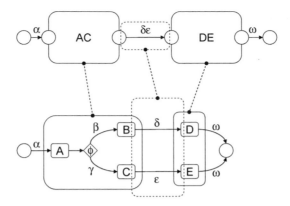

Fig. 5.21. Simple example for parallel decomposition of activities and transitions.

either for a start of a D-activity or the start of a E-activity in the lower flat diagram.

Even if the selection of the ϕ-gateway is not unique, because it is a parallel fork, it is still fair to say that the data type $\delta\epsilon$ is a sum type, because the single trigger of an interface event will transfer always only either a δ-item or a ϵ-item. Things change, if the δ-transition and the ϵ-transition are synchronized in the business process. If the synchronization takes place in the DE-activity the data type $\delta\epsilon$ can remain the sum data type of δ and ϵ. However, if the synchronization takes places in the AC-activity an instance of a $\delta\epsilon$-transition should be considered to transfer a combination, i.e., a tuple, of a δ-item and an ϵ-item as a single, joint object. Then, it is fair to say that $\delta\epsilon$-type is the product type of the type δ and the type ϵ. To say it differently, if a modeler uses a product type for an aggregate transition that is constructed out of the types of the aggregated transitions, this product type introduces a synchronization constraint onto the control flow of the business process. This insight is capable of shedding some new light on the way data dictionaries are built in structured analysis.

5.4 Towards Parallel Abstraction of Activities and Constraints

In Sect. 5.3 we have discussed the parallel abstraction of activities and data. We have said that it is possible to pose a constraint on the behavior of the system by the selection of the data type. Now we consider the hierarchical decomposition of flow charts that are annotated with explicit constraints on the control flow. Business process models are flow charts with constraints. The formcharts introduced in form-oriented analysis [89] are state transition diagrams with annotated dialogue constraints – see Sect. 7.3. For the sake of this discussion it is possible to consider formcharts as flowcharts. The same is for the workflow charts that we introduce in Sect. 9.2 as a domain-specific language for workflow specification. We consider flow charts that allow for parallelism.

We concentrate on flow conditions in this section. Other constraints on the behavior expressed with a flow chart, e.g., the side effect specifications, enabling conditions and activation conditions that we discuss for workflow charts, are also interesting against the background of hierarchical decomposition. However, we concentrate on flow conditions in this section. In business process modeling languages there are usually explicit gateways for case distinctions, parallel split of control and synchronization. For our discussion we do not need to consider extra gateways. We consider flow charts that are graphs and have flow conditions attached to the edges. Gateways for case distinction, parallel split and synchronization can be appropriately expressed in a flow chart language without extra gateways. We discuss this in the setting of workflow charts for the parallel split gateway in Sect. 9.2.4 – see Fig. 9.5 – and for synchronization in Sect. 9.2.10 – see Fig. 9.7.

Consider the following case. Given is a business process model that consists of four activities A, B, C and D and three edges β, γ and δ from A to B, C resp. D at the base level. The edges β, γ and δ are annotated with flow conditions f_1, f_2 resp. f_3. At the second level in the hierarchy the model consist of three activities A^2, BC^2 and D^2 and two edges $\beta\gamma^2$ and δ^2 from A^2 to BC^2 resp. D^2. The activity A^2 encapsulates the sub diagram that consists merely of the base activity A. The activity BC^2 consists of the activities B and C and the activity D^2 consist of the activity D. Now it makes sense to annotate the edge $\beta\gamma^2$ with the flow condition $(f_1 \vee f_2)$ and to annotate the edge δ^2 with the flow condition f_3.

At the base level flow conditions can be considered as operational specifications. This is so, for example, for formcharts and workflow charts. At the base level the flow conditions play a role in the operational semantics. In our example, the flow conditions have the following semantics. After completion of the activity A the flow conditions are evaluated. For all the edges for which the corresponding flow condition has been evaluated to true the targeted activity is triggered. At the higher levels of the hierarchy a flow condition is not an operational specification. It is derived information. You can say that it is a derived post condition. This is so because the operational semantics of a hierarchical flow chart is determined only and completely by the flat diagram of the base level of the hierarchy. This means, if you look at the behavior of the business process from the viewpoint of the second level in our current example, the decision whether activity BC^2 or activity D^2 is started next is not done after completion of the activity A^2 but inside the execution of activity A^2 after completion of activity A, which is a slight but crucial difference. The difference will become clearer when we consider another example, which is a bit more complex, in due course. However, as an effect of the operational semantics that is given by the flow conditions f_1, f_2 resp. f_3 it is possible to derive that after completion of the activity A^2 the post flow conditions $(f_1 \vee f_2)$ and f_3 hold.

Now, let us consider the following case. Given is a business process model that consists of five activities A, B, C D and E, two edges γ and δ_1 from A to C resp. D , plus two further edges δ_2 and ϵ from B to D resp. E at the base level. The edges γ, δ_1, δ_2 and ϵ are annotated with flow conditions f_1, f_2, f_3 resp. f_4. At the second level in the hierarchy the model consist of four activities AB^2, C^2, D^2 and E^2 and three edges β^2, $\gamma_1\gamma_2^2$ and ϵ^2 from AB^2 to C^2, D^2 resp. E^2. The activity AB^2 encapsulates the sub diagram that consists of the base activities A and B. The activities C^2, D^2 and E^2 consist of the activities C, D resp. E. Now it makes sense to annotate the edges β^2, $\gamma_1\gamma_2^2$ and ϵ^2 with the flow conditions f_1, $(f_2 \vee f_3)$ resp. f_4.

Let us assume that the activities A and B are always triggered in parallel. Now, an interpretation of the flow conditions at the second level as operational specifications makes no sense any more. The completion of the activity AB^2 can be caused by the completion of either the activity A or the activity B. Let us assume, for example, that the completion of the activity AB^2 has been caused by the completion of activity B. In this case the condition f_1 may hold. However, whether the condition f_1 evaluates to true or not in this case, the activity C^2 must not be triggered. This means that the operational semantics of flow conditions at the base level must not be applied to the second level. However, the derived flow conditions provide useful information for the system analyst.

5.5 Seamless Business Process and Enterprise Application Modeling

In projects that introduce IT support for business processes, there are typical two kinds of overlapping system specification, one kind that models the business processes from a business perspective, and another kind that models the enterprise IT systems from a technological viewpoint. The following situation is a typical one for a business software vendor. Typically, there are to group of experts in a software vendor company, one group of software engineers responsible for the development of the system, and one group of business experts responsible for selling the software and conducting projects in which the services are adapted to customer needs and introduced at the customer site. In a typical software introduction project a business expert conducts requirement elicitation efforts with the user because the existing software product does not fit totally. Then, the business experts communicate change requests or requests for entirely new functionality to the software development team.

Have a look at Fig. 5.22. There is only one system, with one undebatable, observable behavior of the system – made of the system dialogues provided by the service applications to the user. However, the problem is that business experts and software engineers have a different view on this system. The

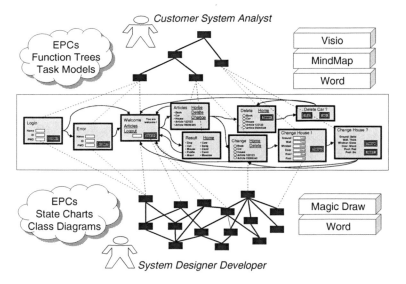

Fig. 5.22. Tyical structural frictions in a combined business process and system model.

business experts model a functional hierarchy that is oriented towards sales and communicating of how the system supports business tasks at the user side. The developers decompose the system dialogues into a component hierarchy in order to deal with complexity, i.e., they map the activities of the dialogues to software entities and decompose those software entities further. However, they not only decompose. Like the business people they also compose dialogues to hierarchies, however, sometimes with a different result, because their efforts are driven by technical issues.

Furthermore, the different groups usually use different tools and notations due to their different background as show in Fig. 5.22. The business experts might use, for example, event-driven process chains (EPCs) [312], function trees and task models as notations and Visio, MindMap, and Word as tools. The software developers might use, for example, UML statecharts and class diagrams but partly also EPCs as notation and MagicDraw and Word as tools. In this way, models of the same system evolve in separated notations and in separated tools. As a result there can be a huge gap when looking at all models as a whole, a gap that is located in Fig. 5.22 exactly there, were the system dialogues are visualized in the box in the middle. Try to understand the problem from the perspective of traceability. If a developer changes some code in some module, he could indeed derive the impact on business processes, but only in terms of the software developer models. However, for the business experts it is not so easy to understand a code change in terms of their business models. Furthermore, there is an overlap in specified phenomena exactly there, where the two worlds meet, at the level of business processes and beyond, i.e., there where also the software developers compose hierarchies bottom-up. Often the same piece of business process is modeled as an EPC by one expert and as a UML statechart by another. This situation can give rise to inconsistencies and communication problems between the two groups.

So, the problem is often not quality of the models and system descriptions – often, these are high both in the business expert and the software developer group. Typically, the problems are the notational heterogeneity and tool heterogeneity. How to approach these problems? As a first step you can select a canonical set of modeling notations, in particular, a single business process notation, and select a single integrating tool for all models and system descriptions – see Fig. 5.23. Selecting notations and tools sounds easy, but it is not, because in selecting you must respect the stakeholders' expectations and attitudes. For the notation of the business processes BPMN (Business Process Modeling Notation) [265] might be a good choice, because the notational element set of BPMN very much resembles EPCs that many business experts are used to. Furthermore, BPMN is maintained by the OMG (Object Management Group) which guarantees a certain sustainability of the notation and therefore might convince the software developing team.

As a next step you can fix a style guide for seamless modeling, so that the gap described above disappears. For example, in [357] system modeling with form-oriented analysis [89] is brought together with modeling of systems based on service-oriented architecture. We propose to exploit the workflow charts that are elaborated in Sects. 9.2.2 through 9.2.10 as a basis for developing such a style guide.

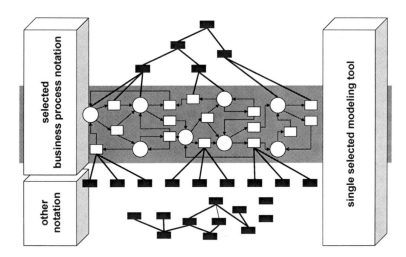

Fig. 5.23. Mitigating structural frictions in a combined business process and system model.

5.6 Modeling Variants

Getting a variety of models under control, see Fig. 5.24, is a concrete and severe problem in lot of software engineering and maintenance projects that is worth discussing here. Actually, it is an issue that is orthogonal to the main discussion strand of this book, but the problem is sometimes so pervasive in projects and finding a smart solution to this problem is such a central question in these projects that it is sometimes overlooked that the management of many varieties is an extra problem independent from the need for frictionless modeling.

Therefore the targeted discussion of this topic in this book can help to keep these two important issues separate and this can help to keep considerations on the design of a frictionless modeling approach focused. This is not a minor issue, because, in real-world projects we observe that people that are under pressure to deal with the complexity of system variants introduce ad-hoc concepts to deal with the problem. As a result, these ad-hoc concepts are actually redundant to existing concepts in the existing project's modeling apparatus, introducing new frictions in places where a disciplined, e.g., simply glossary-based introduction of new terms or viewpoints on the basis of existing concepts would be sufficient and efficient. And this is a pitfall not only for ad-

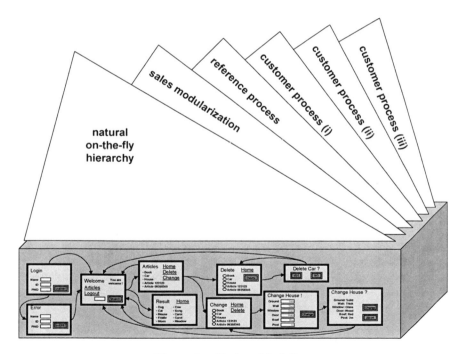

Fig. 5.24. Variant Modeling.

hoc notations in real-world projects this is a pitfall, but also for the designer of a standard notation.

5.6.1 Variants in Software Service Support Scenarios

The need for a systematic approach to modeling variants of a system typically arises in what we call software service support scenarios in this book. This means that there is a software vendor that sells some software product to a customer. However, though the product is a standard product in the product portfolio of the vendor, selling the product to the customer is not enough. The vendor cares also for the deployment and maintenance of the software product and, most importantly, for the adaptation of the product to concrete customer needs. This adaptation involves requirement elicitation activities with the customer, in particular, an analysis of existing and future business processes. If the necessary customer processes are not fully supported, new functionality has to be implemented. Often, existing functionality must be changed, so that the necessary processes are supported. Eventually, a new version of the product, i.e., a customer version, results. The choice to name the described scenario a software service support scenario is a particular good one, because it is very close to the problems addressed by the IT Infrastructure Library (ITIL) [56, 267] service support process. Actually, the standardization of this scenario by a defined process is also an important issue for the software vendor. However, it is a different issue from the one discussed here and must not be mingled into this discussion.

For the described scenario, it is not important whether the resulting customer version is actually deployed at the customer site or is run by the data centre of the vendor, i.e., it is not important whether the vendor is a software service provider. Similarly, it is not important whether the vendor is an independent software vendor (ISV) or a full-service commercial-off-the-shelf (COTS) software house. An independent software vendor is a software house that offers development of individual software solutions on an individual project basis. Actually, successful ISVs are often specialized in a certain sector. Then they usually have a proven code base for the solutions they develop. Often, there is no exact means to distinguish such a code base from a COTS product and sometimes it may be only a question of the vendor's marketing strategy whether to mention this code base as an asset or not, and if so, whether to sell it as a framework solution or as a COTS product.

The variant problem is indeed also an issue for classical COTS vendors. This might puzzle the reader, because it is common sense that one of the disadvantages of COTS software is the assumption that it completely rules the business processes of the customer that deploys that software – as if there is no room for an adjustment of the COTS product. Actually, the converse is true. Part of the business model of a COTS software house is to sell the COTS product, but for some COTS software houses the services offered on basis of the COTS product has become the more important part of the business model, and so is the adjustment of the COTS product to the customer's needs.

5.6.2 Product Variants and Versions

A variant of a product is a version of a product. However, it is not a version in the usual sense of versioning, i.e., a product state in a software product lifecycle. Versioning is about the maintenance of deprecated versus actual versions of a software product, but variants in the described scenario are versions that fulfill different customer needs.

With respect to modeling, the situation can become even more complex, because it is sometimes important to maintain different viewpoints on the same variant of a product, each viewpoint represented by a different model. As an example, Fig. 5.24 shows a typical scenario. As in Fig. 5.22 the deployed system is depicted as some system dialogues in a gray box. Modelers have defined a reference process that corresponds to the initial product that is sold to a customer. Then in each customer project the product starts its own life. It is enhanced and parts of it are changed. These enhancements and changes are documented resulting in this example in an individual business process model for the customer. However, there exist even more models in this example. There exists a sales modularization of the system dialogues used by the sales persons. The sales modularization is a mere functional hierarchy of the system features and is used for pricing. For each module and sub module in the hierarchy a price is fixed.

Furthermore, in the example, there is another hierarchy, called the natural or ad-hoc hierarchy. This ad-hoc hierarchy is also a mere modularization but is oriented towards building modules with high functional cohesion. The sales modularization encapsulates experience of sales efforts and its concrete hierarchy is the result of strategic decisions to optimize income. Therefore, the sales modularization is not optimal with respect to complexity governance; it is not necessarily optimal with respect to understanding of the system functionality, nor is it optimal to get a quick overview of the system features. These latter qualities are also a driving force for building the sales modularization in order to have a solid base for discussion with a lead or new customer. However, the optimization of income along customer needs and customer behavior is the eventual target of the sales modularization. The natural hierarchy is free from these concerns. It is optimized with respect to the governance of the system and model complexity. It typically stems from an ad-hoc, bottom-up process to get the system under control. It is a document that is independent from the reference process and the customer processes; however, it is not orthogonal to them and must be maintained consistent with them. It can serve as a base for the design of these other documents. Furthermore, it serves as a functional view on the reference process, abstracting from control flows and data flows.

Because every product variant is the result of a new independent project with a customer, the need for mutual maintenance of the differences might not seem to be a key success factor for the single project and this might be the reason that it is not done in a lot of projects. It is simply not regarded as an urgent problem from the single project manager's point of view. Furthermore it is overhead. However, maintenance of variants pays off for two reasons, i.e., avoiding redundant efforts in product adoption projects and keeping variants consistent with versioning.

6

Structured Business Process Specification

Isn't it compelling to apply the structured programming arguments to the field of business process modeling? Our answer to this question is 'no'.

The principle of structured programming emerged in the computer science community. From today's perspective, the discussion of structured programming rather had the characteristics of a maturing process than the characteristics of a debate, although there have also been some prominent skeptical comments on the unrestricted validity of the structured programming principle. Structured programming is a well-established design principle in the field of program design like the third normal form in the field of database design. It is common sense that structured programming is better than unstructured programming – or let's say structurally unrestricted programming – and this is what is taught as foundational knowledge in many standard curricula of many software engineering study programmes. With respect to business process modeling, in practice, you find huge business process models that are arbitrary nets. How come? Is it somehow due to some lack of knowledge transfer from the programming language community to the information systemcommunity For computer scientists, it might be tempting to state that structured programming is a proven concept and it is therefore necessary to eventually promote a structured business process modeling discipline, however, care must be taken.

We want to contribute to the understanding in how far a structured approach can be applied to business process modeling and in how far such an approach is naive [113]. We attempt to clarify that the arguments of structured programming are about the pragmatics of programming. Furthermore, we want to clarify that, in our opinion, argumentations in favor of structured programming often appeal to evidence. Consequentially, our reasoning is at the level of pragmatics of business process modeling. We try to avoid getting lost in superficial comparisons of modeling language constructs but trying to understand the core problems of structuring business process specifications. As an example, so to speak as a taster to our discussion, we take forward one of our arguments here, which is subtle but important, i.e., that there are some

D. Draheim, *Business Process Technology: A Unified View on Business Processes, Workflows and Enterprise Applications*, DOI 10.1007/978-3-642-01588-5_6,
© Springer-Verlag Berlin Heidelberg 2010

diagrams expressing behavior that cannot be transformed into a structured diagram expressing the same behavior solely in terms of the same primitives as the original structurally unrestricted diagram. These are all those diagrams that contain a loop which is exited via more than one path to the end point, which is a known result from literature, encountered [37] by Corrado Böhm and Guiseppe Jacopini, proven for a special case [206] by Donald E. Knuth and Robert W. Floyd and proven in general [208] by S. Rao Kosaraju.

On a first impression, structured programs and flowcharts appear neat and programs and flowcharts with arbitrary jumps appear obfuscated, muddle-headed, spaghetti-like etc. [76]. But the question is not to identify a subset of diagrams and programs that look particularly fine. The question is, given a behavior that needs description, whether it makes always sense to replace a description of this behavior by a new structured description. What efforts are needed to search for a good alternative description? Is the resulting alternative structured description as nice as the original non-structured description?

Furthermore, we need to gain more systematic insight into which metrics we want to use to judge the quality of a description of a behavior, because categories like neatness or prettiness are not satisfactory for this purpose if we are serious that our domain of software development should be oriented rather towards engineering [256, 51] than oriented towards arts and our domain of business management should be oriented rather towards science [144]. Admittedly, however, both fields are currently still in the stage of pre-paradigmatic research [223]. All these issues form the topic of investigation of this chapter.

For us, the definitely working theory of quality of business process models would be strictly pecuniary, i.e., it would enable us to define a style guide for business process modeling that eventually saves costs in system analysis and software engineering projects. The better the cost-savings realized by the application of such a style-guide the better such a theory. Because our ideal is pecuniary, we deal merely with functionality. There is no cover, no aesthetics, no mystics. This means there is no form in the sense of Louis H. Sullivan [332] – just function.

6.1 Basic Definitions

In this section we explain the notions of program, structured program, flowchart, D-flowchart, structured flowchart, business process model and structured business process model as used in this chapter. The focus of this section is on syntactical issues. You might want to skip this section and use it as a reference, however, you should at least glimpse over the formation rules of structured flowcharts defined in Fig. 6.1, which are also the basis for structured business process modeling.

In the course of this chapter, programs are imperative programs which may contain 'go to'-statements, i.e., they consist of basic statements, sequences, case constructs, loops and 'go to'-statements. Structured programs are those

programs that abstain from 'go to'-statements. Loops, i.e., explicit programming constructs for loops, do not add to the expressive power of a programming language with 'go to'-statements – in presence of 'go to'-statements loops
are syntactic sugar. Flowcharts correspond to programs. Flowcharts are directed graphs with nodes being basic activities, decision points or join points.
A directed circle in a flowchart can be interpreted as a loop or as the usage
of a 'go to'-statement. In general flowcharts it allowed to place join points
arbitrarily, which makes it possible to create spaghetti structures, i.e., arbitrary jump structures, like the 'go to'-statements allows for the creation of
spaghetti code.

It is a matter of taste whether to make decision and joint points explicit
nodes or not. If you strictly use decision and joint points the basic activities always have exactly one incoming and one outgoing edge. In concrete
modeling languages like event-driven process chains, there are usually some
more constraints, e.g., a constraint on decision points not to have more than
one incoming edge or a constraint on join points to have not more than one
outgoing edge. If you allow basic activities to have more than one incoming
edge you do not need join points any more. Similarly, you can get rid of a
decision point by using several outgoing edges by directly connecting the several branches of the decision point as outgoing edges to a basic activity and
labeling the several branches with appropriate flow conditions. For example,
in formcharts [89] we have chosen the option not to use explicit decision and
join points. Our discussion is independent from the detail question of having explicit or implicit decision and join points, because both concepts are
interchangeable. Therefore, we feel free to use both options.

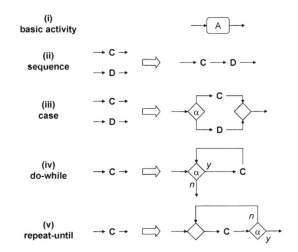

Fig. 6.1. Semi-formal formation rules for structured flowcharts.

6.1.1 D-Charts

It is possible to define formation rules for a restricted class of flowcharts that correspond to structured programs. In [208] these diagrams are called Dijkstra-flowcharts or D-flowcharts for short, named after Edgser W. Dijkstra. Figure 6.1 summarizes the semi-formal formation rules for D-flowcharts.

Actually, the original definition of D-flowcharts in [208] consists of the formation rules (i) to (iv) with one formation rule for each programming language construct of a minimal structured imperative programming language with basic statements, sequences, case-constructs and while-loops with basic activities in the flowchart corresponding to basic statements in the programming language. We have added a formation rule (v) for the representation of repeat-until-loops and call flowcharts resulting from rules (i) to (v) structured flowcharts in the sequel.

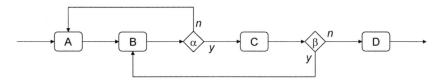

Fig. 6.2. Example flowchart that is not a D-flowchart.

The flowchart in Fig. 6.2 is not a structured flowchart, i.e., it cannot be derived from the formation rules in Fig. 6.1. The flowchart in Fig. 6.2 can be interpreted as consisting of a repeat-until-loop exited via the α-decision point and followed by further activities C and D. In this case, the β-decision point can lead to a branch that jumps into the repeat-until-loop in addition to the regular loop entry point via activity A, which infringes the structured programming and structured modeling principle and gives raises to spaghetti structure. Thus, the flowchart in Fig. 6.2 visualizes the program in Listing 6.1

Listing 6.1 Textual presentation of the business process in Fig. 6.2 with a jump into the loop.

```
01 REPEAT
02   A;
03   B;
04 UNTIL alpha;
05 C;
06 IF beta THEN GOTO 03;
07 D;
```

The flowchart in Fig. 6.2 can also be interpreted as consisting of a while-loop exited via the β-decision point, where the while-loop is surrounded by a preceding activity A and a succeeding activity D. In this case, the α-decision point can lead to a branch that jumps out of the while-loop in addition to the regular loop exit via the β-decision point, which again infringes the structured modeling principle. Thus, the flowchart in Fig. 6.2 also visualizes the program in Listing 6.2

Listing 6.2 Alternative textual presentation of the business process in Fig. 6.2 with a jump out of the loop.

```
01 A;
02 REPEAT
03   B;
04   IF NOT alpha THEN GOTO 01
05   C;
06 UNTIL NOT beta;
07 D;
```

Flowcharts are visualization of programs. In general, a flowchart can be interpreted ambiguously as the visualization of several different program texts, because, for example, on the one hand, an edge from a decision point to a join point can be interpreted as a 'go to'-statement or, on the other hand, as the back branch from an exit point of a repeat-until loop to the start of the loop. Structured flowcharts are visualizations of structured programs. Loops in structured programs and structured flowcharts enjoy the property that they have exactly one entry point and exactly one exit point. Whereas the entry point and the exit point of a repeat-until loop are different, the entry point and exit point of a while-loop are the same, so that a while-loop in a structured flowchart has exactly one contact point. That might be the reason that structured flowcharts that use only while-loops instead of repeat-until loops appear more normalized. Similarly, in a structured program and flowchart all case-constructs has exactly one entry point and one exit point. In general, additional entry and exit points can be added to loops and case constructs by the usage of 'go to'-statements in programs and by the usage of arbitrary decision points in flowcharts. In structured flowcharts, decision points are introduced as part of the loop constructs and part of the case construct. In structured programs and flowcharts, loops and case-constructs are strictly nested along the lines of the derivation of their abstract syntax tree.

Business process models extend flowcharts with further modeling elements like a parallel split, parallel join or non-deterministic choice. Basically, we discuss the issue of structuring business process models in terms of flowcharts, because flowcharts actually are business process model diagrams, i.e., flowcharts form a subset of business process models. As the constructs in the formation rules of Fig. 6.1 further business process modeling elements can also be introduced in a structured manner with the result of having again only such diagrams that are strictly nested in terms of their looping and branching constructs. For example, in such a definition the parallel split and the parallel join would not be introduced separately but as belonging to a parallel modeling construct.

6.1.2 A Notion of Equivalence for Business Processes

Bisimilarity has been defined formally in [273] as an equivalence relation for infinite automaton behavior, i.e., process algebra [249, 250]. Bisimilarity expresses that two processes are equal in terms of their observable behavior. Observable behavior is the appropriate notion for the comparison of automatic processes. The semantics of a process can also be understood as opportunities of one process interacting with another process. Observable behavior and experienced opportunities are different viewpoints on the semantics of a process, however, whichever viewpoint is chosen, it does not change the basic concept of bisimilarity. Business processes can be fully automatic; however, business processes can also be descriptions of human actions and therefore can also be rather a protocol of possible steps undertaken by a human. We therefore choose to explain bisimilarity in terms of opportunities of an actor, or, as a metaphor, from the perspective of a player that uses the process description as a game board – which neatly fits to the notions of simulation and bisimulation, i.e., bisimilarity.

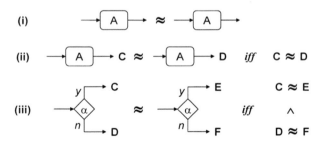

Fig. 6.3. Characterization of bisimilarity for business process models.

In general, two processes are bisimilar if starting from the start node they reveal the same opportunities and each pair of same opportunities lead again to bisimilar processes. More formally, bisimilarity is defined on labeled transition systems [3] as the existence of a bisimulation, which is a relationship that enjoys the aforementioned property, i.e., nodes related by the bisimilarity lead via the same opportunities to nodes that are related again, i.e., recursively, by the bisimilarity. In the non-structured models the opportunities are edges leading out of an activity and the two edges leading out of a decision point. For our purposes, bisimilarity can be characterized by the rules in Fig. 6.3.

6.2 The Pragmatics of Structuring Business Processes

6.2.1 Resolving Arbitrary Jump Structures

Have a look at Fig. 6.4. Like Fig. 6.2 it shows a business process model that is not a structured business process model. The business process described by the business process model in Fig. 6.4 can also be described in the style of a program text as in Listing 6.3.

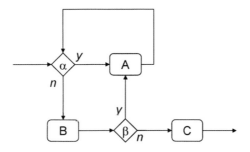

Fig. 6.4. Example business process model that is not structured.

In textual representation or interpretation in Fig. 6.4, the business process model in Fig. 6.4 consists of a while-loop followed by a further activity B, a decision point that might branch back into the while-loop and eventually an activity C. Alternatively, the business process can also be described by structured business process models. Fig. 6.5 shows two examples of such structured business process models and Listings 6.4 and 6.5 show the corresponding program text representations that are visualized by the business process models in Fig. 6.5.

Listing 6.3 Textual presentation of the business process in Fig. 6.4.

```
01 WHILE alpha DO
02   A;
03 B;
04 IF beta THEN GOTO 02;
05 C;
```

The business process models in Figs. 6.4 and 6.5 resp. Listings 6.3, 6.4 and 6.5 describe the same business process. They describe the same business process, because they are bisimilar, i.e., in terms of their nodes, which are, basically, activities and decision points, they describe the same observable behavior resp. same opportunities to act for an actor – we have explained the notion of equality and the more precise approach of bisimilarity in more detail in Sect. 6.1.2.

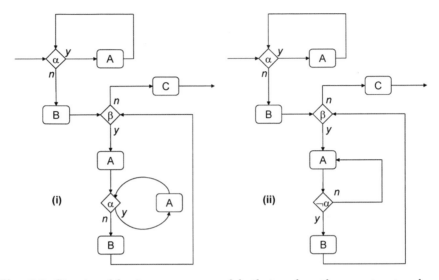

Fig. 6.5. Structured business process models that replace the non-structured one in Fig. 6.4.

The derivation of the business process models in Fig. 6.5 from the formation rules given in Fig. 6.1 can be understood by looking at its abstract syntax tree, which appears at tree ψ in Fig. 6.6. The proof that the process models in Figs. 6.4 and 6.5 are bisimilar is left to the reader as an exercise. The reader is also invited to find structured business process models that are less complex than the ones given in Fig. 6.5, whereas complexity is an informal concept that depends heavily on the perception and opinion of the modeler. For example, the model (ii) in Fig. 6.4 results from an immediate simple attempt to reduce the complexity of the model (i) in Fig. 6.5 by eliminating the A-activity which follows the α-decision point and connecting the succeeding 'yes'-branch of the α-decision point directly back with the A-activity preceding the decision point, i.e., by reducing a while-loop-construct with a preceding statement to a repeat-until-construct. Note, that the model in Fig. 6.5 has been derived from the model in Fig. 6.4 by straightforwardly unfolding it behind the β-decision point as much as necessary to yield a structured description of the business process. In what sense the transformation from model (i) to model (ii) in Fig. 6.5 has lowered complexity and whether it actually or rather superficially has lowered the complexity will be discussed in due course. We will also discuss another structured business process model with auxiliary logic that is oriented towards identifying repeat-until-loops in the original process descriptions.

Listing 6.4 Textual presentation of business process (i) in Fig. 6.4.

```
01 WHILE alpha DO
02   A;
03 B;
04 WHILE beta DO BEGIN
05   A;
06   WHILE alpha DO
07     A;
08   B;
09 END;
10 C;
```

Listing 6.5 Textual presentation of business process (ii) in Fig. 6.4.

```
01 WHILE alpha DO
02   A;
03 B;
04 WHILE beta DO BEGIN
05   REPEAT
06     A;
07   UNTIL NOT alpha;
08   B;
09 END;
10 C;
```

The above remark on the vagueness of the notion of complexity is not just a side-remark or disclaimer but is at the core of the discussion. If the complexity of a model is a cognitive issue it would be a straightforward approach to let people vote which of the models is more complex. If there is a sufficiently precise method to test whether a person has understood the semantics of a process specification, this method can be exploited in testing groups of people that have been given different kinds of specifications of the same process and concluding from the test results which of the process specifications should be considered more complex. Such an approach relies on the preciseness of the semantics and eventually on the quality of the test method. We will suggest to consider such a test method approach again in Sect. 6.3 in the discussion of structured programming, because program have a definite semantics as functional transforms.

It is a real challenge to search for a definition of complexity of models or their representations. What we expect is that less complexity has something to do with better quality, and before we undertake efforts in defining complexity of models we should first understand possibilities to measure the quality of models. The usual measures by which modelers and programmers often judge complexity of models like understandability or readability are vague concepts themselves. Other categories like maintainability or reusability are more concrete than understandability or readability but still vague. Of course, we can define metrics for the complexity of diagrams. For example, it is possible to define that the number of activity nodes used in a business process model increases the complexity of a model. The problem with such metrics is that it follows immediately that the model in Fig. 6.5 is more complex than the model in Fig. 6.4. Actually, this is what we believe.

6.2.2 Immediate Arguments For and Against Structure

We believe that the models in Fig. 6.5 are more complex than the models in Fig. 6.4. A structured approach to business process models would make us believe that structured models are somehow better than non-structured models in the same way that the structured programming approach believes that structured programs are somehow better than non-structured programs. So either less complexity must not always be better or the tenets of the structured approach must be loosened to a rule of thumb, i.e., the belief that structured models are in general better than non-structured models, despite some exceptions like our current example. An argument in favor of the structured approach could be that our current example is simply too small, i.e., that the aforementioned exceptions are made of small models or, to say it differently, that the arguments of a structured approach become valid for models beyond a certain size. We do not think so. We rather believe that our discussion scales, i.e., that the arguments that we will give below also apply equally and even more so for larger models. We want to approach these questions more systematically.

In order to do so, we need to answer why we believe that the models in Fig. 6.5 are more complex than the model in Fig. 6.4. The immediate answer is simply because they are larger and therefore harder to grasp, i.e., a very direct cognitive argument. But there is another important argument why we believe this. The model in Fig. 6.4 shows an internal reuse that the models in Fig. 6.5 do not show. The crucial point is the reuse of the loop consisting of the A-activity and the α-decision point in Fig. 6.4. We need to delve into this important aspect and will actually do this later. First, we want to discuss the dual question, which is of equal importance, i.e., we must also try to understand or try to answer the question, why modelers and programmers might find that the models in Fig. 6.5 are less complex than the models in Fig. 6.4.

A standard answer to this latter question could typically be that the edge from the β-decision point to the A-activity in Fig. 6.4 is an arbitrary jump, i.e., a spaghetti, whereas the diagrams in Fig. 6.5 do not show any arbitrary jumps or spaghetti-like phenomena. But the question is whether this vague argument can be made more precise. A structured diagram consists of strictly nested blocks. All blocks of a structured diagram form a tree-like structure according to their nesting, which corresponds also to the derivation tree in terms of the formation rules of Fig. 6.1. The crucial point is that each block can be considered a semantic capsule from the viewpoint of its context. This means, that once the semantics of a block is understood by the analyst studying the model, the analyst can forget about the inner modeling elements of the block. This is not so for diagrams in general. This has been the argument of looking from outside onto a block in the case a modeler want to know its semantics in order to understand the semantics of the context where it is utilized. Also, the dual scenario can be convincing. If an analyst is interested in understanding the semantics of a block he can do this in terms of the inner elements of a block only. Once the analyst has identified the block he can forget about its context to understand it. This is not so easy in a non-structured language. When passing an element, in general you do not know where you end up in following the various paths behind it. It is also possible to subdivide a non-structured diagram into chunks that are smaller than the original diagram and that make sense to understand as capsules. For example, this can be done, if possible, by transforming the diagram into a structured one, in which you will find regions of your original diagram. However, it is extra effort to do this partition.

With the current set of modeling elements, i.e., those introduced by the formulation rules in Fig. 6.1, all this can be seen particularly easy, because each block has exactly one entry point, i.e., one edge leading into it. Fortunately, standard building blocks found in process modeling would have one entry point in a structured approach. If you have, in general, also blocks with more than one entry points, it would make the discussion interesting. The above argument would not be completely infringed. Blocks still are capsules, with a semantics that can be understood locally with respect to their appearance in a strictly nested structure of blocks. The scenario itself remains neat and tidy; the difference lies in the fact that a block with more than one entry has a particular complex semantics in a certain sense. The semantics of a block with more than one entry is manifold, e.g., the semantics of a block with two entries is threefold. Given that, in general, we also have concurrency phenomena in a business process model, the semantics of block with two entry points, i.e., its behavior or opportunities, must be understood for the case that the block is entered via one or the other entry point and for the case that the block is entered simultaneously. But this is actually not a problem; it just means a more sophisticated semantics and more documentation.

Despite a more complex semantics, a block with multiple entries still remains an anchor in the process of understanding a business process model, because it is possible, e.g., to understand the model from inside to outside following the strict tree-like nesting, which is a canonical way to understand the diagram, i.e., a way that is always defined. It is also always possible to understand the diagram sequentially from the start node to the end node in a controlled manner. The case constructs make such sequential proceeding complex, because they open alternative paths in a tree-like manner. The advantage of a structured diagram with respect to case-constructs is that each of the alternative paths that are spawned is again a block and it is therefore possible to understand its semantics isolated from the other paths. This is not so in a non-structured diagram, in which there might be arbitrary jumps between the alternative paths, in general. Similarly, if analyzing a structured diagram in a sequential manner, you do not get into arbitrary loops and therefore have to deal with a minimized risk to loose track.

The discussion of the possibility to have blocks with more entry points immediately reminds us of the discussion we have seen within the business process community on multiple versus unique entry points for business processes in a setting of hierarchical decomposition. The relationship between blocks in a flat structured language and sub diagrams in a hierarchical approach and how they play together in a structured approach is an important strand of discussion that we will come back to in due course. For the time being, we just want to point out the relationship between the discussion we just had on blocks with multiple entries and sub diagrams with multiple entries. A counter-argument against sub diagrams with multiple entries would be that they are more complex. Opponents of the argument would say that it is not a real argument, because the complexity of the semantics, i.e., its aforementioned manifoldness, must be described anyhow.

With sub diagrams that may have no more than one entry point, you would need to introduce a manifoldness of diagrams each with a single entry point. We do not discuss here how to transform a given diagram with multiple entries into a manifoldness of diagrams – all we want to remark here that it easily becomes complicated because of the necessity to appropriately handle the aforementioned possibly existing concurrency phenomena. Eventually it turns out to be a problem of transforming the diagram together with its context, i.e., transforming a set of diagrams and sub diagrams with possibly multiple entry points into another set of diagrams and sub diagrams with only unique entry points. Defenders of diagrams with unique entry points would state that it is better to have a manifoldness of such diagrams instead of having a diagram with multiple entries, because, the manifoldness of diagrams documents better the complexity of the semantics of the modeled scenario.

For a better comparison of the discussed models against the above statements we have repainted the diagram from Fig. 6.4 and diagram (ii) from Fig. 6.5 with the blocks they are made of and their abstract syntax trees resp. quasi-abstract syntax tree in Fig. 6.6. The diagram of Fig. 6.4 appears to the left in Fig. 6.6 as diagram Φ and diagram (ii) from Fig. 6.5 appears to the right as diagram Ψ. According to that, the left abstract syntax tree ϕ in

Fig. 6.6 corresponds to the diagram from Fig. 6.4 and the right abstract syntax tree ψ corresponds to the diagram (ii) from Fig. 6.5. Blocks are surrounded by dashed lines in Fig. 6.6.

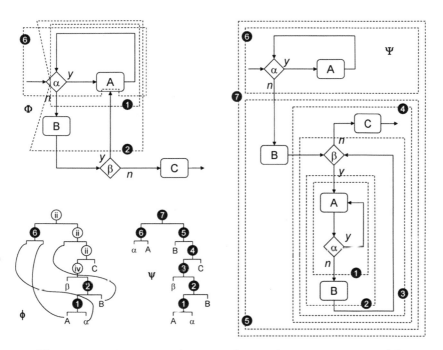

Fig. 6.6. Block-structured versus arbitrary business process model.

If you proceed in understanding the model Φ in Fig. 6.6 you first have to understand a while-loop that encompasses the A-activity – the block labeled with number '5' in model Φ. After that, you are not done with that part of the model. Later, after the β-decision point you are branched back to the A-activity and you have to re-understand the loop it belongs to again, however, this time in a different manner, i.e., as a repeat-until loop – the block labeled with number '1' in model Φ. It is possible to argue that, in some sense, this makes the model Φ harder to read than model Ψ. To say it differently, it is possible to view model Ψ as an instruction manual on how to read the model Φ. Actually, model Ψ is a bloated version of model Φ. It contains some modeling elements of model Φ redundantly, however, it enjoys the property that each modeling element has to be understood only in the context of one block and its encompassing blocks. We can restate these arguments a bit more formally in analyzing the abstract syntax trees ϕ and ψ in Fig. 6.6. Blocks in Ψ correspond to constructs that can be generated by the formation rules in Fig. 6.1. The abstract syntax tree ψ is an alternate presentation of the nesting of blocks in model Ψ. A node stands for a block and for the corresponding construct according to the formation rules. The graphical model Φ cannot be derived from the formation rules in Fig. 6.1. Therefore it does not possess an abstract syntax tree in which each node represent a unique graphical block and a construct the same time. The tree ϕ shows the problem. You can match the region labeled '1' in model Φ as a block against while-loop-rule (iv) and you can subsequently match the region labeled '2' against the sequence-rule (iii). But then you get stuck. You can form a further do-while loop with rule (iv) out of the β-decision point and block '2' as in model Ψ but the resulting graphical model cannot be interpreted as a part of model Φ any more. This is because the edge from activity B to the β-decision point graphically serves both as input branch to the decision point and as back branch to the decision point. This graphical problem is resolved in the abstract syntax tree ϕ by reusing the activity B in the node that corresponds to node '5' in tree ψ in forming a sequence according to rule (ii) with the results that the tree ϕ is actually no longer a tree. Similarly, the reuse of the modeling elements in forming node '6' in the abstract syntax tree ϕ visualizes the double interpretation of this graphical region as both a do-while loop and repeat-until loop.

6.2.3 Structure for Text-based versus Graphical Specifications

In Sect. 6.2.2 we have said that an argument for a structured business process specification is that it is made of strictly nested blocks and that each identifiable block forms a semantic capsule. In the argumentation we have looked at the graphical presentation of the models only and now we will have a look also at the textual representations.

This section needs a disclaimer. We are convinced that it is risky in the discussion of quality of models to give arguments in terms of cognitive categories like understandability, readability, cleanness, well-designedness and well-definedness. These categories tend to have an insufficient degree of definedness themselves so that argumentations based on them easily suffer a lack of falsifiability. Nevertheless, in this section, in order to abbreviate, we need to speak directly about the reading ease of specifications. The judgments are our very own opinion, an opinion that expresses our perception of certain specifications. The reader may have a different opinion and this would be interesting in its own right. At least, the expression of our own opinion may encourage the reader to judge about the readability certain specifications.

As we said in terms of complexity, we think that the model in Fig. 6.4 is easier to understand than the models in Fig. 6.5. We think it is easier to grasp. Somehow paradoxically, we think the opposite about the respective text representation, at least at a first sight, i.e., as long as we have not internalized too much all the different graphical models in listings. This means, we think that the text representation of the models in Fig. 6.4, i.e., Listing 6.3, is definitely harder to understand than the text representation of both models in Fig. 6.5, i.e., Listings 6.4 and 6.5. How comes? Maybe, the following observation helps, i.e., that we also think that the graphical model in Fig. 6.5 is also easier to read than the model's textual representation in Listing 6.3 and also easier to read than the two other Listings 6.4 and 6.5. Why is Listing 6.5 so relatively hard to understand? We think, because there is no explicitly visible connecting between the jumping-off point in line '04' and the jumping target in line line '02'. Actually, the first thing we would recommend in order to understand Listing 6.5 better is to draw its visualization, i.e., the model in Fig. 6.5, or to concentrate and to visualize it in our mind. By the way, we think that drawing some arrows in Listing 6.3 as we did in Fig. 6.7 also help. The two arrows already help despite the fact that they make explicit only a part of the jump structure – one possible jump from line '01' to line '03' in case the α-condition becomes invalid must still be understood by the indentation of the text.

```
01  WHILE alpha DO
02     A;
03  B;
04  IF beta THEN GOTO 02;
05  C;
```

Fig. 6.7. Listing enriched with arrows for making jump structure explicit.

All this is said for such a small model consisting of a total of five lines. Imagine, if you had to deal with a model consisting of several hundreds lines with arbitrary 'go to'-statements all over the text. If it is true that the model in Fig. 6.4 is easier to understand than the models in Fig. 6.5 and at the same time Listing 6.3 is harder to understand than Listings 6.4 and 6.5 this may lead us to the assumption that the understandability of graphically presented models follows other rules than the understandability of textual representation. Reasons for this may be, on the one hand, the aforementioned lack of explicit visualizations of jumps, and, on the other hand, the one-dimensional layout of textual representations. The reason why we have given all of these arguments in this section is not in order to promote visual modeling. The reason is that we see a chance that they might explain why the structural approach has been so easily adopted in the field of programming.

The field of programming was and still is dominated by text-based specifications – despite the fact that we have seen many initiatives from syntax-directed editors through to computer-aided software engineering to model-driven architecture. It is fair to remark that the crucial characteristics of mere textual specification in the discussion of this section, i.e., lack of explicit visualization of jumps, or, to say it in a more general manner, support for the understanding of jumps, is actually addressed in professional coding tools like integrated development environments with their maintenance of links, code analyzers and profiling tools. The mere text-orientation of specification has been partly overcome by today's integrated development environments. Let us express once more that we are not promoters of visual modeling or even visual programming. In [89] we have de-emphasized visual modeling. We strictly believe that visualizations add value, in particular, if it is combined with visual meta-modeling [159, 160, 115]. But we also believe that mere visual specification is no silver bullet, in particular, because it does not scale. We believe in the future of a syntax-direct abstract platform with visualization capabilities that overcomes the gap between modeling and programming from the outset as proposed by the work on AP1 [226, 227] of the Software Engineering research group at the University of Auckland.

6.2.4 Structure and Decomposition

The models in Fig. 6.5 are unfolded versions of the model in Fig. 6.4. Some modeling elements of the diagram in Fig. 6.5 occur redundantly in each model in Fig. 6.4. Such unfolding violates the reuse principle. Let us concentrate on the comparison of the model in Fig. 6.5 with model (i) in Fig. 6.5. The arguments are similar for diagram (ii) in Fig. 6.5. The loop made of the α-decision point and the activity A occurs twice in model (i). In the model in Fig. 6.5 this loop is reused by the jump from the β-decision point albeit via an auxiliary entry point. It is important to understand that reuse is not about the cost-savings of avoiding the repainting of modeling elements but about increasing maintainability.

Imagine, in the lifecycle of the business process a change to the loop consisting of the activity A and the α-decision point becomes necessary. Such changes could be the change of the condition to another one, the change of the activity A to another one or the refinement of the loop, e.g., the insertion of a further activity into it. Imagine that you encounter the necessity for changes by reviewing the start of the business process. In analyzing the diagram, you know that the loop structure is not only used at the beginning of the business process but also later by a possible jump from the β-decision point to it. You will now further analyze whether the necessary changes are only appropriate at the beginning of the business process or also later when the loop is reused from other parts of the business process. In the latter case you are done. This is the point where you can get into trouble with the other version of the business process specification as diagram (i) in Fig. 6.5. You can more easily overlook that the loop is used twice in the diagram; this is particularly true for similar examples in larger or even distributed models. So, you should have extra documentation for the several occurrences of the loop in the process. Even in the case that the changes are relevant only at the beginning of the process you would like to review this fact and investigate whether the changes are relevant for other parts of the process.

It is fair to remark, that in the case that the changes to the loop in question are only relevant to the beginning of the process, the diagram in Fig. 6.5 bears the risk that this leads to an invalid model if the analyst oversees its reuse from later stages in the process, whereas the model (i) in Fig. 6.5 does not bear that risk. But we think this kind of weird fail-safeness can hardly be sold as an advantage of model (i) in Fig. 6.5. Furthermore, it is also fair to remark, that the documentation of multiple occurrences of a model part can be replaced by appropriate tool-support or methodology like a pattern search feature or hierarchical decomposition as we will discuss in due course. All this amounts to saying that maintainability of a model cannot be reduced to its presentation but depends on a consistent combination of presentational issues, appropriate tool support and defined maintenance policies and guidelines in the framework of a mature change management process.

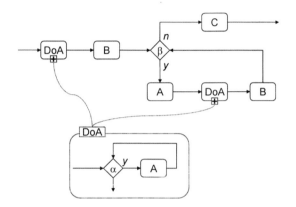

Fig. 6.8. Example business process hierarchy.

We now turn the reused loop consisting of the activity A and the α-decision point in Fig. 6.5 into its own sub diagram in the sense of hierarchical decomposition, give it a name – let us say 'DoA' – and replace the relevant regions in diagram (i) in Fig. 6.5 by the respective, expandable sub diagram activity. The result is shown in Fig. 6.8. Now, it is possible to state that this solution combines the advantages of both kinds of models in question, i.e., it consists of structured models at all levels of the hierarchy and offers an explicit means of documentation of the places of reuse. But caution is necessary. First, the solution does not free the analyst to actually have a look at all the places a diagram is used after he or she has made a change to the model, i.e., an elaborate change policy is still needed. In the small toy example, such checking is easy, but in a tool you usually do not see all sub diagrams at once, but rather step through the levels of the hierarchy and the sub diagrams with links. Remember that the usual motivation to introduce hierarchical decomposition and tool-support for hierarchical decomposition is the desire to deal with the complexity of large and very large models. Second, the tool should not only support the reuse-direction but should also support the inverse use-direction, i.e., it should support the analyst with a report feature that lists all places of reuse for a given sub diagram.

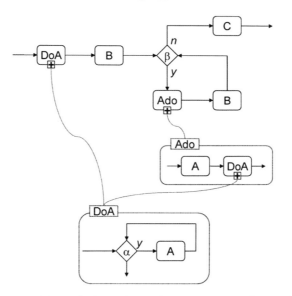

Fig. 6.9. Example for a deeper business process hierarchy.

Now let us turn to a comparative analysis of the complexity of the modeling solution in Fig. 6.8 and the model in Fig. 6.5. The complexity of the top-level diagram in the model hierarchy in Fig. 6.8 is no longer significantly higher than the one of the model in Fig. 6.5. However, together with the sub diagram, the modeling solution in Fig. 6.8 again shows a certain complexity. It would be possible to neglect a reduction of complexity by the solution in Fig. 6.8 completely with the hint that the disappearance of the edge representing the jump from the β-decision point into the loop in Fig. 6.5 is bought by another complex construct in Fig. 6.8 – the dashed line from the activity 'DoA' to the targeted sub diagram. The jump itself can still be seen in Fig. 6.8, somehow, unchanged as an edge from the β-decision point to the activity A. We do not think so. The advantage of the diagram in Fig. 6.8 is that the semantic capsule made of the loop in question is already made explicit as a named sub diagram, which means added documentation value.

Also, have a look at Fig. 6.9. Here the above explanations are even more substantive. The top-level diagram is even less complex than the top-level diagram in Fig. 6.8, because the activity A now has moved to its own level of the hierarchy. However, this comes at the price that now the jump from the β-decision point to the activity A in Fig. 6.5 now re-appears in Fig. 6.9 as the concatenation of the 'yes'-branch in the top-level diagram, the dashed line leading from the activity 'Ado' to the corresponding sub diagram at the next level and the entry edge of this sub diagram.

6.2.5 Business Domain-Oriented versus Documentation-Oriented Modeling

In Sects. 6.2.1 through 6.2.4 we have discussed structured business process modeling for those processes that actually have a structured process specification in terms of a chosen fixed set of activities. In this section we will learn about processes that do not have a structured process specification in that sense. In the running example of Sects. 6.2.1 through 6.2.4 the fixed set of activities was given by the activities of the initial model in Fig. 6.4 and again we will explain the modeling challenge addressed in this section as a model transformation problem.

First, as a further example and for the sake of completeness, we give the resolution of the model in Fig 6.2 into a structured equivalent in Fig. 6.10.

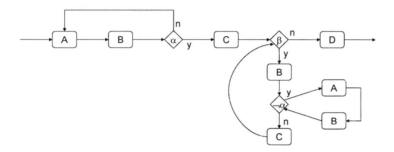

Fig. 6.10. Structured business process model that replaces the non-structured one in Fig. 6.2.

Consider the example business process models in Fig. 6.11. Each model contains a loop with two exits to paths that lead to the end node without the opportunity to come back to the originating loop before reaching the end state. It is known [37, 205, 206, 208] that the behaviors of such loops cannot be expressed in a structured manner, i.e., by a D-chart as defined in Fig. 6.1 solely in terms of the same primitive activities as those occurring in the loop. Extra logic is needed to formulate an alternative, structured specification. Fig. 6.12 shows this loop-pattern abstractly and we proceed to discuss this issues with respect to this abstract model.

Assume that there is a need to model the behavior of a business process in terms of a certain fixed set of activities, i.e., the activities A through D in Fig. 6.12. For example, assume that they are taken from an accepted terminology of a concrete business domain. Other reasons could be that the activities stem from existing contract or service level agreement documents. You can also assume that they are simply the natural choice as primitives for the considered work to be done. We do not delve here into the issue of natural choice and just take for granted that it is the task to model the observed or desired behavior in terms of these activities. For example, we could imagine

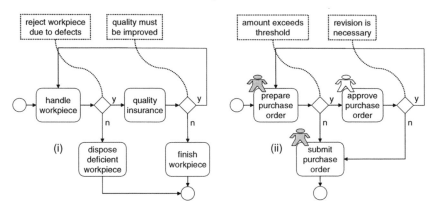

Fig. 6.11. Two example business processes without structured presentation using no other than their own primitives.

an appropriate notion of cohesion of more basic activities that the primitives we are restricted to, or let's say self-restricted to, adhere to. Actually, as it will turn out, for our argumentation to be conclusive there is no need for an explanation how a concrete fixed set of activities arises. What we need for our current argumentation to be conclusive is to demand that the activities are only about actions and objects that are relevant in the business process.

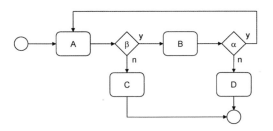

Fig. 6.12. Business process with cycle that is exited via two distinguishable paths.

Fig. 6.13 shows a structured business process model that is intended to describe the same process as the specification in 6.12. In a certain sense it fails. The extra logic introduced in order to get the specification into a structured shape do not belong to the business process that the specification aims to describe. The model in Fig. 6.13 introduces some extra state, i.e., the Boolean variable δ, extra activities to set this variable so that it gets the desired steering effect and an extra δ-decision point. Furthermore, the original δ-decision point in the model of Fig. 6.12 has been changed to a new $\beta \wedge \delta$-decision point. Actually, the restriction of the business process described by Fig. 6.12 onto those particles used in the model in Fig. 6.12 is bisimilar to this process. The problem is that the model in Fig. 6.13 is a hybrid. It is not only a business domain-oriented model any more, it now has also some merely documentation-related parts. The extra logic and state only serve the purpose to get the diagram into shape. It needs clarification of the semantics. Obviously, it is not intended to change the business process. If the auxiliary introduced state and logic would be also about the business process, this would mean, for example, that in the workshop a mechanism is introduced, for example a machine or a human actor that is henceforth responsible for tracking and monitoring a piece of information δ. So, at least what we need is to explicitly distinguish those elements in such a hybrid model. The question is whether the extra complexity of a hybrid domain- and documentation-oriented modeling approach is justified by the result of having a structured specification.

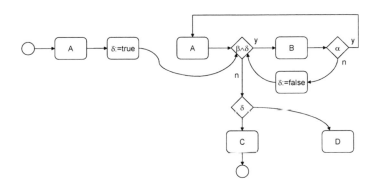

Fig. 6.13. Resolution of business process cycles with multiple distinguishable exits by the usage of auxiliary logic and state.

6.3 Structured Programming

Structured programming is about the design of algorithms. It is about looking for an alternative algorithm that has a somehow better design than a given algorithm but has the same effect. Usually, in the discussion of structured programming the considered effect of algorithms is a functional transformation, i.e., the computation of some output values from some input values. If the effect of a considered algorithm is the behavior of a reactive system things become significantly more complex and the argumentation becomes harder.

6.3.1 An Example Comparison of Program Texts

Let us have a look at an example program of Donald E. Knuth and Robert W. Floyd in [204]. The program is given in Listing 6.6. The functionality of the program is to seek the position of a value x in a global variable array A. If the value is not yet stored in the array, it is appended as a new value at the end of the array. Furthermore, the program maintains the length of the A-array as a global variable m. Furthermore it maintains for each value in the A-array the number of times the value has been searched for. Another global array B is used for this purpose, i.e., for each index i the value stored in $B[i]$ equals to the number of searches for the value stored in $A[i]$.

Listing 6.6 'go to'-Program for seeking the position of a value in an array according to [204].

```
for i:=1 step 1 until m do
  if A[i]=x then go to found fi;
not found: i:=m+1; m:=i;
  A[i]:=x;B[i]:=0;
found: B[i]:=B[i]+1;
```

The program in Fig. 6.6 is not a structured program. Listing 6.8 shows a structured program, which is an alternative implementation of the program in Listing 6.6. The program in Listing 6.8 is also taken from [204]. Knuth compares the programs in Listing 6.8 and Listing 6.6 in order to argue about structured programming. The formulation of the program in Listing 6.8 slightly differs from the original presentation of the program text in [204] with respect to some minor changes in the layout. For example, we have put each statement on a different line and have given line numbers to the lines. Similarly, we have reformulated the program in Listing 6.6 resulting in the program in Listing 6.7. Despite the changes to the program layout, which can be neglected, the version of the program in Listing 6.7 uses a while-loop instead of a deterministic for-loop and therefore needs an incrementation of the loop variable i in the loop body. However, these changes make no difference to the discussion conducted in the following. We have used a formulation with a while-loop to make the program more directly comparable to the program alternative in Listing 6.8.

Listing 6.7 Reformulation of the 'go to'-Program in Listing 6.6

```
01 i:=1;
02 WHILE i<=m DO BEGIN
03   IF A[i]=x THEN GOTO 10
04   i:=i+1;
05 END;
07 m:=i;
08 A[i]:=x;
09 B[i]:=0;
10 B[i]:=B[i]+1;
```

The program in Listing 6.7 is realized with a while-loop that steps through the values in array A. In the loop the program compares the current value in the array with x and if the value equals x the while-loop is exited with a 'go to'-statement. The while-loop is exited with a 'go to' because the loop variable i holds the index of the first field that equals x, which is then exploited in the update of the corresponding field in the B-array in line '10'. Furthermore, the 'go to' is needed to circumvent the execution of lines '07' through '09' in case the value x actually exists in array A, because these lines are only there for handling the case when the value has not been found.

If x exists in A, the program in Listing 6.7 actually finds the first position of x in the A-array. However, only under the assumption that the following pre-condition and side-condition hold the values occur at unique positions in the array, i.e., a value's first position in the array is a value's single position. The necessary side-condition is that the piece of code in Listing 6.7 is the only means to update the A-array and the variable m. The necessary pre-condition is that the variable m holds the length of the array A, in particular, this means that the variable m must be set to zero and the array A is considered as empty before the first run of the program in Listing 6.7. The arrays A and B together can also be interpreted as a hash map data structure with array A holding the keys and array B holding the values. In that sense the program has the functionality of incrementing a key's value if applied to an existing key x, or inserting a key and initializing its value to 1 if applied to a key not yet existing in the hash map.

Listing 6.8 is a reformulation of the program in Listing 6.7 as a structured program, i.e., an alternative implementation without a 'go to'-statement. The condition that leads to an early exit from the loop in Listing 6.7, i.e., an exit before the loop condition has become false, has now been made part – in its negated form – of the loop condition in Listing 6.8. Then, after the loop, it is tested whether the loop has not been ended early by testing for the negation of the loop condition from Listing 6.7. The test guarantees that the code lines that are reserved for cases in which value x does not exist in array A are actually not executed whenever the loop has been exited early.

In [204] Donald E. Knuth argues that the program in Listing 6.7 is an example of a functionality for which structured programming is inadequate. In [204] Knuth gives two reasons for the asserted inadequacy. The first reason is the argument that the program in Listing 6.8 is slightly slower, because of the extra test of the loop condition after the loop in line '05'. Let us assume that the program is not part of some absolutely time critical application, i.e., we do not argue here at the level of machine programming but rather at the level of application programming. Then we can neglect this first aspect against the background of today's computing power. We think that for the most application domains the overhead of this single statement can be considered as marginal. Actually, we do not precisely know which of the programs is faster, because it could be, for example, that the realization of the 'go to'-mechanism

Listing 6.8 Structured Program for seeking the position of a value in an array according to [204].

```
01 i:=1;
02 WHILE (i<=m and (NOT (A[i]=x))) DO BEGIN
03   i:=i+1;
04 END;
05 IF NOT (i<=m) THEN BEGIN
06   m:=i;
07   A[i]:=x;
08   B[i]:=0;
09 END;
10 B[i]:=B[i]+1;
```

of the concretely used compiler and run-time environment is inefficient so that it avoidance outweighs the drawback of the extra test.

The second reason given by Knuth in [204] why he believes that the program in Listing 6.8 is less adequate than the program in Listing 6.7 is much more interesting for our discussion here. The reason given is Knuth's opinion that the program of Listing 6.8 is less readable than the program in Listing 6.7. The problem with this argument is that the better readability of Listing 6.7 is in our opinion not evident. We delve into a discussion of readability of program texts in general and the readability of the program texts in the Listings 6.6 through 6.8 now in Sects. 6.3.2 and 6.3.3.

6.3.2 Readability of Program Texts

Readability is a concept that is hard to grasp. Readability is a concept that inherently is about the perception of a person, i.e., about a person's disposition. A concept close to readability is the concept of understandability. It is possible to define some measure for the understandability of a program text. The question whether such a defined measure is actually objective is another question. One could instruct the test taker to read the program text and say 'stop' immediately when he thinks that he has understood the meaning of the program. Then, it must be determined whether the person has actually understood the program. If he has actually understood the program, the test is valid, otherwise it is not. The defined measurement is not feasible to compare the understandability of a program by a single person. Once, the person has read and understood the first version of the program, he has learned something and this will very likely impact the speed of understanding the second version of the program positively. But the measurement can be used at a statistical scale [13] by running the test with several groups to collect the average understanding periods for the several investigated program versions. Still, the defined measure is flawed. How to judge fair whether a person has actually understood the program? If a person simple describes in natural language the step-by-step operation of the algorithm this may not be sufficient in order to be convinced that the person has understood what the algorithm does. What if people who answer particularly quickly tend to not really understanding the program?

We think that it is hard to tell whether the program in Listing 6.7 is more readable or more understandable then the program in Listing 6.8 or vice versa. Listing 6.6 shows the original version of the program in Listing 6.7. In our version the line number '10' serves as a label of the statement in line '10' when it is referenced in the 'go to'-statement. In the original version the statement has an explicit label 'found:'. Furthermore, the statements in lines '07' through '09' in Listing 6.7 are placed together in a single line in the original version, which visually emphasizes that these statements logically belong to the block of logic which is executed in cases where the value x is not yet stored in the array A. The readability of a program text can be improved by several means, e.g., line indentation, proper comments, or telling names. Such actions are usually best if they adhere to a style guide defined for a project. We think it is hard to tell whether the explicit exit from the loop with a 'go to' in Listing 6.7 or the exit via the loop condition in Listing 6.8 is more understandable. Actually, we are somewhat biased in favor of the exit via the loop condition.

Further Attempts to Improve the Readability of a Program Text

Various attempts can be undertaken to improve the readability or understandability of the program in Listing 6.8 further. In the program in Listing 6.9 we have made the usage of the logic that is needed to handle the single cases of loop exit unique. In Listing 6.8 the statement in line '10' is used in the case that the value x occurred in array A to increase the number of times it has been searched for the value x by one. However, the statement is also used in the other case, i.e., when the value x has not occurred in the array. Therefore, the number of times of searches for x is initially set to zero in line '08' in those cases so that it can be increased correctly to one afterwards. We think that it is somehow artificial to set the value of search times to an incorrect value first. Therefore we made the blocks for handling the two cases under consideration unique in the sense that there is no overlap in case handling any more.

In Listing 6.9 the lines '06' through '08' are only used if x has not occurred in the array and line '11' is only used if x has occurred in the array. Furthermore, lines '06' through '08' in Listing 6.9 completely handle the case that x has not occurred in the array, because we changed line '08' so that it immediately sets the value of search the time to the finally correct value of one. We did something else that improves the readability further in our opinion. In lines '07' and '08', which assign values to fields of the arrays A and B we have used the variable m instead of the variable i to index the wanted field. We think that the usage of m indicates better that we currently access the last element of each field, which fits better to the containing block.

Listing 6.9 Making unique the finalizing actions that react on the single conditions of a composed loop condition.

```
01 i:=1;
02 WHILE i<=m and (NOT (A[i]=x)) DO BEGIN
03   i:=i+1;
04 END;
05 IF NOT (i<=m) THEN BEGIN
06   m:=i;
07   A[m]:=x;
08   B[m]:=1;
09 END ELSE BEGIN
10     B[i]:=B[i]+1;
11 END;
```

Listing 6.10 shows yet another program solution for the discussed functionality. Here we moved all the specific code that is needed to handle the two cases leading to the exit of the loop inside the loop. We have done that at the price of an auxiliary variable 'stop' which has the sole purpose to signalize that the loop should be exited. Both cases that lead to an exit of the loop are detected and handled completely inside the loop. In the program version in Listing 6.9 each condition is tested twice, once as part of the complex loop condition and once again after the loop has been exited. The complex condition in Listing 6.9 necessarily says something about the reasons why the loop is eventually exited, because it conducts the respective test. The loop condition in Listing 6.10 is merely about encoding a control flow issue, however, it is also possible to introduce a comment explaining why the loop stops after the statement in line '03' or it is also possible to encode this comment in the naming of the loop condition variable, e.g., by using a name like

- 'NotYetCompletelyScannedAndNotYetFound' or
- '((i<=m) AND (NOT A[i]=x))'

instead of the straightforward name 'stop'. It is up to the reader to decide whether the program design pattern used in Listing 6.10 is more counterintuitive or more intuitive than the one used in, e.g., Listing 6.9 – we do not really have an opinion about that. The program in Listing 6.10 is important for another reason. It hints at a general solution to resolve program cycles that have more than one exit by the introduction of extra state and extra logic.

6.3.3 Structured Programming and Denotational Semantics

In Sect. 6.3.2 we have discussed the concept of readability of program texts. We want to talk about readability of programs further but from a more for-

Listing 6.10 Moving special actions that react on the single conditions of a composed loop condition into the loop.

```
01 stop:=false;
02 i:=0;
03 WHILE (NOT stop) BEGIN
04   i:=i+1;
05   IF i>m THEN BEGIN
06     m:=m+1;
07     A[m]:=x;
08     A[m]:=1;
09     stop:=TRUE;
10   END ELSE BEGIN
11     IF A[i]=x THEN BEGIN
12       B[i]:=B[i]+1;
13       stop:=true;
14     END;
15   END;
16 END;
```

mal viewpoint this time. We take forward the main argument of this section, which is vague or informal, but, nevertheless, is an argument. It is fair to consider programming languages with a standard denotational semantics and their programs as better understandable than programming languages with a continuation-based semantics. Imperative programming languages with a standard denotational semantics are those that are completely block-structured, i.e., those that do not allow for arbitrary jumps, whereas programming languages with 'go to'-statements must be treated with a continuation-based semantics.

The discipline of formal semantics of programming languages could encourage us to argue further in favor of the program in Listing 6.8 as better understandable as the program in Listing 6.7. The program in Listing 6.8 can be given a standard denotational semantics [328, 285], whereas the program in Listing 6.7 cannot be given a standard denotational semantics but only a continuation-based denotational semantics [329, 330].

Basically, there are three different approaches to the formal semantics of programming languages, i.e., operational semantics [211, 351], axiomatic semantics [161] and denotational semantics [328, 285] which is also called the Scott-Strachey-approach to the semantics of programming languages. We do not want to delve into a distinction of these three approaches to semantics of programming languages. We just give a short statement about the essence of each of the three approaches. An operational semantics describes the effect of a program as its interpretation by a machine or, more abstractly, through the application of a reduction system to it. An axiomatic semantics tries to characterize the impact of the single building blocks of a program onto the program state logically by identifying pre- and post-conditions for them. A denotational semantics directly assigns a mathematical object to a program as its semantics. Even in the standard case of functional programming languages or imperative programming languages without jumps, these mathematical objects cannot be just functions between ordinary sets. The mathematical objects are more complex, because in general a semantics for such a language has to deal with recursion, non-termination and higher-order functions. Therefore the mathematical objects are complete partial orders – or lattices [317] in the original work on denotational semantics – and continuous functions. Again, we do not want to delve into a complex discussion of formal semantics here, in particular, we do not want to delve into the technical aspects of denotational semantics. What counts is an understanding that denotational semantics is a mature apparatus in understanding the programs of a programming language directly as mathematical objects. When we say that the quality of denotational semantics lays in its direct understanding we mean that the semantics of a program is given by semantic composition of the semantics of its direct parts.

A major aspect of the denotational semantics of a programming language is that it is decompositional. As we have said, the semantics of a program can be understood directly by the application of a semantic function on the semantics of its sub programs. The semantics of an imperative program is the transformation of a store. Given an arbitrary store, it transforms it into another store. A store is a mapping that maps variables to values. The transformation on stores that is specified by a program can be considered mathematically as a function between sets. The sets must be special sets, i.e., complete partial orders, and the function must be special functions, i.e., continuous function, so that the denotational semantics works, however, for us it is sufficient to understand here that the transformations are functions. Stores are also functions. The source domain of a store is the set of variables and the target domain is the set of possible values.

The difference between the programs in Listings 6.7 and 6.8 is the following. For the program in Listing 6.8 a semantics can be given as a transformation of stores for all of its sub programs and recursively all the sub programs of sub programs. This is not so for the program in Listing 6.7, because of the 'go to'-statement that jumps out of the loop. In order to deal with this the sub programs must be described relatively to an extra notion of continuation [329, 330], which binds semantics of exploited programs to labels used in the exploiting program. The continuation of a program is a second argument in addition to the store – it is a kind of environment. A continuation-based semantics transports the operational concept of jumps to the mathematical structures that denote programs and therefore brings the operational complexity of them to these structures. The current discussion can be considered as a reformulation of the discussion on decompositional semantics of block-structured versus arbitrary business process models that we have conducted in Sect. 6.2.2 and illustrated Fig. 6.6 for the field of programming languages,

$$[[01]] = \lambda\sigma.\lambda v. \begin{cases} 1 & , v = i \\ \sigma(v) & , else \end{cases} \tag{6.1}$$

$$[[03]] = \lambda\sigma.\lambda v. \begin{cases} \sigma(i) + 1 & , v = i \\ \sigma(v) & , else \end{cases} \tag{6.2}$$

$$[[02..04]] = \nu\lambda F.\lambda\sigma. \begin{cases} ([[03]] \circ F)\sigma & , \sigma(i) \leq \sigma(m) \wedge (\sigma(A))(i) \neq \sigma(x) \\ \sigma & , else \end{cases} \tag{6.3}$$

$$[[06]] = \lambda\sigma.\lambda v. \begin{cases} \sigma(i) & , v = m \\ \sigma(v) & , else \end{cases} \tag{6.4}$$

$$[[07]] = \lambda\sigma.\lambda v. \begin{cases} \lambda p. \begin{cases} \sigma(x) & , p = \sigma(i) \\ (\sigma(A))(p) & , else \end{cases} & , v = A \\ \sigma(v) & , else \end{cases} \tag{6.5}$$

$$[[08]] = \lambda\sigma.\lambda v. \begin{cases} \lambda p. \begin{cases} 0 & , p = \sigma(i) \\ (\sigma(B))(p) & , else \end{cases} & , v = B \\ \sigma(v) & , else \end{cases} \tag{6.6}$$

$$[[06 \cdots 08]] = [[06]] \circ [[07]] \circ [[08]] \tag{6.7}$$

$$[[05 \cdots 09]] = \lambda\sigma \begin{cases} [[06 \cdots 08]]\sigma & , \sigma(i) > \sigma(m) \\ \sigma & , else \end{cases} \tag{6.8}$$

$$[[10]] = \lambda\sigma.\lambda v. \begin{cases} \lambda p. \begin{cases} \sigma(B)(\sigma(i)) + 1 & , p = \sigma(i) \\ \sigma(B)(\sigma(p)) & , else \end{cases} & , v = B \\ \sigma(v) & , else \end{cases} \tag{6.9}$$

$$[[01 \cdots 10]] = [[01]] \circ [[02 \cdots 04]] \circ [[05 \cdots 09]] \circ [[10]] \tag{6.10}$$

however, this time against the background of a more formal treatment which is available for programming languages, i.e., denotational semantics.

As an illustration of what we have just explained we glimpse over the denotational semantics of the program in Listing 6.8 in a step-by-step fashion now. The denotational semantics of the program in Listing 6.8 is given by the Eqns. 6.1 through 6.10.

The statement in line '01' assigns the value 1 to the variable i. This is also expressed by the denotation of the statement that we have given in Eqn. 6.1. The expression $[[01]]$ is a shorthand notation for the semantics of the line '01', in which we have used so-called semantics brackets $[[$ and $]]$. The denotation of line '01' is a function that takes a store σ – the input store – as an argument and yields a new result store. The input store and the result store are both functions that map each variable to a value. The result store maps each variable v to the value that it is mapped to by the input store σ except for the variable i which is mapped to the value 1 by the result store independent of the value it is mapped to by the input store. This is exactly what the semantics of an assignment statement is about, i.e., manipulating the left-hand variable and keeping all other variables of the store as they are.

The semantics of line '03' is given in Eqn. 6.2. Line '03' is similar to line '01'. Here, the variable that is manipulated is again the variable i, however, this time it is increased by one, which means that the result store maps the variable i to the value that it is mapped to in the input store σ plus 1. The semantics of the while-loop in lines '02' through '04' is given in Eqn. 6.3. The semantics of $[[02 \cdots 04]]$ is defined recursively. It is defined as a function F that takes a store σ as an input argument. The function first evaluates the loop condition with respect to the input store. If the loop condition evaluates to false, the function yields the input store as it is as the result store, which represents adequately the termination of the while-loop. In the case that the loop condition evaluates to true, the function F is unfolded one time by applying the semantics of the inner block of the while-loop, i.e., $[[03]]$ in our case, to the input store, taking the result of this application of $[[03]]$ and then applying F recursively to this result. You might want to use the explicit notation $F\big([[03]](\sigma)\big)$ for this sequenced application of first $[[03]]$ and than F, however, we have decided to express it by a function concatenation $\big([[03]] \circ F\big)$ which is then applied to the input store σ as a whole.

You might also want to use a more direct notation for recursive definition like $\big(F \equiv_{DEF} G(F)\big)$ instead of the $\nu\lambda$-notation $\big(\nu\lambda F.G(F)\big)$ that we have used in Eqn. 6.3. However, the $\nu\lambda$-notation expresses better that recursive definitions have no operational semantics but the so-called fixed point semantics in the denotational approach to the semantics of programming languages. Without further elaboration and explanation the understanding of a recursive definition is operational, i.e., it relies on a notion of reduction of the program text which is reduced until a token is reached that leads to the next reduction of the entire program text. The fixed point semantics is another viewpoint on recursion. It defines the recursive function $\big(F \equiv_{DEF} G(F)\big)$ as the smallest fixed point of the higher oder function $\big(\lambda F.G(F)\big)$. At a first sight, the fixed point semantics is less operational, however, it is also somehow operational by the way the smallest fixed point is constructed as the limit of the endlessly repeated application of the considered higher order function to the bottom element $\bot$ of its input domain – see the fixed point theorem of Knaster-Tarski [336] and, e.g., [145] for further reference.

We have said that the stores that are transformed by programs are mappings that map variables to values. In our case the store is nested for some variables, i.e., the array variables. First the application of the store to an array name yields a further function that maps position indexes to result values. Then, the application of this function to a concrete position index yields the array value. For example, the expression $(\sigma(A))(i)$ in Eqn. 6.3 stands for the concrete array value $A[i]$. According to this, the updates to array values are modeled in Eqns. 6.5, 6.6, and 6.9. The semantics of the program lines '06' through '08' should be self-explaining now.

The semantics of a sequence of program statements is given by the concatenation of the function that they denote. The semantics of the program that consists of the lines '06' through '08' in Eqn. 6.7 is an example for this. The semantics of the lines '05' through '09' is now defined by Eqn. 6.8. The lines '05' through '09' form a case construct. Equation 6.8 checks the case condition on the store. If it evaluates to false the result store remains the same, otherwise the result store is yielded by the application of the semantics of the lines '06' through '08' to the store. The semantics of the program line '10' in Eqn. 6.9 should be again self-explaining. Finally, the semantics of the whole program is defined as the concatenation of the semantics of its direct program parts in Eqn 6.10.

In the example we have constructed the program semantics bottom up. The example has shown that program semantics can be given by composition of the semantics of its program parts. In the case of programs without 'go to'-statements the semantics of all program parts can be given homogenously as transformation of stores. This is not so for programs with 'go to'-statements. This means that this is not so for programs with 'go to'-statements in general. Some programs with 'go to'-statements can also be given a standard semantics. We call a semantics that is given homogenously as transformation of stores for all program parts a standard denotational semantics or standard semantics for short. If a program with 'go to'-statements has only such circles that can be exited by no more than one means, it can also be given a standard semantics. The program in Listing 6.7 has no standard semantics, because the circle realized by the program while-loop in lines '02' through '05' is a circle that can be exited by two means, i.e., the loop-condition in line '02' and the 'go to'-statement in line '03'. Therefore, the program in Listing 6.7 must be interpreted as a program of a programming language with 'go to'-statements and, as we have said earlier, a programming language with 'go to'-statements does not have standard denotational semantics but must be given a non-standard denotational semantics, e.g., a continuation-based denotational semantics.

6.4 Frontiers of Structured Business Process Modeling

We are not able to characterize the subset of business processes for which we believe that structured process descriptions, i.e., structured business process models, are better. However, we have argued against the hypothesis that this subset equals the set of all business processes. This means, we say that the postulation that all business processes should be structured [162] is arguable. We do not say that the statement is false; this would be to harsh, because the message that all business processes should be structured is not a statement with a truth value but a postulation. Furthermore, we argue in a yet informal setting, which is the pragmatics of system specification methodology. For the same reason, we would say that it is not appropriate to say that the message is true.

However, eventually we dare to say: It should not be postulated that all business processes should be structured. This is a negative result. Nevertheless, it is an important result, because it can help modelers in preventing pitfalls.

Structuring is considered a proven concept in program design. We have discussed structured programming in Sect. 6.3. The overall question behind the discussion in Sect. 6.3 is whether structured programming is actually as proven as it is considered. We have discussed an example program of the established computer science author Donald E. Knuth that he actually considers as a counter-example for structured programming. What interests us here is merely the fact that an established computer science author argues against the general validity of the structured programming paradigm. Actually, Knuth has argued that the non-structured program in Listing 6.7 is somehow better than the structured program version in Listing 6.8, in particular also because, in his opinion, it is slightly better readable than the program version in Listing 6.8. We have said that we do not think so and that we actually feel that the structured program version in Listing 6.8 is better readable. In that sense we have actually defended structured programming. For us, it is important to show, that the standing of structured programming should not be used without care in the argumentation for a structured approach to business process modeling.

The arguments that are given in favor of structured programming:

- Improved readability.
- Improved maintainability.
- Improved testability.

With respect to validation the arguments have different levels of formality. The longer the structured approach is used as the best practice in real-world projects, the more we rely as a software engineering community in the validity of its claims. Empirical software engineering [36] with its experiments could offer tools for the more systematic evaluations of a software engineering approach, pattern, method and so on. The arguments in favor of a structured approach must be basically the same for the domain of programming languages and the domain of business process modeling language. And the same holds for the claims of structured business process modeling as holds for the claims of structured programming. Without systematic investigation they must be proven through experience in real-world projects and feedback from software engineers in real-world projects.

However, what we have tried to argue in this section is that the standing of structured programming can not simply be transferred to a structured business process modeling approach, even if it would be taken for granted that structured programming is without doubt the best practice in program design. We summarize the reasons for this in the following. The semantics of programming languages is different from the semantics of business process modeling languages. The semantics of a program is a state transformation. The state transformation of a program is achieved compositionally by the parts of the program which again have state transformations as semantics. It does not matter, how a program achieves the overall state transformation with its inner state transformations. This fact opens a space for program design. A program with better design, i.e., with improved readability, maintainability, testability and the like can be taken to replace a program with a weaker design. Business processes may also manipulate state and therefore may cause a state transformation as a side-effect. However, they have an observational semantics. In particular, two business process descriptions are considered as equal if they are observational equivalent. For a program, the processing does not count – as long as we have not to deal with reactive programming and the like. What counts for a program is the result. Two programs are equal if they evaluate to the same result; they are equal if they stand for the same state transformation.

Two business process descriptions may not be interchangeable even if they always have the same effect with respect to a business objective. This is because each modeling element stands for a real-world activity and a business process is a plan for doing work. Therefore, the opportunities for reshaping a given business process description are in general much more restricted than the possibilities for reshaping a program. You can reshape a program as much as you want and, in particular, as much as you think it improves the design of the program text, as long as you ensure that the resulting reshaped program has the same semantics. It is even a best practice to abstract from the implementation, to hide the implementation of functionality. All this does not immediately hold also for business process modeling. We give a further small example for the limitation in freedom for reshaping in Fig. 6.14 that works even without a discussion of structuring principles and structured modeling languages.

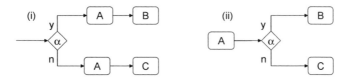

Fig. 6.14. Two business processes that are not behavioral equivalent.

Figure 6.14 shows two processes. In process algebraic notation [249, 250] process (i) is $\alpha.A.B + \neg\alpha.A.C$ and process (ii) is $A.(\alpha.B + \neg\alpha.C)$. Now, let us assume that A has no impact on the outcome of the decision α. If we interpret the two processes (i) and (ii) as programs of a usual programming language with A, B and C being statements, this would mean that A is not manipulating those parts of the system state that is tested by α. If (i) and (ii) were programs we now could start a discussion on whether we would prefer the program design of (i) over the program design of (ii). For example, the inner reuse of activity A in (ii) is a plus, because it improves maintainability. But (i) and (ii) are business process description and the discussion about which one has the better design is limited even if α is independent of A and, therefore, A and B have the same effect with respect to the business objective. The problem is that also α describes an activity, i.e., a test that is conducted, that occurs in the real world. And it might be a huge difference whether you conduct the test at the beginning of the process or conduct it in the middle after activity A for several reasons. One such reason might be that α tests some property of a good that flow through A and the good occurs at another location after A than before A and the location of the good before A is much more suited for conducting the α-test than the location after the processing of A.

The described problem of reshaping a business process description – against the fact that business process modeling must be in first place domain-oriented and only in second place artifact-oriented – is the basic motive also in the other examples of this section.

7

Workflow Technology and Human-Computer Interaction

The purpose of this chapter is to characterize workflow-intensive systems from a human-computer interaction viewpoint, i.e., it explains how a typical IT application is experienced by a user. It explains how a typical IT application structures the work of its user. Therefore the notion of worklist is explained and how current workflow technology orchestrates applications and programs that implement system dialogues on the basis of a worklist paradigm. As an important by-product the chapter contributes to the understanding of the gap between workflow definition and application programming. The chapter also discusses how workflow technologies can support the assignment of actors to tasks. Again, we try to conduct the discussion as product-independent as possible. What interests us are the basic concepts behind concrete role models found in today's workflow technologies.

7.1 Two HCI Styles of Workflow Systems

We distinguish between two kinds of possible workflow systems and coin the following terms for them:

- Terminal/server-style workflow systems
- Windows-style workflow systems

The two kinds of workflow technologies are distinguished by the degree of parallelism they reveal to the user of the workflow system. The two workflow systems styles are not about implementation technology as the chosen names of terminal/server-style and windows-style might suggest. They are about the capabilities to visit and arrange the dialogues that make up the workflow system as experienced by the users. The implementing technology is not the point. A terminal/server-style workflow system can be implemented with a windowing toolkit. However, it remains a terminal/server-style workflow system. This is similar to the many form-based application generators which

D. Draheim, *Business Process Technology: A Unified View on Business Processes, Workflows and Enterprise Applications*, DOI 10.1007/978-3-642-01588-5_7,
© Springer-Verlag Berlin Heidelberg 2010

generate rich clients and allow for further development of them usually in an object-oriented, event-based technology. With these application generators the resulting rich client nevertheless only realizes a strict submit/response-style system and not a highly interactive user interface that really exploits the capabilities of the underlying event-based technology. Also vice versa, what we will define as windows-style workflow system or windows-experience of workflow consumption can be implemented in a terminal/server-fashion of user interaction. Also other names for the two workflow styles like single-user-single-task for the terminal/server-style and single-user-multiple-tasks for the windows style would be appropriate, however, we think that terminal/server-style and windows-style are highly suggestive terms once the technology-independence of the notions they represent has been understood.

7.1.1 Degree of Parallelism Revealed to the User

In a workflow system process instances are initially started by a user via a process instantiation menu. Activity instances are launched to be started upon the completion of other tasks. The activity that are ready to start are presented to the user in a worklist, also called activity list or task list. The worklist allows the user to select an activity instance and to start it. The process instantiation menu and the worklist structures the work of the user at the human-computer interface. Further structure is provided by the dialogues that support the running activities.

Parallelism in workflow systems as experienced by a single user stems from the possibility to start several process instances as well as from parallel sub processes in workflow definitions. All workflow systems allow the user to experience parallelism by arbitrarily intertwining the activities from different process instances or different sub process instances, or, to say it more precisely to intertwine the dialogues that support the activities. However, in general the granularity of such intertwining is at the granularity of starting and completing a dialogue supporting an activity. This means it is necessary to distinguish between such coarse-grained states that are made of the activities that are ready to be executed and the fine-grained states that are made of the state of screens of the dialogues of the workflow system. According to these different kind of states it can also be distinguished between coarse-grained and fine-grained user interactions. Coarse-grained user interaction creates new process instances and starts or completes activity instances. Fine-grained user interactions edit forms and trigger server actions that lead to new screens.

In form-oriented analysis [89] we have considered the single user working in a single user session of a submit/response-style system. In form-oriented analysis we have characterized the user interaction as following a two-staged interaction paradigm. The interactions that trigger server actions and lead to new screens are considered as coarse-grained in systems that implement a two-staged interaction and the interactions with the single screens are considered as fine-grained. In the modeling of form-oriented analysis this distinction between coarse-grained and fine-grained interactions is exploited to describe the system navigation and behavior in terms of the coarse-grained interactions and to abstract away from the fine-grained interactions wherever suitable. Here, in the current strand of discussion we further consider a third kind of interaction which has been described as more coarse grained and deals with the navigation via the worklist yielding a three-staged interaction. The fine-grained user interactions of this discussion, i.e., navigations between screens and screen interactions are than again distinguished as coarse-grained and fine-grained as in form-oriented analysis.

The distinctions between the different kinds of interaction help to structure and develop the discussion on parallelism revealed to the user in the sequel. In Sect. 7.1.2 we start with a workflow system that is restricted to two out of the three kinds of interactions just described, i.e., the coarse-grained navigation via the worklist and the most fined grained interactions with single forms. This means, that we consider the special case of a workflow system in which each activity is supported by only one screen and not yet by a complex dialogue or application. This special case is not merely interesting for didactical purposes but has practical relevance. Workflow management system products and today's business process management suites combine a rapid development tool for screen and form composition with the executable specification of workflows. If such a technology is not used as a means of meshing together existing applications but as a software development environment to build a new information system from scratch this typically results in this special case of workflow system. In any case you will be able to identify crucial portions of the workflow system that adhere to this special case. Then in Sect. 7.1.3 we consider workflow systems that contain all of the three described kinds of user interaction.

7.1.2 Dialogues Realized by Single Form Screens

Figure 7.1 shows a simple workflow definition. The workflow consists merely of a pure sequence of activities to be scheduled on after the other. Most importantly for the current considerations is the fact that all the activities are assigned to the same user. Each of the activities is realized by a single screen that typically includes a form to be filled out and submitted by the user. In general, an activity can also be realized by a complex dialogue consisting of several screens to be invoked. The considered case with only one form screen for each activity is particularly simple but is already sufficient to discuss the distinction between terminal/server-style and windows-style workflow systems. In currently used workflow definition languages the specification of the implementing dialogues usually does not belong to the workflow definitions. In Fig. 7.1 activities are depicted in the style of usual event-driven process chain notation by rounded rectangles embedded into a start and end event depicted by a hexagon.

The screens and forms that make up the activity support of the workflow system are depicted by bubbles and rectangles, i.e., in the style of the concrete formchart notation discussed in [89]. Activities in Fig. 7.1 are labeled with uppercase letters. Each screen is labeled with the same letter as the activity it belongs to in lowercase and a form that appears on one of those screens gets the same letter as the screen it appears on. We have mingled together freely a notation for workflow definition and the formchart notation for user interaction definition into one diagram in Fig. 7.1. The forms that the user can fill out and submit on the various activity screens are not the only user interaction capabilities that we have depicted in Fig. 7.1. Also the start button of start link that appears on the worklist page and leads to the selected activity page is always shown. In the sense of formchart notation all the activities of the workflow definition part of the diagram in Fig. 7.1 together stand for the worklist page of the workflow system.

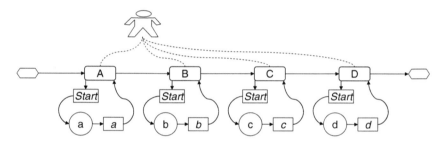

Fig. 7.1. Process definition with one form for each activity as implementing system dialogue.

Terminal/Server-style Realization

Figure 7.2 shows a human-computer interaction with a terminal/server-style workflow system that realizes the workflow defined in Fig. 7.1. Let us assume that, initially, three process instances have been launched and the user can select to start the first activity of one of the process instances. Yet another synonym for activity, i.e., task, has been used as a headline of the worklist in Fig. 7.1. Each of the process instances that has been launched has a unique identifier ranging from '01' to '03' in the current example. The worklist always shows all the next possible activity instances of each active process instance. Each activity instance appears in the worklist with the name of its corresponding activity concatenated to the identifier of its process instance.

Initially, the user in the current example selects the activity 'A02' and starts it by pressing the start button. As a result the corresponding page and form are represented to the user. The user can edit the form and submit it. As a result of this he is redirected back to the worklist where he can select

the next activity. In the worklist the label of the completed activity instance
has been replaced by that of the next activity in the process instance that
is now ready for activation. If an activity is started and the corresponding
form is presented to the user the worklist is inactive, i.e., it is not possible for
the user to start yet another activity in parallel to a started one. Actually, in
the current example presented in Fig. 7.2 it is meant in such a way that with
the selection and start of an activity the worklist really disappears from the
computer screen.

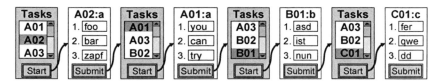

Fig. 7.2. Strictly chained forms of a terminal-server style workflow system.

Drawbacks of Terminal/Server-style Workflow Systems

In Fig. 7.2 the user must wait with the selection and start of a new activity
instance until he has fully filled out the form belonging to the current activity
instance. The work is a strict interchange of selecting from the worklist and
completely finishing activity dialogues. We call this kind of workflow-system
a terminal/server-style of workflow system. The drawback of such workflow
systems is that with the structuring of the workflow into activities the degree
of parallelism revealed to the user is fixed once and forever. If a form is very
long the user might want to start another form in parallel. Actually, this is
not a real strong argument against the terminal/server-style workflow system.
However, it is at least a soft argument against it. It is an argument against
it in the sense of good human-computer interaction principles. For example,
controllability is a dialogue principle of good human-computer interface design, which is, e.g., described in part 110 on dialogue principles of the ISO
standard 9241 on ergonomics for human-system interaction, i.e., ISO 9241-
110:2006 [185], formerly very well known as ISO standard 9241 on ergonomic
requirements for office work with visual display terminals, part 10, i.e., ISO
9241-10:1991 [176]. In terms of ISO 9241 controllability stands for the ability
of the user to control the direction and pace of the dialogues of a system. The
user interface guidelines [358] of the Microsoft Developer Network (MSDN)
have an even more narrative description of this principle for which they coin
the term 'user in control', i.e., a user is in control of the dialogues if he feels
in control of them rather than feeling controlled by them. With respect to
the terminal/server-style workflow system it is fair to state that a user might
rather feeling controlled by a dialogue if he cannot escape from it but rather
is obliged to fully complete it.

The blocking of the user from visiting other dialogues in a terminal/server-style workflow system can easily be experienced as limiting the user's controllability. On the other hand, it can be also experienced as inefficient by a user to be directed back too often to the worklist where he is able to select the next dialogue to enter. The ability to select a subsequent activity instance can not only be a benefit in terms of controllability but also a burden in terms of efficiency. Therefore, in a terminal/server-style workflow system it is a challenge to find the appropriate balance between controllability and efficiency, i.e., to find the appropriate granularity of workflow states.

At least if a business process management suite is not used as an enterprise application integration technology, there is usually a design space in partitioning the system into dialogues eventually resulting into workflow states. In order to give an impression of what has been said, Fig. 7.3 visualizes the fact that in our current example depicted in Fig. 7.1 it might be possible to mingle all the dialogues together by simply combining the reports of the several pages and connecting the forms to one superform without loss of functionality. We do not delve into the topic of general commensurability or interchangeability of dialogues here, however, as a side remark to Fig. 7.3 it should be said that the combination of dialogues might not always be possible as easily as depicted. For example, it becomes hard if the report on one page depends on the user's input to one of the preceding pages in Fig. 7.1.

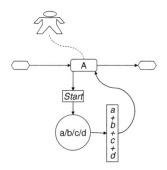

Fig. 7.3. Alternative activity support by a superform-based dialogue.

A strong argument against the terminal/server-style of workflow systems is that the blocking of the user imposed by the dialogues can lead to hard delays. The user should have all information needed to finish a dialogue supporting an activity ready before he starts it, otherwise he is forced to gather it after he has started. This means he has to finish all business processes or tasks in the context of the workflow system supported activity before he can actually proceed with other activities of the workflow system. In the worst case the user is blocked by waiting for the opportunity to finish a certain task and to gather the information necessary to complete the dialogue.

Parallelism Revealed by Terminal/Server-style Workflow Systems

The explained drawbacks of terminal/server-style workflow systems stem from limited support for parallelism. In terms of the discussed three-staged inter-action model terminal/server-style workflow systems prevent parallelism at the level of screen interaction and the level of triggering new screens inside an activity supporting dialogue. Nevertheless, terminal/server-style workflow systems allow for some degree of parallelism. They allow for quasi-parallelism at the level of completed dialogues. This means, through the concept of work-list the user has the freedom of choice in how he intertwines the activities of the various activated process instances against each other. At the one extreme, he can choose to finish all the activities of one process instance one after the other before he starts an activity of another process instance. At the other extreme he could choose a round-robin style. In our example this amounts to starting the same kind of activity instance of all of the activated process instances one after the other before proceeding with another kind of activity instance.

The statements on the limited support for parallelism only hold for the single user working in a single user session at the terminal/server-style work-flow system. With respect to the dialogues supporting different users even a terminal/server-style workflow system allows for full parallelism. The execu-tion of a dialogue supporting one user is completely independent from the execution of all the dialogues supporting other users unless special coordi-nation efforts are implemented. As we will see in due course, the limitations on parallelism experienced by the single user can be overcome, however, the parallelism by a single user will always be a kind of quasi-parallelism. This is so, because in every solution the finest granularity of quasi-parallelism is the level of single key strokes – the single user is able to operate at most one keyboard.

Allowing for More Parallelism

Figure 7.4 shows the human/computer interaction with a system that also re-alizes the workflow defined in Fig. 7.1. The system supports with its dialogues the same functionality as the system shown in Fig. 7.2, however, it allows for more parallelism to be experienced by the user. The difference is in a detail, i.e., in an additional save button on the pages supporting the single dialogues. Again, the user starts by selecting and starting the first activity instance of the process instance with identifier '02'. Again, as a consequence, the worklist disappears from the computer screen and the page supporting the activity appears.

Then the user partly fills out the form provided on the page but suddenly decides not to complete filling out the form with all necessary data. Instead he decides to suspend the work on the current activity and to proceed with an activity instance of another process instance first. He does so by clicking the save button on the page. As a result the current activity supporting page disappears and the worklist reappears on the computer screen. However, unlike the system depicted in Fig. 7.2, the activity 'A02' has not disappeared from the worklist, i.e., in terms of its members the worklist has remained the same as before the invocation of the activity instance. The only difference is that the currently visited activity instance is shaded in the worklist, i.e., it is visualized in a thinner font as well as in italic letters. This means that activity instances that have never been started are visualized in a different manner than those that are suspended by the user. These different visualization are not necessary for the user to achieve his tasks but might help him in structuring his work and selecting the next activity to work on.

As the next step the user selects and starts the first activity instance of another process instance, i.e., the process instance with identifier '03'. He completes the appearing form and submits it. As a result the activity instance 'A03' is replaced by the next activity instance 'B03' of process instance '03'. Now, the user chooses to resume the previously suspended activity instance 'A02'. He selects it in the worklist and restarts it by pressing the start button – the slight misnomer of the start button with respect to its usage as a restart or resume button should be no problem here. The page supporting the activity reappears in the same state it was in when it disappeared when the activity was suspended by the user. This means that the workflow system has preserved the result of the fine-grained user interaction on that page. In particular the data that the user has entered into the form so far are there again and the user can proceed with working with the page as if it has never been suspended. After finally submitting the form the activity instance 'A02' is replaced by an activity instance 'B02' in the worklist.

Fig. 7.4. Workflow system that allows for saving screen states.

Exploiting Windowing in Allowing for More Parallelism

Figure 7.5 shows the human/computer interaction with yet another system that realizes the workflow defined in Fig. 7.1. The realizing system exploits a standard windows engine in its implementation to allow for the desired amount of parallelism. The worklist does not occupy the whole screen anymore, it is shown in a window that resides on the root pane of the windows interface.

As in the example presented in Fig. 7.4 the user chooses to start activity instance '02' as the first action. As a result a new window that shows the activity supporting page pops up. However, the window with the worklist does not disappear. Furthermore, as a result of starting the activity instance its label in the worklist immediately becomes shaded to signal that it has been started. As in the example presented in Fig. 7.1, the user starts working on the activity instance '02' but decides to suspend it in order to work on activity instance '03' first. However, because windows technology is exploited no explicit save button is needed on the activity pages any more. The user just starts the activity instance '03' and a respective windows pops up and becomes active. In the example, activity instance windows that are active have a black horizontal bar at the top, whereas activity instance windows that are currently inactive have a white bar at the top.

Unlike the example in Fig. 7.1 the user also decides not to completely finish with activity instance '03' but to resume it like activity instance '02'. As a next step, he resumes activity instance '02'. He does so by selecting activity instance '02' and starting it via the worklist. As a result the window of activity instance '03' becomes inactive and the window of activity instance '02' becomes active. The user can switch between the two activity instance windows back and forth to intertwine the work on the single activity instances at arbitrary fine level of granularity, i.e., down to the level of single key strokes as already mentioned.

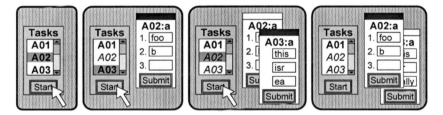

Fig. 7.5. Exploiting windowing for saving screen states of a workflow system.

The system presented in Fig. 7.5 allows for as much as parallelism as the system represented in Fig. 7.4. However, it does not allow for more parallelism. The same schedules in terms of key strokes on different activity instance pages can be realized with both systems. The only difference is a slight change in comfort. With the system in Fig. 7.4 the user always needs one more click in order to suspend the current activity and to invoke a new activity instance page, i.e., the click onto the save button of the current page. In that sense the system in Fig. 7.4 implements a windows mechanism, which becomes clear if one perceives the single activity instance pages of the dialogue as maximized windows, i.e., windows that occupy the whole screen, and the save button as a window minimizing or shrinking button.

The Windows Metaphor

Windowing as described in Alan Kay's work on the reactive engine [195] consists of two concepts, i.e., virtual screens, and windows management – see Fig. 7.6. A virtual screen is a screen that is actually too large to be displayed on a computer terminal. With windowing it is possible to experience a virtual screen with a viewport that is small enough to be displayed on the computer terminal. With the viewport's scrollbars it is possible to scroll through the virtual screen. Because of this feature it is fair to say that the computer terminal is already a graphical user interface, even if it is only used to run, e.g., text manipulating applications. On the other hand, the viewport can be even smaller than the actual computer terminal, so that it can be placed arbitrarily on the computer terminal allowing for displaying other things, in particular other viewports. The containers used to display a viewport on the computer display are called windows. A virtual screen can be used to display the page of an application's dialogues, so, windows can be used to run applications or sub applications. Many windows can be displayed and managed on the graphical user interface. Windows management is about direct manipulation of the windows on the computer terminal, i.e., it provides a means to move a window around, to minimize a window, i.e., to shrink it to an icon, to restore it, i.e., to bring back a window from an icon it has been shrunken to, and the like.

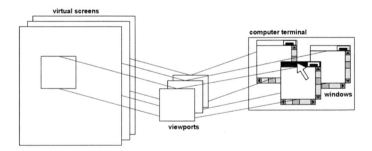

Fig. 7.6. Virtual screens versus viewports versus windows.

If an application or sub application is running inside a window, shrinking a window completely keeps the window's screen state for later restoring. Therefore a window is a virtualization, i.e., a window is virtual computer terminal. The term virtual screen was reserved by [195] for the background screens that is larger than the real computer terminal, but a window is actually also a virtual screen in its own right. We have chosen the term windows-style workflow system for all workflow systems that allow its dialogues to be suspended and resumed in the restored fine grained screen state they were in when they were suspended. We have chosen the name because the shrinking and restoring of windows, which accomplishes exactly this, is such a characteristic feature of the windows management part of the windows paradigm. We use the name even for those systems that do not fully realize a windowing experience with all its window management features but at least those that are needed to reveal the crucial amount of added parallelism to the user.

The insight that windowing is a virtualization concept also shows us the potential for exploiting application virtualization technology like currently emerging appliance execution engines to hook together existing applications in interplay with business process management technology.

Root Pane Serving as Worklist

In the example in Fig. 7.5, an activity instance window can be activated via the worklist, i.e., by selecting and starting or restarting it. But this is not the only way to resume an activity instance. Also the built-in feature for activating windows of the underlying windowing engine can be exploited. An activity instance window can be activated in the example simply by clicking on it. Clicking on a currently inactive window, of course, also deactivates the currently active window. This shows that there is a level of redundancy between the concept of worklist and the windowing features. Actually it is possible to get rid of the explicitly implemented worklist completely. This is expressed by Fig. 7.7. The system represented in Fig. 7.7 is a variant of the system discussed in Fig. 7.5 that works without an worklist. The idea is simply that the root pane itself can serve as the worklist.

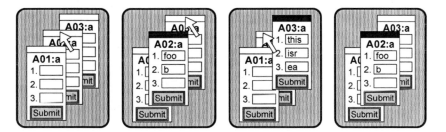

Fig. 7.7. Exploiting the root pane of a windowing system as worklist.

In the system of Fig. 7.7, starting a process instance means that the window or possibly the windows of its first activity instance resp. instances pop up on the root pane. In our case three process instances have been started and therefore three initially inactive activity instance windows reside on the root pane. Starting or resuming an activity instance is always done by simply clicking at and this way activating the corresponding window. Suspending an activity instance is the result of starting or resuming a different activity instance.

The explicit worklist has its justification from a human-computer interaction viewpoint. It provides the user with an overview of all open tasks and a means to navigate between them at a single designated spot. In the system Fig. 7.7, we have not yet made use of the standard windows management features of shrinking and restoring a window. If all of the activity instance windows in Fig. 7.7 are shrunken to icons this actually results into a kind of worklist similar to the ones in Figs. 7.4 or 7.5. This is what is actually done by the system realized in Fig. 7.8. Unlike the system in Fig. 7.7 the system does not generate the full activity instance windows at the beginning but only iconized versions of them. Then clicking on the iconized window of an activity instance resembles very much the selection and start of an activity instance via an explicitly implemented worklist. The respective activity instance window pops up and is ready for form editing.

Unlike the windows in Fig. 7.7 the activity instance windows in Fig. 7.8 have a minimizing button at the top-right corner. In the user interaction of Fig. 7.8 the minimizing button plays the same role as the save button in the user interaction shown in Fig 7.4.

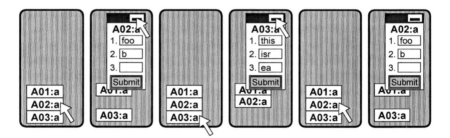

Fig. 7.8. Fully exploiting windowing for saving screen states of a workflow system.

The discussion here is not about proposing that workflow systems should be realized without an explicitly implemented worklist. The purpose of the discussion is to clarify the semantics of the worklist concept from a human-computer interaction viewpoint, i.e., it is about explaining that the essential functionality of a worklist has the semantics of a root pane gathering activity instance windows or iconized windows in the framework of a windowing technology. An explicitly implemented worklist can be made subject to sophisticated features for organizing the task items. We have already seen one such feature in the examples of Figs. 7.4 or 7.5, i.e., the different appearance of activity instances that have been started in the past and those that have never been started. The worklist is also the natural place for administrative task management features like the rescheduling of a task to another role or person in the organization.

7.1.3 Dialogues Realized by Multiple Screens

So far, in Sect. 7.1.2 we have discussed the difference between terminal/server-style and windows-style systems merely against the background of the special case of workflow systems with single page and single form dialogues, i.e., systems where each of the dialogues that support the activities consists of exactly one page and form only. Fortunately, all the crucial arguments given in the discussion so far generalize more or less immediately to the full case of three-staged interaction.

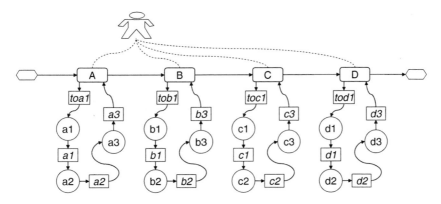

Fig. 7.9. Process definition with complex activity implementing system dialogues.

Figure 7.9 shows a workflow system description similar to the one in Fig. 7.1. The actual workflow definition with its activities and the single user attached to them is the same in Fig. 7.9 and Fig. 7.1. The difference is in the implementing dialogues. In Fig. 7.9 the dialogues are complex, i.e., they do not consist of just one page and form each but of three pages and forms each. The user has to trigger page changes in order to step through the dialogues.

Figure 7.10 shows an example user interaction of a terminal/server-style workflow system that realizes the workflow description in Fig. 7.9. Once a user has started a dialogue that belongs to a certain activity instance via the worklist, the user must step through the entire dialogue. He must completely fill in all required data in all the forms on all pages of the dialogue. Only when the user has reached the last page of the dialogue and submitted the last form is he routed back to the worklist again where he can select and start a new dialogue.

In the current example we have to deal with all three kinds of user interaction that we have identified for workflow systems, i.e., navigation via the tasks list, navigation across the pages of a dialogue, and interaction with the single pages of the dialogues. In the examples of Sect. 7.1.2 we only had to deal with two kinds of user interaction, i.e., navigation via the tasks list and interaction with the single pages of the dialogues. The blocking of the user encountered in the terminal/server-style of the workflow definition in Sect. 7.1.2 now spawns all kinds of interactions of a user with the dialogue in Fig. 7.10. Despite that, there is no crucial difference. The drawback of blocking seems to be more severe in the case other work is blocked with a complex dialogue than blocked by work on a single supporting page and form. However, in general it depends on the design of the dialagues compared. A large, i.e., typically scrollable page and form with, e.g., hundreds of input fields is even more complex than a concrete complex dialogue, which may simply consist of two very small pages and forms.

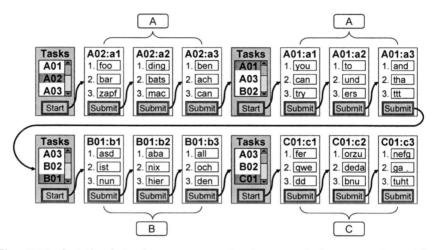

Fig. 7.10. Strictly chained process execution in a terminal-server style workflow system.

With respect to windows-style workflow, systems with complex dialogues differ from systems with single page dialogues in the complexity of the state that must be saved and restored when a dialogue is suspended and resumed. In the examples discussed in Figs 7.5 through 7.8 each of the popped up windows is the first window of a started sub application. Whether the whole started dialogue is experienced in the initial window, or the sub application itself makes heavy use of windowing with popping up dialogues for its own sub application principally does not matter. However, with activity instance supporting dialogues that extensively use windowing subtle issues may arise with respect to the user expectations.

For example, if a dialogue opens several windows it should be enforced that they are all closed on completion of the dialogue. This could be achieved by deactivating those buttons that stand for final data submission, i.e., that stand for the completion of the activity instance, as long as they are auxiliary windows open in that dialogue. Another solution is to implicitly shut down these windows and therefore implicitly accept the data gathered by the user within these windows whenever such a final button is pressed. Both solutions are kinds of sub dialogue synchronizations. As a pattern, such synchronization techniques can also be applied to the entire design of the dialogue so that there are no auxiliary windows open whenever a window contains a final button. A further option to achieve rich dialogues in terms of windowing and avoiding the issue to have multiple windows open at the end of the dialogue is the appropriate exploitation of modal dialogues.

7.1.4 Overall Workflow System Design

A workflow system is a system that allows for the execution and coordination of workflows of several users. In general, the software design of a workflow system can be freely chosen. However, if workflow technology is reused, the workflow technology imposes a certain software structure onto the whole workflow system. In particular, if workflow systems have no enterprise application integration background but are built from scratch to support part of an organization's business processes, different non-standard software designs often emerge. This is especially true for how the entirety of workflow rules, i.e., the workflow definition, is actually enforced in the system.

In a very straightforward workflow system implementation the knowledge about which further activities have to be followed by which users after completion of a given activity can be completely distributed over the whole workflow system implementation code. Such an implementation consists of a bunch of dialogue implementations for the several activities that have to be supported. Upon completion of a dialogue the code of that dialogue triggers the next activities. The code may invoke a dialogue implementation directly enforcing a certain user to do a certain thing. Most probably, however, the code accesses the worklist software component responsible for structuring a certain user's work and pushes a concrete activity instance to it. Or, equally probably, it accesses a general worklist manager software component and pushes an activity instance together with a responsible user to it. With knowledge on workflow reference models like that of the Workflow Management Coalition [164] in mind you might want to rule out the described system architecture approach from the outset. However, you will find this design pattern in enterprise resource planning systems that have been built from scratch. You will definitely find the pattern in scenarios where several stand-alone workflow-intensive systems are hooked together to fulfill common business processes.

The introduction of workflow enactment service into a workflow system design can be seen as the action of tearing all the distributed activity continuations from the code and gathering them at a single spot. Then, however, a workflow enactment service with its underlying workflow engines is basically much more than a database maintaining the complex runtime state of the workflow system. Because all end-user applications are programmed against this state database and coordinate their coarse-grained dialogue control against it, the coarse grained dialogue control now has got a hub-and-spoke architecture which lowers the overall coupling. However, standard workflow enactment services offer little, or actually nothing, for the more fine-grained interaction control concerning page changes and screen interactions.

7.2 Actor Assignment in Workflow Automation

Actors can be attached to the activities of business process models and work-flow definitions. On the level of business process modeling the assignment of an actor to an activity can have the meaning that the actor is responsible for activity, that he executes the activity, that he does the work of the activity and so on. In general, actors can be human actors but also automatic actors like machines or IT systems. Often, the term resource is used for what we call actors in this section. We prefer to use the term actor, because it fits the term activity. The term actor expresses better that the attached resource is active and that it is responsible for the execution of the activity than the term resource. Resources in general may also be passive, i.e., resources in general may also be processed by an activity instead of executing the activity. The term actor is also used in the Unified Modeling Language. Here it is used in sequence diagrams, and, in particular, also in activity diagrams which are a form of flowcharts and are often considered as business process models and used for business process modeling.

In this section we are interested in human actors and workflow definition. We are interested in the semantics of assigning human actors to activities of a workflow definition. If a business process specification is taken as a workflow definition that is interpreted by a workflow management system, the assignment of an actor to an activity has a very concrete meaning. Whenever an instance of an activity is activated, a link to the dialogue supporting the activity is added to the worklist of the actor that is assigned to the activity. We have given an in-depth explanation of the worklist paradigm and the operational semantics of workflow management technology already in Sect. 7.1.1 on the basis of a three-staged interaction viewpoint.

Actually, concrete workflow technologies offer more than the opportunity to assign a single actor to an activity. Usually, it would not be sufficient to assign a single concrete actor to an activity. Usually, you have many actors working on instances of the same activity. Concrete actors must be scheduled to concrete instances of activities. Often, a high flexibility of this scheduling is desired. For example, what if an employee is not available, for example, because of a business trip? How to achieve a good work load balancing? Concrete workflow management products offer the opportunity to assign a so-called role or working group instead of a concrete actor to an activity. A role can be a set of concrete actors together with a selected pattern of choosing a concrete actor or a subset of concrete actors from this role. Concrete workflow management products propose and offer concrete role models and scheduling patterns. Roles are statically assigned to activities. They restrict the pool of possible actors to an explicitly defined set. Concrete actors are determined dynamically, which is also called dynamic staff scheduling.

7.2.1 Interpretation of Actor Groups

Dealing with roles assigned to activities in business process models has two aspects. The first one is about the dynamic selection of concrete actors for an activity instance, i.e., about dynamic staff scheduling. Typical recurring pattern in dynamic staff scheduling can be identified and turned into rapid development features in concrete workflow management products. We discuss dynamic staff scheduling in Sect. 7.2.2. The second aspect of role models is the orchestration of concrete actors that have been dynamically scheduled for a given activity instance. If only one actor has been selected this is actually not a question. Then, the activated task appears as a link in the worklist of the user. However, if more than one actor has been selected, there are several alternatives in continuing the process that we will discuss in this section. We use the term actor group for a set of concrete actors that have been selected out of a role or working group as the result of dynamic staff scheduling. We do not use working group, because the term working group is already used by some concrete workflow technology products for roles.

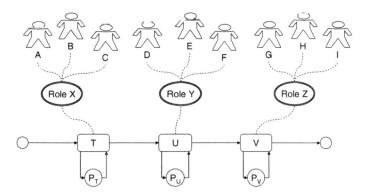

Fig. 7.11. Roles attached to a workflow definition.

Figure 7.11 shows a simple business process model in which roles X, Y and Z are attached to the single activities T, U and V. The programs that are started by the users via their worklists are illustrated as circles P_T, P_U and P_V. Roles consist of concrete actors, e.g., role X consists of the three concrete actors A, B and C.

We identify and explain the following interpretations of actor groups:

- Parallel execution of assigned tasks.
  - Synchronizing parallel execution.
  - Non-Synchronizing parallel execution.
- Preemptive execution of assigned tasks.
  - Preemption with session conservation as a special case.

Parallel Execution of Assigned Tasks

Let us assume that more than on actor is dynamically selected from a role.
This can be can be interpreted as the specification of parallelization, i.e., parallel fork of as many new activity instances as selected actors. It is not the
question here, whether such parallel interpretation is actually implemented
in workflow technology products today. We explain it here for reasons of systematization, because it is an option to be implemented and is the obvious
alternative to the preemptive execution of a task that have been assigned to
multiple actors, which is actually implemented in existing workflow technology products like Lotus and Websphere MQ – we will discuss the preemptive
execution of tasks in due course after the discussion of the parallel execution.

With a parallel interpretation of scenarios like the one shown in Fig. 7.11
a link to a new instance of the considered activity is posted to the worklist
of each actor. There are two options of interpretation with respect to synchronization, i.e., a synchronizing option and a non-synchronizing option. In
the synchronizing option, all actors selected from role X in Fig. 7.11 must
finish the task T before a link to new instances of activity U is attached to
the worklists of the actors selected for role Y. In the non-synchronizing option
new actors are selected from the role Y and new instances of the activity U
are posted to the selected actors whenever one of the instance of activity T
has been finished.

In order to visualize the difference between the synchronizing and the
non-synchronizing option, let us assume for a moment that the dynamic staff
scheduling mechanism selects always all concrete actors of a role upon activation of an activity instance – actually, the selection of all of the statically
given actors of a role is the most basic actor scheduling pattern that can
be supported easily by concrete workflow management technologies. Then,
it would be possible to repaint the diagram in Fig. 7.11 without roles but
single actors attached to the activities directly as shown in diagram (i) for
the synchronizing option and diagram (ii) for the non-synchronizing option in
Fig. 7.12.

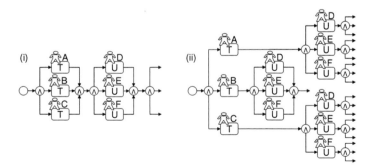

Fig. 7.12. Repaintings of the workflow definition in Fig. 7.11.

An example in which the synchronizing option of a parallel interpretation could be used is a content or document management system with a staged content creation. In a staged approach to content creation there are authors and reviewers. After an author has initially created content it is not immediately published but reviewed first. As the outcome of a reviewing stage the content is either accepted or passed back to the author with hints on revisions. It is even possible that there are several levels of review and reviewers. During a reviewing stage it can be useful that more than one reviewer have a look at the content in parallel and the several comments and remarks are gathered at the end of the review stage.

There is even another means to exploit the selection of multiple actors for a given activity and this is the joint execution of the activity by the actors. It is possible to imagine a workflow product that enables the simultaneous work on documents, reports and forms scheduled to several actors. It is the CSCW community (computer-supported collaborative work) that has discussed – among other topics – means of simultaneous editing of documents and computer conferencing.

Preemptive Execution of Assigned Tasks

The preemptive execution of a task that has been assigned to multiple actors is actually implemented in concrete workflow management products. Let us assume that all actors of role X has been selected for task T a link to it appears in the worklists of each actor. If one of the actors picks the task it is disabled for the other actors. This means, if another actor chooses a task that has already been started he is not led to the dialogue supporting the task T but to a dialogue that informs him that this task is obsolete because it is already in progress by another actor. When the actor returns to his worklist, the link to the task should deleted as if he has been executing it. In addition to this it is possible to imagine that a link to an activity is disabled in a worklist immediately after it has been selected by another actor for execution. Here, human-computer interaction aspects come into play. The disabling of a link from a worklist should not be realized as a removal of the link which, in general, would provoke a restructuring of the worklist that might confuse a user that is currently looking at the worklist. The disabling of a link should be rather realized as a shading of the link.

7.2.2 Selection of Actors

It is possible to identify patterns in the selection of actors from a role and turn them into a specification feature of a workflow product, i.e., a modeling element of the product's workflow definition language or other means of specification with the product's workflow definition tool.

For example, a workflow designer might want to specify priorities for the actors of a role with the semantics that the system first tries to schedule the activity to the actor or actors with the highest priority. If the actors of one level of priority are not available, the task is scheduled to actors of the next lower priority. The system can have the information on whether an actor is available or not from the enterprise resource planning systems. For example, an employee is not available when he is on a business trip or certified ill. The workflow management system might maintain its own explicit data whether an actor is available or not. It is also possible to provide a means for users to decline tasks in a worklist explicitly. In this case a task is scheduled to actors of a certain priority and then, if all of these actors decline to execute the activity, it is scheduled to actors of a lower level priority.

As another example, the workflow system could try to support load balancing. An easy approach would follow a round-robin style of scheduling, i.e., tasks are assigned to actors sequentially, one after the other. Another approach could try to apply assumptions on current work loads of actors. For example, the task could be assigned to the actor with the shortest worklist – or even better – to the actor with the smallest number of started process instances plus number of items in the worklist. Such assumptions can only be fair if knowledge about typical work times of activity instances can be taken into account. This might not be easy, because in general there are a lot of different kinds of activities that are posted to worklists and even the work time of activities of the same kind may vary significantly depending on the circumstances. Furthermore, all of these heuristic-based approaches of workload balancing are necessarily flawed if the workload of employees that work with a workflow management system does not stem alone from the workflow management system and is not tracked completely and in real-time by an appropriate time recording system. The automatic scheduling can be supplemented with human scheduling. This means a workflow management system could send tasks to a meta-worklist or scheduling list of an employee who has the responsibility to schedule the task to the worklists of the actors. A human scheduler can apply more rules and up-to-date information about the real workload of employees.

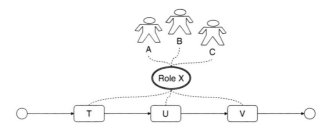

Fig. 7.13. Business process model with the same role attached to multiple activities.

Other important patterns of actor scheduling exploit knowledge of the business process state history, in particular, information about who has worked on a certain activity in the past. Figure 7.13 shows a business process model in which the same role consisting of more than one actor has been attached to more than one activity. Let us assume for a moment that the diagram is actually a general business process model and not yet a workflow definition given in the concrete visual workflow definition language of a workflow management tool. What the modeler actually might wanted to express with the business process model is the fact that the whole business process consisting of the activities T, U all V is either executed by one and only one of the actors A, B or C. Unfortunately, this is not what is expressed by the business model in Fig. 7.13, although it is natural to understand the model in that way. This means that this is a source for misunderstanding and mistakes, in particular if the model is translated into a workflow definition.

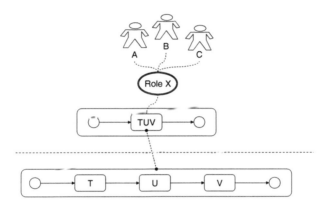

Fig. 7.14. Attempt to detail the meaning of the process model in Fig. 7.13.

An attempt to express better what the modeler might wanted to express is given with the business process model in Fig. 7.14 which exploits the notation for decomposition of business processes that we have used throughout Chapt. 5. Anyhow, also this pattern of re-scheduling an activity to an actor that has executed also the preceding activities can be supported by appropriate workflow definition features by a workflow management tool.

7.2.3 On General Actor Assignment in Workflow Automation

Figure 7.15 illustrates the business model for conducting a business trip. Actually, what is shown in Fig. 7.15 is a crucial cutout of such a business process. A more complete description of business trip planning and execution is used as an example in Sect. 9.2.1 which is illustrated in Fig. 9.2. Actually, the business process model in Fig. 7.15 is a cutout of the business process model in Fig. 9.2. In Sect. 9.2.1 the assignment of roles and their treatment is not too important for the discussion so that the complexity of this issue is not discussed there. Here, in this section, it is actually the complexity of the actor assignment that interests us.

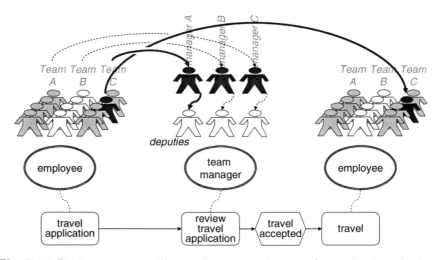

Fig. 7.15. Business process with complex actor assignment for conducting a business trip.

At the beginning of a business trip process instance an employee applies for the travel. Then, the travel application is reviewed by a team leader. After the team leader has accepted the travel application, the employee receives a notification that he is allowed to make the business trip and actually travels. The employee and team manager connected to the activities of the described business trip do not stand for single concrete persons but persons out of groups of persons. There are many employees and there are also many team managers. Therefore an employee role which consists of multiple employees is attached to the activities of travel application and traveling in Fig. 7.15 and similarly a team manager role that consists of many team managers is attached to the activity of reviewing a travel application. The problem is that the set of employees has an internal structure. The set of all employees consists of teams A, B and C. If a member of a certain team is applying for a business trip the corresponding team manager must review the travel application.

This means that an ordinary role mechanism is not sufficient to handle this scenario. The set attached to the travel application activity is not a role in the above described sense but rather a role of a role, because it consists of teams. A team is also a role which consists of concrete team members. However, the business process is not described for a single team but for all teams.

Furthermore, also the role of team managers has an internal structure. For each team manager there is a deputy. In case the team manager is not available his deputy should overtake the task of reviewing dangling travel applications.

In Sect. 7.2.2 we have described the actor scheduling pattern of prioritization which applies here.

Then, after the travel application has been accepted, the employee is informed. The crucial point is that only the correct employee must be informed, i.e., the employee that initially has applied for the travel. This is an example of actor scheduling that is based on the knowledge of the business process state history that we have also discussed in Sect. 7.2.2. The difference to the concrete example pattern described in Sect. 7.2.2 is that the information about the correct actor cannot be taken from the directly preceding activity but must be taken from an elder activity.

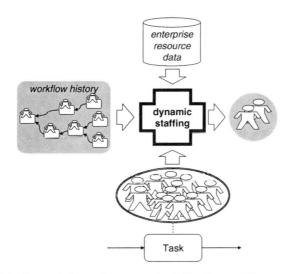

Fig. 7.16. General dynamic actor scheduling in workflow automation.

Based on our discussion of possible interpretations of groups of actors in Sect. 7.2.1, the selection of actors in Sect. 7.2.2 and the business process in Fig. 7.15 we now come to the following conclusion. Dynamic staff scheduling in workflow automation depends on available enterprise resource data, the state history of the running and run business processes instances and the definition of roles – see Fig. 7.16 for an illustration. Conceptually, the defined roles are less important for the determination of the concrete actors for the next activity than the enterprise resource data and the workflow history. From a general viewpoint, a defined role forms a bound onto which actors can be selected. In that sense they are an extra constraint that is not strictly necessary, but can be considered as useful.

In general role definitions are as useful as type systems are in programming languages. In particular roles are as useful as the actor scheduling patterns that are supported by extra workflow definition mechanisms in concrete workflow products. However, independent of how many concrete patterns in actor selection you identify and explicitly support in a workflow technology product, in general there is still need for the opportunity to arbitrarily specify or program the selection of next actors. A workflow technology must provide such opportunity through appropriate hooks in its workflow definition tool or application programming interface.

7.3 Form-Oriented Analysis

In form-oriented analysis we consider certain kinds of submit/response-style systems that occur very often in practice, in particular in the domains of enterprise computing and e-commerce and that range, in terms of technology, from legacy terminal/server-based systems, over form-based client-server systems in the technology family of Oracle Forms, to web applications [102, 85]. The kind of submit/response-style systems that we consider in form-oriented analysis appear to the user through dialogues consisting of reports and forms. It is a repeated game of a client page showing up and offering navigation capabilities leading again to new client pages. In more detail, it works the following way. A client page shows up. This client page consists of a report that presents data to the user, one or more forms and one or more links to other client pages. In form-oriented analysis we have a unified view of forms and links, i.e., we consider links as forms that offer no input capability. Actually, if you have a closer look at links as programming language constructs in concrete technologies, like web links, i.e., HTML links, you will encounter that links can also carry data in the form of hidden parameters and that it is very common to realize selections of items, i.e., form-like interaction capabilities by the means of links. Therefore, we foster a unified view of forms and links in form-oriented analysis and will not distinguish between them in the following unless necessary. Submitting a form triggers a server action that has a side effect on the system data state and eventually leads to one out of more possible client pages.

Form-oriented analysis is a typed-approach to the specification of human-computer interaction. Both the client pages and the server actions have types. The type of the client page describes the kind of data that is shown as a report on the client page. The type of a server action describes the input capabilities of the form triggering this server action. A form is a user-editable function or method. The type of a server action describes the kind of data that the user can submit to it by a form. The types of client pages and server actions are accompanied by types of an information model that describes the inner state of an information system model. Server actions manipulate the inner data of the information system and reports are written against this data. It is a proven pattern to specify an information system as a separation of those data that are exchanged between the user and the system at the system boarder and those data that are persistently held by the system. In [89] we have discussed so-called message system models as an alternative that work without an information system model, partly in order to understand the reasons for the success of full information system models. In this text, we always assume that the dialogue model given by a formchart is accompanied by an information model, even if an information model is not explicitly given or even needed in the concrete examples. Furthermore, the notion of dialogue constraints as a means to completely specify the human-computer interaction on top of the dialogue type structure and also the relationship between the information model types and the message model types have been elaborated in form-oriented analysis – see [89] for further reference.

We can summarize Sect. 7.3 as follows. The submit/response-style systems considered by form-oriented analysis are bipartite state-machines. The state of a submit/response style system permanently alternates between client states, also called dialogue states, that are processed by the user and server states that are processed automatically. Formcharts are typed bipartite directed graphs consisting of client pages representing client states and server actions representing server states.

8

Service-Oriented Architecture

There have always been two strands of research to improve development and maintenance of software – both in practice and in academia: executable specification and reusable components. In the domain of enterprise applications the issue of executable specification is currently addressed by business process execution initiatives, the issue of reusable components is currently addressed by service-oriented architecture.

Actually, motivated by the promises of each of these current mainstream approaches we see a lot of projects where people try to bring them together, see e.g. [58, 243, 110]. But then people encounter tensions between the two paradigms, because they were not designed for each other. How to exploit service-oriented architecture in a workflow-intensive information system scenario? How to implement workflow logic in a service-oriented manner? Then – though in principle service-oriented architecture is a technology-independent paradigm – in concrete projects these questions are sometimes approached very directly by asking where to establish web service layers in a workflow-based enterprise application. Basically, there are two alternatives. You can use web services to wrap units of logic that are controlled by the workflow engine. In current business process management suites web services are the usual invocation mechanism for business logic. Similarly, you can use web services to integrate system dialogues into the workflow logic. For example, with business process management suites like the Oracle SOA suite it is possible to hook together system dialogues – typically developed with a rapid report and forms development tool – that bridge the workflow states. The other alternative is to reveal a whole workflow enactment service as a web services layer. Then, a fat client implements both the worklist as well as the system dialogues that bridge the workflow states. As you can see, such discussions easily lead to quite detailed technical questions. At the same time the question arises, whether wrapping of some code units in the one or other way really brings the speed ups and cost savings that one might expect from establishing a new paradigm – service-orientation in this case. So, let us approach the question

D. Draheim, *Business Process Technology: A Unified View on Business Processes, Workflows and Enterprise Applications*, DOI 10.1007/978-3-642-01588-5_8,
© Springer-Verlag Berlin Heidelberg 2010

what service-orientation is about and how it can be exploited for business process technology more conceptually and in particular more systematically.

It is a commonplace now that service-oriented architecture is the natural candidate to bring the flexibility, agility and adaptivity to business process management suites and eventually to the enterprises that are supported by it. How come? Service-oriented architecture emerged as a kind of meta architecture for enterprise computing foreseeing a new more generalized, flexible role of single applications in an enterprise. On the technical side, service-oriented architecture is exposed as clusters of design rationales and architectural principles. The problem is that the single design rationales and architectural principles are motivated from several different strands of thinking, for example, an overall system architecture viewpoint, a system management and maintenance viewpoint, a rather step-wise enterprise application integration viewpoint, and, very importantly, an electronic data interchange viewpoint.

8.1 The Evolution of Service-Oriented Architecture

One of the mainstream perceptions of service-oriented architecture is that it is a technology independent meta architecture for large-scale enterprise computing [255]. There are other communities that use the service-oriented architecture metaphor for their technology, for example, OSGi – note that OSGi stand for Open Service Gateway initiative. Standard applications of OSGi technology are in the area of embedded systems. Another such example is Jini [353]. Jini technology has discoverability of services, which is considered as a key characteristics of service-oriented architecture, as a crucial asset and indeed Jini is often said to establish a service-oriented architecture [231]. Jini targets the level of network-connected devices, whereas service-oriented architecture as discussed in this book targets the creation of information utilities in large-scale enterprises. We believe that an architectural paradigm should be discussed always with its domain objectives in mind in order to have a context to appreciate or criticize the several design principles it imposes. The currently discussed OASIS reference model for service-oriented architecture [230] mentions large-scale enterprise applications as a main driver of service-oriented architecture, however, it does not mention other drivers and the reference model in [230] abstracts away from enterprise computing.

Another perception of service-oriented architecture is that it is connected to the concrete web services stack technology stack. Actually web services technology has substantially contributed to the wide-spread adoption of service-oriented architecture. We will delve into the topic of web services based service oriented architecture in Sect. 8.4.

Nonetheless, once more it is important to point out that service-oriented architecture began as a technology-independent discussion, e.g., CORBA technology can be very well used to build a concrete service-oriented architecture [239]. For example, the architecture described in [286] – see Fig. 8.3 –

is based on the notion of a service bus that is implemented with CORBA technology. Actually, the system discussed in [286] is a very typical example of a service-oriented architecture as described in [316, 315] – Fig. 8.2. When we talk about service-oriented architecture in this book we talk about system architecture concepts for enterprise computing.

As should now have become clear, service-oriented architecture is not a single paradigm. There are several service-oriented architecture visions and concepts that emerged over time as depicted in the overview of Fig. 8.1. Service-oriented architecture emerged as a three-tier architecture for enterprise application integration as we will explain in Sect. 8.2. Then the term service-oriented architecture was hyped by the concrete web-service technology establishing the vision of creating a new lightweight, ubiquitous and open electronic data interchange platform based on this web-services technology. As a result web-services technology has become a synonym for service-oriented architecture for many stakeholders in the enterprise computing community. This is the reason why service-oriented architecture is now recognized as an enabler for flexible, adaptive business processes, i.e., simply by the wide-spread usage of web-services technology in state-of the art commercial business process management technology products. We deal with the several facets and usages of web-services technology in Sect. 8.4.

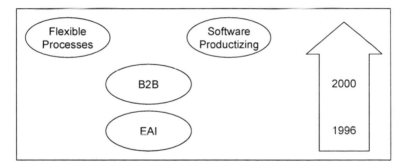

Fig. 8.1. The evolution of SOA paradigms and visions.

Another strand of argumentation in service-oriented architecture is in the area of software development methodology and systematics. Here, inspired by the new tools for component maintenance, and in particular those that deal with service discoverability, innovators where thinking about new opportunities to accelerate the software development process. For example, the systematic integration of massive reuse of software components into software development projects was envisioned. Recently, the massive reuse of software components stemming from the multitude of projects in a large enterprise are considered, typically in the realm of SOA governance.

Services as Information Utility

In [28] a trend of enterprise computing facilities becoming a utility was identified. The vision of an information utility is about decoupling information services from appliances that can consume these services. It is about overcoming silo system landscapes and creating a new degree of freedom in using enterprise applications and databases. In [28] this information utility vision is discussed from the viewpoint of an implementing middleware. Similarly, in [316, 315] the concept of a service-oriented architecture is described as being about avoiding the tight coupling of processinglogic and the data it processes to concrete applications or processing modesmode.

Only later, a concrete pattern of service-oriented architecture emerged with the inherent rationale to create some kind of enterprise-wide information utility. We will discuss these characteristics in Sect. 8.3. In another strand of work service-oriented architecture evolved into the vision of creating not only enterprise-wide information utilities but also a world-wide information utility, i.e., an inter-enterprise-wide information technology. We will discuss this electronic data interchange aspect in Sect. 8.4 on web-services-based service-oriented architecture.

Service-Component Architecture

The original vision of service-oriented architecture with its three tiers of services, applications and clients – see Sect. 8.2 – is rather a hub-and spoke architecture. The original service-oriented architecture is not a component metaphor, i.e., it is not about building arbitrary composition hierarchies or to, say it differently; it is not about assembling – wiring – services. This is where the Service-Component Architecture (SCA) [354, 24] steps in.

The Service Component Architecture addresses heterogeneous distributed computing. Heterogeneity is twofold in the case of the Service Component Architecture, it accounts for both several different implementation technologies and several different service binding technologies. Supported implementation technologies encompass languages of quite different style like C, C++, Java, PHP, COBOL, BPEL, XSLT, XQuery, SQL. Supported service binding technologies are, for example, web services, JMS (Java Messaging Service), and CORBA IIOP.

Furthermore, the Service Component Architecture systematically cares for the specification of quality of service. In its collection of standards profiles [25] are defined for security, reliability, personnel responsibilities, i.e., developer, assemblers, deployers, profile administrators and ACID transactionality [299].

8.2 Three-Tier Service-Oriented Architecture

Figure 8.2 shows Gartner's original tier terminology of service-oriented architecture from [316]. The architecture in Fig. 8.2 should be understood as one out of many service-oriented architectures in the sense of [316]. According to the many possible different software clients, it is possible to build different service-oriented architectures. As always with the notion of "architecture", the term architecture can be used for the structure of a concrete system with all its considered components at the chosen appropriate level of abstraction, but can also be used for the common, i.e., generalized, structure of all the concrete systems that adhere to a certain architectural concept. In that sense service-oriented architecture as intended by [316] is rather characterized by the distinction between tiers A through B and their explanation and Fig. 8.2 with all its concrete clients is an example architecture.

Tier A in Fig. 8.2 is a tier of services that realize business logic and access to data that are common to several applications in the enterprise. Tiers B and C together consists of the enterprise applications that are software clients to the tier A of services. We do not delve into the distinction between B and C here, in [316] it is somehow used to explain the difference between batch and online users. We want to discuss the role of the service-tier and the options to build it instead.

In general we want to decide between the following kinds of service-oriented architecture:

- Fat service hub hub-and-spoke architecture, fat hub-and-spoke architecture for short,
- Thin service hub hub-and-spoke architecture, thin hub-and-spoke architecture for short.

In the fat hub-and-spoke architecture the service-tier actually implements some business logic and holds some data. With this architecture business logic that is necessary for several applications can be realized and maintained at a single spot, i.e., the service tier. In its extreme form, however, the fat hub-and-spoke architecture does not allow the service-tier to reuse business logic or data from the other software applications of tiers B and C. Here, all the logic and data that is provided by the service tier A must be implemented by the service tier. In its extreme form the fat hub-and-spoke architecture is therefore not about the mutual reuse of business logic and data that reside in the several applications of the enterprise. It is about this mutual reuse only in the sense that these logic and data can be taken from the several applications and be brought to the service tier A in a kind of overall system refactoring and system landscape refactoring step.

The obvious interpretation of the arrows labeled (i) and (ii) in Fig. 8.2 leads us to the conclusion that the service-oriented architecture introduced in [316] is actually of the described extreme form of fat hub-and-spoke architecture. In Fig. 8.2 updates and queries, which are represented by arrow (i), can be made by the software applications of tier B to the service tier A but not vice versa. Similarly, as depicted by arrow (ii), results and error messages can be delivered from the service tier to the applications in the other tiers but not vice versa. We therefore call this form of fat hub-and-spoke architecture also uni-directional hub-and-spoke architecture. Also in the uni-directional hub-and-spoke architecture there are message flows back and forth between the service tier and the other tiers. However, with respect to both of the two kinds of different message flows, i.e., update or query, on the one hand, and result or error feedback, on the other hand, the message flow is actually uni-directional. Or to put it the other way round: with respect to a complete cycle consisting of an update or query and a result or error message all message flows are uni-directional.

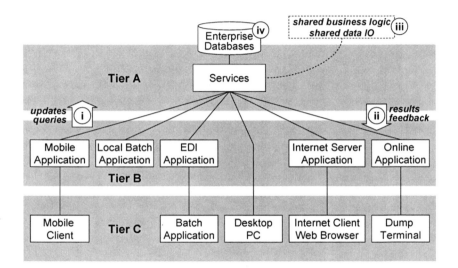

Fig. 8.2. Gartner Group tier terminology for service-oriented architecture.

In a thin hub-and-spoke architecture, the service tier does not implement any business logic and does not hold any data itself. Here, the service tier is merely a broker for the reuse of logic and data between the several applications in an enterprise. This means, a thin hub-and-spoke architecture is about dropping box (iii) and database (iv) from Fig. 8.2. Consequentially, both of the arrows i and (ii) have to be replaced by bidirectional message flows in Fig. 8.2.

The discussed thin and fat hub-and-spoke architectures are extremes, however. In practice a mixture of both styles can be applied in an enterprise application integration project. Some of the business logic and data is then realized in the service tiers, other business logic and data access is just realized by appropriate wrappers in the service tier. The thin hub-and-spoke architecture leads to bidirectional message flow both for updates and queries and for results and messages. We therefore call it also a bidirectional hub-and-spoke architecture. A thin hub-and spoke architecture implies bi-directionality, however, the converse is not true. If the service-tier realizes some business logic merely by being a broker, there can also be some direct realization of business logic in the service-tier. That distinguishes the bidirectional from the uni-directional hub-and-spoke architecture. A fat hub-and-spoke architecture does not imply uni-directionality, but vice versa.

A bidirectional hub-and-spoke architecture is the one that is found most often in practice. In concrete companies other names for the service tier are often used, for example, 'data wheel', 'business logic pool' or the like. Even names that contain a reference to EDI are often used, the term 'EDI pool' is a good example for this. If the service tier is only used for in-house software reuse purposes, a name containing EDI is strictly speaking incorrect, because electronic data interchange usually stands for inter-enterprise data interchange. However, in the true sense of the word electronic data interchange is a correct characterization of the functionality of a service tier. Business logic can be triggered by sending a data message via a so-called EDI pool and the answer of triggered business logic is also just data send back to the requester. Business logic can be understood very broad. Even functionality that deals with application workflow like a workflow system's task list can be revealed by a purely data interchanging message interface to the other applications in an enterprise. From that somehow low-level viewpoint every interaction among applications can be understood merely as data interchange. Furthermore, often one of the products that are in the B2B gateway market segment [220] like Microsoft BizTalk or TIBCO Software, just to name two, are used to build a service-tier, even, if it is only used for intra-enterprise data communication purposes.

A bidirectional hub-and-spoke architecture is also a common approach to the integration of legacy systems with emerging new systems, which is a common theme in enterprise application integration. Also the currently discussed enterprise service busses are bidirectional message-oriented middleware products. Figure 8.3 depicts an architecture that has been described in [286]. The system landscape has been built in order to expose existing banking applications to new channels imposed by the new e-commerce age, i.e., call centers and the web, and furthermore, to integrate them with new enterprise resource planning systems, both SAP and others. The core of the system landscape consists of legacy systems on the basis of IMS (Information Management System) technology, with IMS hierarchical databases, IMS transaction processing technology and IMS messaging technology that are all eventually exploited in COBOL programs.

The three-tier architecture discussed here must not be mixed up with the widespread known three-tier enterprise application architecture. The three tier architecture discussed here is an architecture for system landscapes, whereas the usual three-tier architecture is almost always an architecture of single enterprise applications. The advantage of a hub-and-spoke architecture for a system landscape is that business logic and data that is shared by several applications is controlled and maintained at a single spot. A hub-and-spoke architecture prevents a uncontrolled growth in the number of connections and interfaces between the various applications. Furthermore, the hub can be made

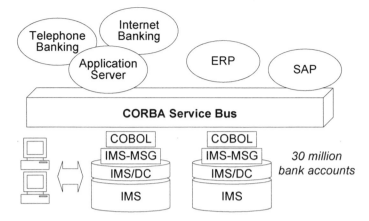

Fig. 8.3. Example CORBA service bus for banking applications.

subject to concrete policies, it can be supported by specialized technology like enterprise service bus products or as mentioned before by B2B gateway products.

Sticking to a legacy system to avoid unjustifiable effort is a common theme that in enterprise application architecture is often called investment protection. The usage of the term investment protection is a bit odd for this. Another and perhaps more obvious usage of the term investment protection is as a synonym for risk management in investment planning. The kind of investment protection that leads to the preservation of an existing system as an integrated legacy system in a new system landscape can be seen as the consideration of an originally planned amortization period of an existing system in the planning of a new system. If the amortization period is not yet over, stakeholders might be biased against replacing an old system. The investment into the old system is then considered somehow as an asset that is worth saving in its own right. This is a bit odd, because the planning of a new system landscape should be done on the basis of systematic total cost of ownership and total economic impact analyses. In such analyses, the existing systems can be considered merely as a pool for software reuse like third-party products that are considered in build-or-buy decisions. A neutral viewpoint is also necessary particularly in presence of existing applications.

8.3 Characteristics of Service-Oriented Architectures

In the beginning of the discussion, service-oriented architecture was rather about the principle of decoupling services from appliances, i.e., the observable trend of some kind of information utilities emerging in large scale enterprise architectures. Some definitions of service-oriented architecture, e.g., the one given in [133] boil down to an explanation of modularization. However, the objective of a certain level of decoupling of enterprise applications is a unique selling point of service-oriented architecture one should be aware of. Over time it has become common sense that there are certain design rules and key characteristics that make up service-oriented architecture. To these belong [49] coarse-grainedness, interface-based design, discoverability of services, single instantiation of components, loose coupling, asynchronous communication, message-based communication. Further such characteristics are strict hierarchical composition, high cohesion, technology independency, idempotence of services, freedom from object references, freedom from context, stateless service design – see, e.g., [60, 120].

Some of the key characteristics usually connected with service-oriented architecture are know from other paradigms like object-oriented design or component-based development, others are unique selling points of service-oriented architecture and others explicitly distinguish service-oriented architecture from other approaches. For example, single instantiation of components explicitly distinguishes service-orientation from component-orientation. Loose coupling, high cohesion and interface-based design are also targeted by object orientation. However, in the context of service-oriented architecture, loose coupling is often understood differently from how it is understood in the object-oriented community. In the object-oriented community it stands for the general pattern of minimizing the overall number of any kind of dependencies between components in a system. In service-oriented architecture it is often understood as the availability of a dynamic binding mechanism.

Discoverability of Services

The issue of discoverability of services is often seen as crucial for service-oriented architecture. What is meant is special support for discovering in the form of appropriate registries and tools [48]. Discoverability of services touches the assembly and eventually the organization of development and maintenance of services, a strand of work that is currently addressed by SOA governance . On the other hand, discoverability is at the core of the business-to-business vision of service-oriented architecture, yet another aspect that is discussed in due course in Sect. 8.4.

Research Potential in Service-Oriented Architecture Principles

The SOA principles can add value to enterprise applications, e.g., discoverability can greatly improve reuse, targeting coarse-grainedness can guide code productizing efforts and message-orientation is the proven pattern in enterprise application integration. The problem is, however, that the SOA principles are by no means silver bullets [45, 46] for enterprise application architecture, least of all the combination of them. This means, the circumstances under which the SOA principles add value and how they can be exploited must be analyzed carefully. It is important to recognize that with respect to enterprise system architecture the promise of SOA, i.e., the creation of an information utility, is an objective rather than a feature of the approach. Best practices have to be gathered in order to make SOA work in projects. There is also a demand for heuristics like SEI's (Software Engineering Institute) SMART (Service-Oriented Migration and Reuse Technique) technique [217] to estimate and mitigate risks of using SOA and SOA technology in concrete projects.

8.4 Web Services based Service-Oriented Architecture

Web services technology helped make service-oriented architecture a mainstream theme. After its huge success, Internet technology seemed to be the natural candidate for the service binding mechanism of service-oriented architecture. Concrete new products of major software vendors like IBM's Websphere and Microsoft's .NET were based on the web services technology stack. These products with their integrated development environments allowed for easy distributed programming via the web. In its original definition, service-oriented architecture is a set of technology independent concepts, in particular, it is independent from the web services stack. However, in practice service-oriented architecture is often discussed with web services in mind. Here, in concrete projects they are often very concrete technical aspects like the easier interplay with firewalls that influence the decision to use service-oriented architecture in favor of another technology.

The web services technology stack – see Fig. 8.4 – has SOAP (Simple Object Access Protocol) [41] on top of HTTP as the basic remote method invocation mechanism. The Web Services Description Language (WSDL) is used for the specification of web services signatures, i.e., it provides the web services type system in terms of programming language technology.

The crucial point with the web services technology stack is that it goes beyond WDSL. It has UDDI (Universal Description, Discovery and Integration) on top. The UDDI standard was intended to build global yellow pages for subscription and description of services by enterprises. With UDDI, service-oriented architecture became an electronic data interchange (EDI) initiative. The term business-to-business was coined with Internet technology and typically B2B is used for web services based electronic data interchange, whereas EDI is used for electronic data interchange based on established formats like the X12 transaction sets or UN/EDIFACT [174] – EDIFACT (Electronic Data Interchange For Administration, Commerce, and Transport) for short. As an EDI initiative, the goal of the web services stack was to create a lightweight, open alternative to existing, established value-added networks. It is this new envisioned EDI the term B2B is used for. Established EDI scenarios are often asymmetric from a business-to-business viewpoint. A very typically example is provided by large manufacturers or large retailers that requests their smaller supplierssupplier to be connected to them by EDI. At the same time established EDI is known to be quite heavyweight – technologically and organizationally [118] – to adopt.

However, improved inter-organizational EDI is currently addressed more visibly by other standardization bodies like UN/CEFACT (United Nations Centre for Trade Facilitation and Electronic Business)and OASIS [348, 347] (Organization for the Advancement of Structured Information Standards), which are experienced in the EDI domain. In the original strand of work on B2B, i.e., with UDDI as a world-wide yellow pages mechanism for service-enabled enterprises, B2B did not take off.

The problem with EDI is that parts of its heavyweightedness cannot be overcome simply by a new technology stack. This is the issue of pre-negotiations between EDI participants before an EDI connection is actually established. These negotiations are business related and cannot be automated, they encompass the negotiation of prices, quality of servicesof service, and contract penalties. Furthermore the results of these negotiations must be made justifiable. Paper-based trading has a long legal tradition but electronic trading had to become mature before a robust legal foundation for it could be provided. Furthermore, it must not be overlooked that the success of established EDI was only partly due to the creation of a technological infrastructure for electronic data interchange. Another success factor of established EDI initiatives was the standardization of business messages, which is a technology independent asset for the community. The original B2B initiative forgot about message standardization in the beginning.

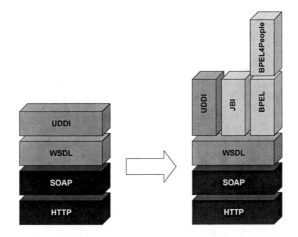

Fig. 8.4. The web services technology stack then and now.

Today more proprietary standards and technologies are based on WDSL representing two aspects of enterprise system architecture, i.e., enterprise application architecture and business process execution. JBI [342] (Java Business Integration) is an attempt to standardize the notion of enterprise service bus

(ESB), which is a currently widely discussed approach to enterprise application architecture. BPEL is a currently discussed language for the execution of automatic workflow.

8.4.1 Web Services-based Business Process Execution

SOA technology and business process technology are converging [219]. The relationship between SOA and business processes has been somehow misrepresented, because despite its name, the SOA-based Web Services Business Process Execution Language [344, 122] (WS-BPEL) – BPEL for short – does not support crucial workflow concepts like user roles needed for business execution in today's business process management suites. BPEL is just a high-level programming language with web services as its primitives. Thus BPEL is a language for the execution of automatic workflow, however, it is not a language for the execution of human workflow. Therefore, concrete BPEL-based business process management products add there own, proprietary workflow concepts to BPEL. This need is also addressed by BPEL4People (WS-BPEL Extension for People) [203, 4]. The current SOA-based business process management suites tackle the problem of how to exploit SOA technology in workflow-intensive applications; however, in doing so they do not towards raising the level of abstraction to executable specification of business processes.

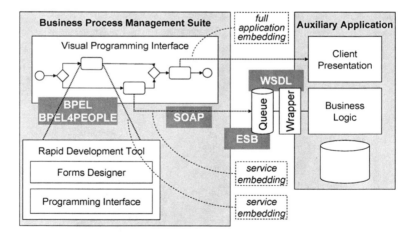

Fig. 8.5. Exploitation of concrete web services technologies for building business process management systems.

Figure 8.5 shows the typical exploitation of concrete web services technologies by contemporary business process management product. We distinguish several means to glue together software components with a business process management suite in Fig. 8.5, i.e., full application embedding, service embedding and dialogue embedding. In the scenario in Fig. 8.5, the business process management suite is used to combine several existing applications to a new one and to enrich them with new system dialogues that are developed with technology provided by the business process management suite itself. The new application logic is developed in the business process management suite with a visual programming language and tool. Here, a visual form of the webservice technology BPEL and a proprietary extension for human workflow is typically used allowing new system dialogues to be hooked into the visual program. For the development of these new system dialogues the business process management suite offers support via a rapid development tool that typically ships with a visual programming tool for form-based computer screens. The new dialogues can also be implemented without the rapid development tool that ships with the business process management suites. They are then new auxiliary applications in the sense of the drawing in Fig. 8.5

Application can be integrated into the new developed application by actually embedding their dialogues. We call this style of application integration 'full application embedding' in order to distinguish it from reusing merely the business logic of an existing application. For dialogue embeddings of auxiliary applications no elaborate high-level standard mechanisms exist. They can be accomplished rather directly with program calls on the operating system level with its low-level program parameter passing mechanisms. Often, auxiliary applications are prepared with message-based application programming interfaces that then can be used to call the desired dialogues. For this, the web-service technology WSDL would be the current language of choice in building the necessary wrappers. We have not depicted this in Fig. 8.5.

It is possible to integrate only the business application into the new developed application – called service embedding in Fig. 8.5. Here WSDL is typically used for building the wrappers and web-services technology SOAP is the transmission protocol of choice. One important issue that leads to a business process management project is often that users are not satisfied any more with the HCI layer of the existing applications. Existing applications are often built with one of the many proprietary rapid development tools of the 1980s. So the goal is then to replace the HCI layer by new web-based dialogues or new state-of-the-art rich client interfaces with a modern look-and-feel. On the other hand, the target of replacing the existing system dialogues is usually not the only reason for a business process management project. Usually, there is actually the need for new application logic. At the same time the programs that make up the dialogues can make up a significant code base that cannot be replaced in one go. Therefore a typical migration path would start with building new application logic around the existing applications on the basis of full application embedding and would then proceed with the step-by-step replacement of the existing dialogues eventually resulting in complete homogenous service embedding.

8.5 Service-Orientation as Development Paradigm

There is yet another facet of service-oriented architecture that is currently widely considered. It is the software development and operations aspect. What many IT stakeholders in enterprises expect from SOA is the transformation of the many software applications into a code base that is open for reuse in their future enterprise application development projects. This expectation is about breaking silo applications into services. And it is about software productizing in current and future software development projects. Software productizing is a term used by Frederik Brooks in citeBro75 – see Fig. 3.2.

8.5.1 Designing Services for Reuse

Software productizing refers to various extra initiatives that can be performed to make software a product, e.g., well-documented, well-tested and therefore deliverable to buyers, and more general in the sense of being prepared for adaptation to different contexts and platforms. We therefore use the term software productizing here for the extra effort needed to make a piece of software more generally usable, i.e., to make it reusable for other software products than the one it is currently developed for. If, at the time development, a developer already has some other concrete applications in mind, for example, some applications that are also currently under development or applications that are planned, the extra efforts in generalizing a piece of software can lead to a quick win. Otherwise, software productizing is about anticipating potential future software development. Then, software productizing must involve analyzing which kind of future applications the several pieces of currently developed software could be useful for. This involves an analysis of how the design of these applications will probably look or it involves efforts for this family of future potential applications. There is an obvious tradeoff between these software productizing efforts and the costs saved by reusing the resulting generalized pieces of software. Software productizing in the discussed sense is somehow conceptually opposite to the current trends of agile software development, which its courage-driven design [20, 80, 81, 146] and continuous refactoring.

   SOA governance [163, 235, 362] is the entirety of efforts that contribute towards making the promises of service-oriented architecture a reality [163]. Definitions of SOA governance contain high-level descriptions of the problems encountered in projects that try to make service-oriented concepts a reality in an enterprise. Typical SOA governance definitions put a focus onto the operations of software services, i.e., monitoring, controlling and measuring services [163]. However, in SOA governance projects it is often expected that a SOA governance expert gives some advise on how to organize the IT development to enable better reuse [363] of existing software across all project boundaries. This heavily affects software process and development team organization issues. For example, initiatives like the Smart SOA [166] best practices catalogue – which by the way must not be mixed up with SEI's SMART (Service-Oriented Migration and Reuse Technique) approach – try to address these issues. In practice, there is often a very straightforward understanding of SOA governance in terms of features of tools that support service-oriented architecture [196]. The most typical tools are service registries and service repositories.

In concrete SOA governance projects there is the need for a diversity of specialized tools, technologies and techniques like an appropriate service development and operations infrastructure, a service versioning concept, a service development and operations process, tools for service analysis, development, profiling and monitoring. A good example for the complex needs in a SOA governance project is the concrete enriched meta-model for web services elaborated in [71], which contains information about the origin of a serive, the developer in charge of a web service, the staging state a of service, versions and releases of services, coupling of services, the usage structure of clients and services, auxiliary text documentation, UML representations of WSDL specifications, UML statecharts for service behavior descriptions, the service deployment structure and documentation of generated Java stubs.

8.5.2 Towards Massive Software Reuse

Figure 8.6 shows what we call silo development. The situation that is shown in Fig. 8.6 is such that there are several software development projects in an organization, however, each of the projects is completely encapsulated and conducted separately from the other projects. At this point we can assume that each single project involves the several distinguishable stages of requirement elicitation, design, implementation and operation without loss of generality. Concrete successful projects have a concrete and usually more sophisticated software engineering process model. But for the purpose of explaining the issue of massive reuse across projects the coarse-grained stagewise model that we use here in the following is appropriate. Once more, we want to emphasize that we always follow a descriptive, informative approach instead of a prescriptive, normative one, in particular, when we are talking about software engineering processes. The point here is that there is typically a long period of operation and maintenance in the whole software lifecycle compared to the relatively short stages of analysis, design and implementation.

Iterative Projects

If the operation phase in a software lifecycle were about keeping the application running, some bug fixing and helping users, the visualization of the software projects in Fig. 8.6 would fit reality quite well. However, in reality the operation phase is actually also a software maintenance phase. And

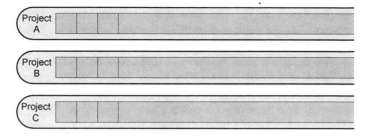

Fig. 8.6. Stagewise development of silo software systems.

maintenance in general covers much more than bug fixing. It involves handling change requests and implementing functionality that fulfils new requirements that emerge during operation. So, there is some fully-fledged software engineering with requirement elicitation, design, and implementation in the operations phase. If there is a critical amount of software engineering during operations the situation is modeled more appropriately by an iterative software development process as shown in Fig. 8.7. Figure 8.7 shows one of the silo projects from Fig. 8.6.

The difference is that the project now consists of several iteration projects. The overall projects starts with some requirement elicitation, design and implementation work until a first stable version can be launched. In parallel to the operation of the first version a new project for the next iteration is started. In that project new requirements are gathered, the design may be refactored, and then existing functionality is changed and new functionality is added according to the new requirements as an implementation step. All this can be seen as a reuse scenario. The new version of the system is actually a new system that reuses parts of the former version. A significant amount of the former system is usually reused. If only a few lines of new code are actually added to a very large software system you might say that this is not really an example of software reuse but just a small change to the system. But for us it is important to insist that we deal with reuse here. We do so because of the setting of our discussion which is iterative software development. Therefore, all arguments concerning reuse in the sense of software engineering and the software system lifecycle in particular apply here, and they do so independently from the question of how large the reused part of software is compared to the new software added. Furthermore, the described scenario is a reuse on the several levels of artifacts. Code is reused as well as existing requirement descriptions and existing design. The crucial point is that once the new version of the system is ready to be launched, the former version of the system is shut down, depicted as a big cross in Fig. 8.7.

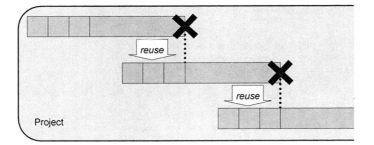

Fig. 8.7. Iterative development of a silo software system.

Mega Projects

We have said that an iterative project consists of several iteration projects as depicted in Fig. 8.7. During the overall lifecycle of the software product more and more iteration projects may be conducted. It would be possible to say that an iteration project is a sub project of the iterative project it stems from. We deliberately do not use the word sub project for an iteration project, because we want to reserve the word sub project for another phenomenon in project management, which is worth considering with respect to the complexity of enterprise-wide software development. Large projects easily become so large that it is necessary to create a number of sub projects, which is depicted in Fig. 8.8. The usual reason is that the project is too large to be handled by the available human resources in terms of number or skills of the company that conducts the project [135]. Then, sub projects have to be defined that can be given away to sub-contractors. Now, a systematic division of labor across several, usually distributed teams must be managed. The lack of resources may not be the only reason for creating a sub project structure. Another reason can be that the project is simply too large to be managed without a leveled management approach. The crucial point is not the distribution of labor over sub teams, but the organization of these sub teams. Sub projects have the characteristics of full-fledged projects. This means, each sub projects has its own project manager and its own project management infrastructure.

After the overall large project in Fig. 8.8 has been started a requirement elicitation takes place as a first phase. Some of the design is done. At least a coarse-grained design which allows for the division of the whole project into sub projects has to be done. Then the sub projects are distributed to sub teams. This distribution means extra efforts. The initial design must be particularly consistent and robust, because once the sub projects are running it is hard to change things. At the same time the sub product description must be sufficiently accurate. In each sub project further design is done and then implementation takes place. Eventually the results of the single sub projects have to be integrated. Again, this integration means extra efforts.

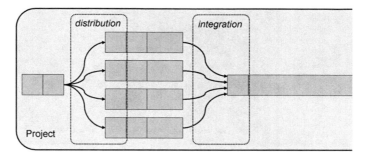

Fig. 8.8. Division of a project into sub projects.

SOA Governance for Ubiquitous Reuse

In an iterative project each iteration project reuses artifacts from the former iteration project. The projects in an enterprise are usually iterative projects, however, the single iterative projects can still be silo projects so that the reuse is limited to all the single projects. Things change fundamentally if we allow for reuse across project boundaries, which is depicted in Fig. 8.9. The reuse across project boundaries must be managed. It is exactly that reuse, which gives rise to SOA governance.

Why is the reuse across project boundaries fundamentally different from the reuse inside a single project? Each of the projects has its own project management, its own software tools and repositories, its own development process and so on. If there should be reuse across project boundaries appropriate projects unifications must be conducted and, furthermore, extra organizational structure must be created. The more there is reuse across project boundaries the more the boundaries actually vanish and eventually the set of different projects must be handled as one huge project. All this is true from the static viewpoint of the mere code base, or more generally, from the viewpoint of the artifact base. Nonetheless it is also true for the dynamic viewpoint of running and evolving systems, which is depicted in Fig. 8.10.

Figure 8.10 depicts a situation where a project reuses software from a product that evolves iteratively in another project. Assume that the new project B reuses some software while the first iteration of the iterative project A is still underneath. Now, assume that a next iteration of project B has been started and has just finished its implementation phase. The code is now to be deployed and made operative. Usually, as shown in Fig. 8.7 the deployment of the new version in an iterative project would mean that the old version is replaced, i.e., that the old version is shut down. However, in the described scenario here this cannot be done without care.

Assume that in the new iteration the application has been changed at a place that effects software that is reused by project B. As a first problem, the stakeholders in project B must become aware that changes to the software in project A have happened and then they must be able to determine whether

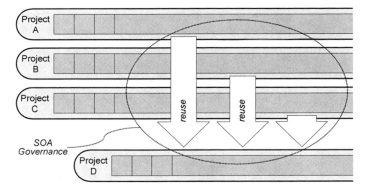

Fig. 8.9. Software reuse across project boundaries.

the changes are relevant to the software of their project. This determination consists of two steps. First, they need to understand whether the changes are in any of the parts that have been reused. Then they have to decide, whether the changes should be adopted or not. For example, if the changes are rather bug fixes, project B very likely wants to adopt them. On the other hand, if the changes have been made on behalf of users of software product A that want the software to behave differently, it can also be, that these changes are not necessary and not appropriate for software product B.

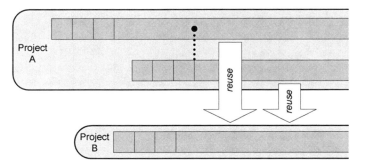

Fig. 8.10. Software reuse from a maintained software product.

Assume that the stakeholders of project B want to adopt a software change in project A. Then they need to distinguish between the two kinds of ways of realizing the reuse. One option is that software of project A was copied to project B where its copy has become a new part of the code base. Then this copy must be renewed by a new copy of the changed piece of software. But that is not all. In general, the product in project B needs also to be refactored. This is obviously so when the interface of the replaced software components has been changed. Beyond merely structural changes product B must also be refactored carefully with respect to the behavioral changes.

The other option for the realization of reuse in Fig. 8.10 is that product B calls the application parts it needs as services. In the case the stakeholders of project B want to adopt a change to the software of project A they do not have to copy code, because it is there and running, but the real part of adoption, i.e., the refactoring of their product so that it fits the new version has still to be done.

We now turn to the really interesting case which makes things completely different from the silo project development. It is the case that stakeholders in project B do not want to adopt a certain change. In that case a version of the old software must be kept running in parallel to the new version. In Fig. 8.10 we have depicted a solution where project A is responsible for the operation of the old version of the software, so that project B can keep using it as service by calling it. With respect to complexity this differs a little from a solution that copies the old version to project B, because the result remains the same, i.e., two versions of a software part are run and maintained henceforth in parallel.

Similarly, things become more complicated if a piece of software copied from product A to B is changed sometime after its deployment by project B. Then a careful co-evaluation of both the changes in project A and project B is necessary and both kinds of changes have to be brought together by the developers in project A. This leads us to yet another observation with respect to reuse. So far, we have only considered the impact of changes to a software component on software that reuses this software. In general, however, also the other direction is relevant. A software piece can also be subject to change because of its usage in another project than the one it originally stems from. All these problems are exactly the problems of software variants as described in Sect. 5.6 from the viewpoint of modeling. To realize the potential of all the software in an enterprise as a common code base for reuse the borders between the projects must be removed. At the next level all the projects with their sub projects and iteration projects can be seen as one huge project as depicted in Fig. 8.11. It is the complexity of this general software development problem that must be properly managed by initiatives like SOA governance that promise to contribute to enterprise-wide software engineering.

8.5.3 Software Use versus Software Reuse

There is a huge potential of software reuse in large companies. On a global scale, there is even more potential for reuse through emerging service-orientation. One of the widely recognized visions of service-oriented architecture was the retrieval of services in global repositories as described in Sect. 8.4. This vision was tightly connected to the concrete UDDI standard of the web-services technology stack. This kind of service retrieval and use had the focus on electronic data interchange, i.e., business-to-business computing. It was not in the

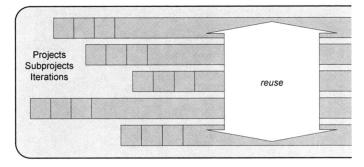

Fig. 8.11. SOA governance as ubiquitous reuse.

first place about software reuse in the sense of SaaS (Software as a Service). It is a promising idea to see the global code base as a repository for reuse – see [7, 8] for a discussion and concrete supporting technology.

The topic of the discussion of Sect. 8.5.2 has been software reuse in development projects and actually IT stakeholders want SOA experts to say something about software reuse. However, the earlier visions of service-oriented architecture concerning the fields of enterprise application integration, electronic data interchange, and flexible business processes were not originally visions about software reuse. In a strict sense the field of reuse is always also about design for reuse, i.e., the discipline of anticipating the reuse of a piece of software. For example, we believe that this viewpoint is wide-spread in the object-oriented software pattern community – note, that according to the subtitle of [130] design patterns are about reusable object-oriented software. SOA governance in the sense of best practices and tools is relevant for all the discussed SOA visions and not only the software productizing vision.

9

Conclusion

Many of today's enterprises consider business process orientation as a key enabler. Due to globalization today's markets are highly competitive. Enterprises must be prepared to react quicker to new threats. They want to be prepared to react quicker to new opportunities. They must react quicker to changing and new customer demands. A mature business process management teamed together with a flexible IT infrastructure becomes more and more important in many successful enterprises.

In Fig. 1.1 we have called the reader's attention to the gaps and tension that exist between business process modeling, workflow definition and application programming. The book analyzed these gaps and tensions. Now, this chapter eventually addresses these gaps and tensions by proposing a typed approach to business process specification. The chapter introduces a concrete typed workflow specification language – the so-called typed workflow charts. These can be exploited as a domain-specific programming language and facilitate tight integration between workflow definition and system dialogue programming. Furthermore, typed workflow chart specification is amenable to integration with business process modeling.

9.1 Business Processes and Workflows

It is common to make a distinction business process modeling and workflow definition. With business process modeling in Fig. 1.1 we mean a system analysis activity, i.e., an 'as is'-analysis or a 'to be'-analysis of the business processes an organization is made of. With a workflow definition in Fig. 1.1 we mean the specification of a workflow created with the workflow definition tool of a workflow system technology. In this sense a workflow definition is a high-level program, which is typically a visual program. This means, a workflow definition is a somehow executable business process model or specification. It is executable in the sense that it can be interpreted by a so-called workflow enactment service teamed together with a so-called workflow engine

D. Draheim, *Business Process Technology: A Unified View on Business Processes, Workflows and Enterprise Applications*, DOI 10.1007/978-3-642-01588-5_9,
© Springer-Verlag Berlin Heidelberg 2010

that maintains workflow state and steps through workflow definitions with the help of a worklist client. The worklist paradigm has been explained in depth in Sect. 7.

9.1.1 Usual Distinctions between Business Processes and Workflows

Just from the meaning of the words the terms business process and workflow can be used as synonyms. And actually, the terms business process and workflow are often used as synonyms. The Workflow Management Coalition (WfMC) cleanly distinguishes between business processes and workflows [356]. In [356] business processes are explained as the more general concept of a net of business activities whereas a workflow is a automation of a business process. Let us have a look at the definitions of business process and workflow as given by the Workflow Management Coalition. The notion of business process is defined as follows:

> *"A set of one or more linked procedures or activities which collectively realize a business objective or policy goal, normally within the context of an organizational structure defining functional roles and relationships."* [356]

The notion of workflow is defined by the Workflow Management Coalition as follows:

> *"The automation of a business process, in whole or part, during which documents, information or tasks are passed from one participant to another for action, according to a set of procedural rules."* [356]

To define a workflow merely as an automation of a business process would be quite an ambiguous definition. The above definition of workflow as given by the Workflow Management Coalition is more elaborate than just stating that a workflow is an automation of a business process but, nevertheless, it remains ambiguous in the following sense. Automation of a business process can be understood as the replacement of an existing, not yet automated business process by a new fully automatic one. For example a handcraft process of a workshop production could be replaced by a fully automatic production-line. What interests us more than the full automation of a business process are certain automatic parts of a business process that deal with supervisory control. This is so for fully-automatic and semi-automatic business processes.

We think that in the view of workflow technology, which is at the center of discussion in the workflow community which the Workflow Management Coalition aims to represent, it is fair to remark that there is a notion of workflow that is not the automation of a business process itself but an automatic process in an enterprise application, i.e., a state-based human-computer dialogue, that supports an otherwise existing business process. A business process does not exist completely independently from the workflows that support it, precisely because it is supported by these workflows. However, in general a business process can be considered independently from its supporting workflow in an enterprise application. Sometimes, the workflow support of the business process speeds up the workflow makes it easier to learn and to follow for humans, makes it more robust against erroneous execution and so on. But all of these important advantages are just quality properties of the concrete semi-automatic implementation of the business process and the business process often could exists without this concrete workflow support, for example, it could exist with another kind of workflow support or even without workflow support at all.

Fortunately, when talking about business process technology and workflow technology in particular, we do not have to think too much about the meaning of automation of business processes in general. We have a concrete meaning of workflow at hand, which stems from the considered technology class, i.e., the workflow management system as given by the workflow management reference model of the Workflow Management Coalition in [356]. We have visualized this workflow management reference model in Fig. 4.3.

9.1.2 This Book's Distinction between Business Processes and Workflows

In this book we use the term business process for the value-adding processes an organization is made of and the term workflow for the automation of such process. Even more concretely, we usually use the term workflow for a certain kind of IT support for a concrete business process, i.e., a piece of software that enables a business process and controls its correct and complete execution. Even more concretely, we usually use the term workflow for such IT support that is realized with a workflow management system.

Anyhow, we do not mind whether you want to distinguish between the terms of business process and workflow or not. However, we want to make clear that it is often important to distinguish between business processes in general and the automation of business processes, independently from the question whether you want to use the terms business process and workflow for this distinction. For example, for us it is very important to distinguish between the activity of understanding and describing business processes in general, on the one hand, and the definition of a workflow in the definition tool of a workflow technology, on the other hand. We use the term business process modeling for the former notion and the term workflow definition for the latter.

It is worth mentioning that the Workflow Management Coalition uses the term process definition for what we call workflow definition. The terms and business model and business definition sound more equal to each other than the terms business process model and workflow definition. Furthermore, the term workflow definition hints at the concept of a workflow management system that interprets workflow definitions as programs in a high-level, visual programming language, i.e., we think that the term workflow somehow brings a flavor of executability. Therefore we prefer the term workflow definition over the term process definition. There are other terms that make sense for what we call a workflow definition, e.g., executable business process model, executable business process specification, workflow specification and so forth.

9.1.3 Tool Support for Business Processes – Business Process Technologies

There is no need to use special-purpose tools and technologies to automate business processes. For example, you can use a general-purpose drawing tool to support your business process modeling efforts. And you do not need workflow management technology to develop a workflow-intensive software application. However, there are special-purpose business process technologies as shown in Fig. 9.1.

There are tools whose purpose is to support business process modeling and others to support business process automation. Actually, Fig. 9.1 shows three kinds of tools, i.e., business process modeling tools, business process management suites and workflow management systems. Business process management suites and workflow systems together stand for the class of special-purpose business process tools explicitly supporting business process automation. You can also use the terms workflow technology or workflow management system technology and the like for the kind of tool named workflow management system in Fig. 9.1. Actually, the term business process management suite and workflow management system in a sense mean the same class of tools. The point is that workflow management system is the traditional name for a similar kind of system. Established workflow technology vendors renamed their products and call them business process management suites today. However, you would usually expect features from a business process management suite that go beyond the automation of business processes. Such features are, for example, advanced capabilities for process analysis like monitoring tools for the executed workflows and simulation tools for the workflow definitions as sketched in Fig. 9.1.

Those tools that support business process automation also offer a means to visually specify business process models, which is given by their workflow definition tool. However, tools for business process automation usually do not count as business process modeling tools. This is justified, if a business process automation tool does not offer the full range of features for business process description that you might except from a business process modeling tool. For example, a typical business process modeling tool might offer support for a lot of different kinds of diagrams, for example, support more than hundred of different kinds of modeling language standards and quasi-standards would be an educated guess. The point is that with a business process modeling tool you usually do not want to model only the narrow aspect of business processes as a net of business activities, but also all other kinds of aspects of the enterprise.

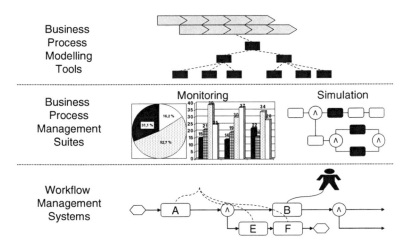

Fig. 9.1. Concrete business process technologies.

Actually, with respect to the needs of analysis and modeling there is no real limitation in flavor or aspects for which system an analyst might want to have integrated support in a business process modeling tool: data, organizational structure, the deployment structure of enterprise applications, strategic plans and so forth. Alone for the aspect of pure business process modeling, you would expect support for the different accepted modeling language standards and quasi-standards, i.e., event-driven process chains like the one in Fig. 4.6, BPMN, UML activity diagrams and so forth. In terms of different types of diagrams in general, you would expect support for: entity-relationship (ER) diagrams, all the different kinds of object-oriented diagrams from different kinds of modeling methods like UML or OMT [306], old-fashioned but nonetheless established and still widely used kinds of diagrams like SADT or IDEF-0 , supply chain diagrams like the uppermost diagram in Fig. 9.1, diagrams for Norton and Kaplan's balanced score cards [194], organization charts and so forth – the list is really open-ended.

A mature business process modeling tool should allow for the modeling of these aspects and should allow the analyst to control the complexity that arises from the interrelationships between the several aspects. A concrete feature that you might except from a mature business process modeling tool is the maintenance of all the models in a way that is independent from concrete syntax, i.e., the maintenance of a model repository, and support for tracking and balancing between the model elements of different kinds of models. Furthermore, against the background of the many kinds of diagrams and concrete modeling elements that are possibly needed in your organization you might except support for meta-modeling so that your business process modeling tool is open for extensions or changes to the offered diagrams or even the addition of an entirely new kind of diagram. Actually, there are some business process modeling tools that offer meta-modeling capabilities, either as a service provided by the tool vendor, or as an explicit feature available to the user, where the latter is rather the case for tools from academia [212, 197] but also for some commercial tools [159, 160, 115, 246].

Actually, there is no reason why a tool for business process automation should not also support the features that you might except from a business process modeling tool. And actually, we believe that these two classes of tools will be unified in the future. However, a distinction between the two classes seems to be here to stay for a while. For example, the Gartner Group distinguishes between two markets, i.e., the market of business process analysis tools, which is just another name for business process modeling tools, and the market of business process management suites resulting in two separate magic quadrants published by Gartner [261, 158].

9.2 Integrating Workflow Definition and Dialogue Programming

In this section we now integrate workflow definition and dialogue programming by the introduction of a typed-approach to business process specification, typed business process analysis for short. The key artifact that we introduce is the typed workflow chart. The typed workflow chart is an extension of the formchart that addresses the needs of workflow definition. Similarly, typed business process analysis is a generalization of form-oriented analysis [89, 82, 83, 95, 94, 96, 97, 105, 106, 92, 87, 107] that addresses the needs of business process specification. The framework of typed business process analysis is also amenable to the integration of business process modeling in general and workflow definition in particular as we will detail in Sect. 9.4. Once more we want to make clear our distinction between business processes modeling and workflow definition that we already discussed in Sect. 9.1 – a workflow definition is a special kind of business process model, usually the most detailed one in a hierarchy of business processes, that specifies the top-level structure of the dialogues of a workflow management system.

9.2.1 An Introductory Example

We have given an example business process model that deals with the tasks of business travel application, review, support and report in Fig. 9.2. The business process model oriented towards an event-driven process chains (EPC) [312] with their typical usage of events to represent case distinctions.

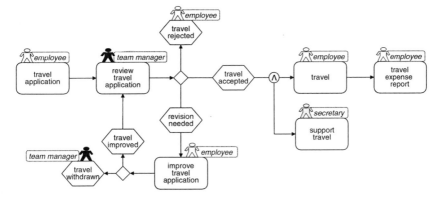

Fig. 9.2. Business process model for conducting a business trip.

Before an employee may travel he must apply for it. The application is reviewed by a responsible team manager. For some employees, the application can be rejected. For other employees the application can not be rejected by the team manager, however, it can be sent back to the applicant for changes and improvement. The rejection of an application is notified to the applicant. The detail information that there is a distinction between employees with respect to rejection and revision of travel applications is absent from the business process model in Fig. 9.2. The rules about how an employee's application has to be treated with respect to rejection and revision are known and applied by the supporting IT system. Also this fact is not represented in the business process model in Fig. 9.2.

If the application is accepted the employee may travel. In parallel to the allowance the secretary will start supporting the employee with travel arrangements and further administrative tasks. After the employee has finished the business trip, he has to declare the travel expenses.

Figure. 9.3 is the workflow definition – given as a workflow chart – of the IT system that supports the above described business process. A workflow chart specifies a human-computer interaction. Circles in the workflow chart stand for computer screens showing information and providing forms for data input. White rectangles stand for forms that appear on computer screens. Gray rectangles stand for links in user worklists or task start menus. An employee starts a workflow instance by clicking on a travel application link in his task start menu. The travel application page is shown to the user. The page has a travel application form. The application page will be reused later for the revision of the application. Then, a travel withdraw form will be shown. Now, the travel withdraw form is not yet shown, because the user is the first time on this page. This fact is expressed by the so-called enabling condition attached to the edge from the travel application page to the withdraw form.

After the employee has submitted the travel application form, a link to the review of the travel application appears in the worklist of the team manager. If the team manager chooses this link from his worklist, the system will determine, whether it is possible to reject or to return the application. This is expressed by the so called flow conditions attached to the outgoing edges of the review travel application link. The flow conditions are mutual exclusive, so that the determination of the next page is unique.

If it is possible to reject the application a page is shown to the manager with a rejection form plus an acceptance form. If it is possible to return the application a page is shown to the manager with a revision form and an acceptance form. Both the rejection and the revision form, as well as the acceptance form provide means to input information necessary like comments, hints, change requests and so on. If the manager rejects the application a link to an appropriate notification message appears in the worklist of the applicant. If the manager returns the application to the user a link to the travel application page appears in the worklist of the employee that allows the employee to revisit his application and to change and improve the application according to the recommendations made by the manager, which are then also shown on the travel application page.

If the manager has submitted the acceptance form, a link to the corresponding travel expenses report task appears in the worklist of the employee and a link to a travel support task appears in the worklist of the secretary. When the secretary selects this link, a client page with all the information about the new travel that he needs to support the traveler is shown to him. He can leave this client page via a 'continue'-link after which the link to the travel support information page reappears in his worklist or via a 'delete'-link which removes the task from the worklist.

After an employee has finished his travel, he selects the link to the corresponding travel expense report task. On the corresponding page he can fill out an appropriate travel expense form. The travel itself is not represented in the workflow chart in Fig. 9.3.

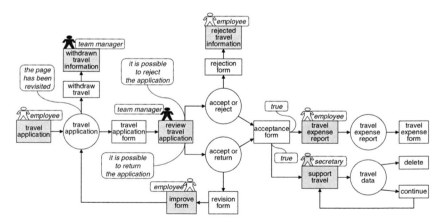

Fig. 9.3. Workflow chart for conducting a business trip.

9.2.2 Typed Workflow Charts

A workflow chart is a tripartite directed graph. There are three kinds of nodes, i.e., client pages, immediate server actions and deferred server actions. Each client page is only followed by immediate server action, each immediate server action is followed only by deferred server actions and each deferred server action is only followed by client pages. Figure 9.4 shows a correct workflow chart. We consider typed workflow charts, which means that a type is assigned to each node in the workflow chart. We assume in the following that all the workflow charts are typed, so that we use the terms typed workflow chart and workflow chart synonymously.

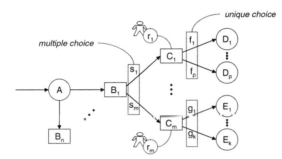

Fig. 9.4. Basic workflow chart.

The types used for the nodes of a workflow chart can be arbitrary complex sum-of-product types, e.g., the class diagrams of usual object-oriented modeling methods serve as a good basis – see Sect. 5.3 for a discussion of sum-of-product types. The types can be arbitrary complex, i.e., they can be arbitrarily nested; however, a type of a node must be at least a product type. It can be an empty product type; however, it must not be a basic type. In our examples, we usually assign a type to a node by giving the type the name of this node – in [101] we went even a step further and directly interpreted a class diagram as a formchart.

The workflow chart is annotated with further specification information of various kinds. As in form-oriented analysis different kinds of dialogue constraints are used, as indicated by the s_i, f_i and g_i in Fig. 9.4. We will not give a comprehensive explanation of all kinds of dialogue constraints that are necessary to completely specify a workflow management system, but refer to form-oriented analysis [89] for a comprehensive reference. However, we will discuss extra concepts in dialogue constraint writing needed for workflow specification in the following. Furthermore, users or user roles are attached to the workflow chart, as indicated by r_1 through r_m in Fig. 9.4. Users or user roles are attached only to deferred server actions as we will again explain in Sect. 9.2.4.

9.2.3 From Client Pages to Immediate Server Actions

A client page of a workflow chart is like a client page in a formchart – see Sect. 7.3 for an introduction to formcharts. The type of a client page describes the report shown to the user in an abstract sense. An immediate server action that is attached to a client page describes a form that appears on that client page. The user can fill out a form and submit it. The type of a server action describes the edit opportunities offered to the user by the corresponding form. For each attribute of a record type a concrete value must be provided before submission of the form. The concrete value must be provided by the user or automatically by a hidden parameter mechanism. It can be elaborated how a concrete type specifies concrete edit opportunities. For example, if an attribute has a basic infinite type, this can be interpreted as an input field in the form that has to be filled out by the user. As another example, if an attribute has a finite type, i.e., an enumeration type this can be interpreted as a selection menu. In [89] we have proposed one concrete means of interpretation of types as edit opportunities.

There may be more than one immediate server action connected to a client pages as shown by the server actions B_1 through B_n in Fig. 9.4. The user can submit only one form. Only the data filled into the submitted form is transferred to the server. Data that has been filled into or selected in forms other than the one submitted is lost after submission.

9.2.4 From Immediate Server Actions to Deferred Server Actions

An immediate server action processes the values it has received upon invocation by the user. In general the server action has a side effect on the information system state. After completion of an immediate server action, the user is led to his worklist. The edges from immediate server actions to deferred server actions are annotated with conditions as shown by the conditions s_1 through s_n in Fig. 9.4. We call edges from immediate server actions to deferred server actions activation edges. We call the conditions annotated to activation edges show conditions or activation conditions. Given an activation edge and its activation condition, the deferred server action targeted by the activation edge is called the corresponding deferred server action of the activation condition, i.e., each C_i is the corresponding deferred server action of each s_i in Fig. 9.4.

The Semantics of Activation Conditions

The semantics of an activation condition is the following. If and only if an activation condition evaluates to true a new link to the corresponding deferred server action is created and added to a user's worklist, i.e., a new link to the corresponding deferred server action is shown to a user – this is the reason why we call activation conditions also show conditions. Which user's worklist the new link is added to? This depends on the role annotated to the targeted deferred server action and the concrete role model used. Let us assume that we are dealing with a single-user role model, i.e., a role model in which each role is actually a single, fixed user. This means, the role annotation assigns a concrete single user to each deferred server action. In the context of such a single-user role model the link of an activated deferred server action is added to the worklist of the user that is annotated to the deferred server action.

Let us assume that we have to deal with a more complex role model in which a role stands for a set of concrete users. If we have to deal with such complex role model we have the choice to fix the semantics of workflow activation. One choice is that a link to the activated deferred action is added to the worklist of each concrete user in the set defined by the user role which is annotated to the deferred action. So, it is indeed not necessary to restrict the semantics to an alternative where an activated workflow is activated uniquely for only one user. However, if we chose to add an activated workflow to more than one worklist we have to fix semantics for this somehow distributed activation link that is created this way. A usual solution would be a preemptive semantics that deletes workflows from worklists once a workflow is actually started. Another possible solution lies in a completely different interpretation of the situation in which more than one copy of workflow instances is actually created and distributed over the users. Another option for dealing with a multiple-user role is to choose one concrete user from the set of users whenever a deferred action is activated. In this case a concrete mechanism for the selection of the concrete user should be defined – see Sect. 7.11.

All this said, we now fix the trivial single-user role model for workflow charts. We do this only for the sake of simplifying the upcoming discussion of workflow charts, i.e., without loss of generality. We therefore speak about a user attached to a deferred server action instead of talking about a user role or role attached to a deferred server action. However, once the semantics of the workflow chart is understood for the single-user role model, workflow charts can be extended by other, more complex user role models and appropriate semantics can be given to them.

With the single-user role model fixed we can now give the following definition. If and only if an activation condition evaluates to true a new link to the corresponding deferred server action is created and added to the worklist of the corresponding user.

Worklist Implementation Issues

The above definition of the semantics of activation conditions does not specify when the newly created link is actually shown to the user. It is fair to state that the new link is shown to the user as soon as possible, but what does that mean? Actually, the question depends on the implementation of the workflow management system. In Sect. 7 we have identified a distinction between terminal/server-style workflow systems and windows-style workflow systems.

In a terminal/server-style workflow system the user has no access to the worklist as long as he is working with a system dialogue. For the workflow chart this means that with a terminal/server-style implementation, the worklist is not available when the user sees and works with a client page. As soon as the user returns to his worklist all new links that has been added to it in the mean time are presented to him. In a window-style implementation the user always has access to the worklist. If the worklist is currently shown to the user the question is whether the links that are added to it are immediately presented to the user or not. This is an issue for both terminal/server-implementations and windows-style implementations. The option that a link is not shown immediately to the user means that we must distinguish between a notion of worklist and a notion of shown worklist. The worklist in general is a conceptually worklist of all activated deferred server action, whereas the shown worklist is the list of deferred actions that are actually shown to the user.

The question of whether to show a new link immediately or not is in the first place a human-computer interaction question, in the second place a technological question. If the user looks at the worklist it might be confusing if the worklist changes, in particular, when links are added relatively often. For example, if links are added at the beginning of the list or, based on some criteria like alphabetical order or task numbers, somewhere in the middle of the worklist, an addition of a link may make it difficult to read the list, because lines can always be re-arranged suddenly. If links are added to the end of the list and the list is too long to be presented on the screen in one go, the addition may not have the desired effect of an immediate addition, i.e., immediate information about new available tasks. A compromise might be to enable a reloading of the worklist and to inform the user with some kind of flag whenever new tasks arrive.

The Multiple Choice of Deferred Actions

After completion of an immediate server action an arbitrary number of the connected activation conditions can evaluate to true. In Fig. 9.4 we have used the term multiple choice for this scenario. The multiple choices give rise to extra parallelism. Parallelism means that the user can influence how to intertwine defined sequences of activities, i.e., sequences of client pages and server actions. The user can influence this intertwining by the selection of the next task from the user list, i.e., by the selection of the next deferred server action. In order to have a choice there must be more than one task in the worklist. Even if the evaluation of activation conditions after immediate server actions were always unique instead of multiple, there would exists parallelism, because the task in a user's worklist may stem also from arbitrary many other users. It is also possible to allow automatic events or events from outside the workflow system to trigger new workflow instances, which would also give rise to parallelism. Therefore we say that multiple choice of deferred actions give rise to extra parallelism, i.e., it is not the only source of parallelism.

The multiple choice of deferred server actions after the completion of an immediate server action is deterministic. The multiple choice is done automatically based on the system state and concrete conditions, it is therefore not an example of non-determinism. It is a common misunderstanding to believe that parallelism always comes with non-determinism. You can have completely deterministic systems that deal with forms of parallelism. The user's choice of the next deferred action from his worklist might be classified as non-deterministic. An observer that knows little about the rules that the user's decision is based on, would classify this selection as non-deterministic. If there exists such rules and the more the outside observer knows about these rules, the observer would tend to classify this selection also as deterministic. The same discussion applies to events that trigger workflow instances from the system's environment. Observers classify choices as non-deterministic if they do not understand the decision rules. If an observer does not understand the decision rules of a choice the user might at least understand the distribution of concrete choices, i.e., the choice is amenable to treatment with probability theory. Even if an observer understands the distribution of concrete choices, he would still classify a choice as non-deterministic, unless he also understands the decision rules behind the choice.

An arbitrary subset of the activation conditions that belong to one immediate server action can evaluate to true after completion of that immediate server action. This means, in particular, that also none of the activation condition may evaluate to true. Indeed, it can happen that a user's worklist becomes empty. Then, the user must start new tasks or must wait for new tasks triggered by other users or external events. We assume that the workflow system provides a start menu, i.e., a list of links to deferred actions that serve as entry points to workflow instances – see also Sect. 9.2.6 for a discussion of the creation of workflow instances. It is possible to introduce a modeling element, a start marker, let's say a small circle, to denote those deferred server actions that should serve as entry points for the initial creation of workflow instances. The information given by the start markers can then be exploited in constructing the user's start menus.

It is not necessary to introduce explicit modeling elements for generating parallelism, called, e.g., fork or split connectors or gateways in common business process modeling languages. You can express all kinds of forking with a set of conditions which are all evaluated independently from each other. Explicit modeling elements can be introduced as syntactic sugar. Fig. 9.5 shows two versions to express the same multiple choice. The first one uses activation conditions only, the second one uses also a fork gateway and a decision gateway. All the activation conditions that are constantly true in the first version are replaced by the introduction of the fork gateway in the second version. The two activation conditions s and $\neg s$ from the first version are transferred to the branches of the decision gateway in the second version.

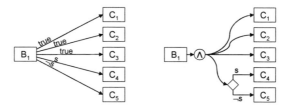

Fig. 9.5. Implicit versus explicit multiple choice.

9.2.5 From Deferred Server Actions to Client Pages

A deferred server action usually appears as a link in worklists. In general, it would be possible to have worklists that consist of forms instead of links, so that the user can enter some initial data before starting the selected next task. However, in today's workflow technologies worklists consist of links that lead to task. This does not mean that the type of a deferred server action is necessarily the empty type. A link can carry hidden parameters as we have discussed in Sect. 7.3 and so is also for those links that trigger deferred server actions.

Like immediate sever actions, a deferred server action also processes some logic and may have a side-effect onto the state of the information system. The edges leading from a deferred server action to a client pages are annotated with so-called flow conditions, see the f_i and g_i in Fig. 9.4. These flow conditions serve the same purpose as the flow conditions in the formcharts of form-oriented analysis. After an deferred server action has been executed, all the connected flow conditions are evaluated. In contrast to immediate server actions, this evaluation must be unique, i.e., exactly one of the flow conditions must be evaluated to true. Basically, there are two options to ensure that exactly one of the flow conditions is evaluated to true. It is possible to require from the workflow designer that he writes the flow conditions in such a way that they are mutually exclusive and complete for each system state. Another option is to introduce a means to specify an order for the flow conditions and a means to specify a default, fall through edge.

9.2.6 The Workflows given by a Workflow Chart

Each deferred server action can be considered the entry point to a workflow; it can be considered the entry point of an automated business process. If an activation condition evaluates to true, an instance of a workflow is activated. What does activation of a workflow instance mean? We have a strict human-computer interaction oriented answer to this question. A workflow instance is activated if it shows up in a worklist. We say that the workflow instance represented by a link in a worklist is activated but not yet started. The user can start a workflow instance by selecting the corresponding link in the worklist. Figure 9.6 shows how workflows are represented by deferred server actions.

Each deferred server action in the large workflow chart at the top of Fig. 9.6 can be interpreted as the start of a sub workflow definition. In Fig. 9.6 we have used small circles as start markers and small double-lined circles as end markers for workflow definitions. The smaller diagrams in Fig. 9.6 each show one sub workflow definition of the large workflow chart.

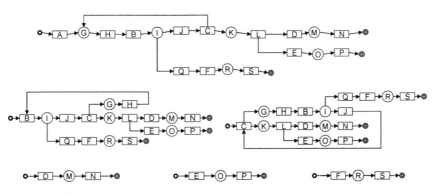

Fig. 9.6. Deferred server actions as entries to workflows.

We have a continuation-based or nested viewpoint with respect to workflows, i.e., workflow definitions and workflow instances. A workflow consists of a starting deferred server action, followed by a client page, followed by an immediate server action, recursively followed by a workflow. A workflow is usually seen as an entity that serves the user to achieve a certain goal. This understanding of workflow – see also the Workflow Management Coalition's definition of business process given in Sect. 9.1 once more – somehow contradicts the just-given definition. Given a concrete workflow definition, in general, you would not see each of its inner workflows in the sense of our definition as independent workflows in the usual sense.

The notion of achievable goal is somewhat vague and depends upon the viewpoint of the observer; however, it should not be neglected. Therefore, the workflow definition language should provide a way to divide the whole flat workflow chart into parts, which are then the top-level workflow or let us say tasks. The usage of start markers and end markers could be used for this purpose.

The specification of tasks could be, for example, exploited in the naming of client pages, so that a user always is aware of the context task he is working in. Similarly, the task name could also be exploited in the naming of the links occurring in worklists. A link could consist, for example, of a task name plus a task identifier plus the name of the targeted deferred server action. The name of the initial deferred server action, i.e., the deferred server action that is the entry point to a task, can be taken as the name of the task. Alternatively, the workflow definition language could provide a means to specify an extra name for a task. The task identifier can be generated whenever a task is started and can be propagated to the subsequent inner workflows of the task. A task can be considered finished when there are no dangling activities of the task, i.e., open client pages or processing server actions that belong to a task specification.

We do not delve further into this topic of task specification. This means that we do not want to elaborate a full task specification mechanism and its effects here. A purpose of the discussion of tasks was to illustrate that further useful notions can be built on top of the workflow chart concept. And indeed, in Sect. 9.2.7 we will discuss a further possible exploitation of the workflow chart in Sect. 9.2.7, i.e., the interpretation of sub workflow charts as complex dialogues, which is very important, because it overcomes the strict separation of workflow definition and application programming.

9.2.7 The Interplay of the Dialogue Client and the Worklist Client

A workflow chart is executed or interpreted by the interplay of two kinds of clients. The first one is the worklist client or worklist processor, the second one is the so-called dialogue client or dialogue processor. The worklist client presents the worklist to the user and enables the selection of a concrete subsequent task in the form of a link to a subsequent deferred server action. Upon selection of a task the worklist client hands over to the dialogue client. The dialogue further processes the workflow chart. The dialogue client renders the report data of the client page and shows the forms connected to it. It enables input to the forms and submits the data to the selected immediate server action. Then, as a default behavior, the dialogue client hands over to the worklist client. In Sect. 7 we have explained that workflow systems follow a three-staged interaction paradigm. The worklist client stands for the first stage of interaction, i.e., selection of a task from the worklist, and the dialogue client stands for the second stage of interaction, i.e., editing of the input capabilities of the client page, and the third stage of interaction, i.e., selection of a navigation path and submission of data.

We have said that the dialogue client hands over to the worklist client as a default. This is not necessarily so however. Let us start with the following scenario. After a user has triggered an immediate server action, and after completion of this immediate server action, an arbitrary number of deferred server actions is selected for further processing. Here, if the selection is unique with respect to the user who triggered the immediate server action this user's dialogue can be continued, i.e., the worklist processor stage can be skipped. It can be skipped, because there is no ambiguity and therefore no need for user intervention from a dialogue processing viewpoint. If the processing stays with the dialogue processing client this means that the uniquely determined deferred server is actually executed immediately. Then the next client page is determined uniquely, which is always the case; because we have said that flow conditions are always uniquely evaluated.

We fix the term dialogue for a single-user human-computer interaction that is two-staged in the sense of form-oriented analysis and formcharts. In a dialogue we consider only the interactions with a client page, i.e., the editing and submission of a client page's forms. This does not mean that you can, in principle, model or program worklist within the two-staged interaction paradigm [15]. It means that we consider a dialogue model as being interpreted by a dialogue processor only. The simplest dialogues consist of one client page and its connected forms. Rapid development tools in some business process management suites support exactly the development of such one-step dialogues leading to a report with a form that leads back to the worklist upon submission.

Complex dialogues consist of many different client pages and server actions wired together. A dialogue model is characterized by the fact that the server processing stage uniquely determines the next client page for the single user. Therefore, those parts of a workflow chart in which the activation conditions that are evaluated uniquely relatively to the triggering user are candidates for being interpreted as mere dialogues. This observation can be exploited in various ways as we will see in due course.

9.2.8 Dynamic Detection of Dialogues

It is possible to detect at run-time whether the evaluation of activation conditions with respect to the current user is unique or not. On the basis of this it can be decided dynamically whether the user is directed to his worklist or to the next client page. With such dynamic scheduling of the two clients, the number of visits to worklists can be reduced significantly for some concrete workflow definitions. Imagine a workflow definition in which the interaction for each user is actually determined completely uniquely with respect to the system responses and the only kind of parallelism stems from forking parallel tasks to other users. In such system all the visits of the worklist are superfluous. At least they are superfluous at first sight. Actually, it is exactly the same example that also shows us the risks of such an approach of dynamic client scheduling. A user might be involved too long in his dialogue before it is finishes and he gets the chance to see tasks that arrived in the mean time.

Another point of criticism against the dynamic scheduling approach is the obvious potential violation of an important dialogue principle, i.e., conformity with user expectations [176]. Imagine a user has been used to being routed to a worklist after a certain client page and is suddenly directed to a subsequent client page. He might be confused or miss the opportunity to select the next concurrent task himself.

The worklist is a tool to reveal parallelism to the user. The interplay between the worklist client and the dialogue client should be designed intentionally. It should be designed with care. Despite its risk, the opportunity of having a dynamic client scheduling shows the potential of dialogues that are contained in the workflow chart. We discuss the explicit specification of dialogues on the basis of workflow charts in Sect. 9.2.9,

9.2.9 Explicit Specification of Dialogues

The dialogues that are contained in a workflow definition open a design space for the system modeler. The system modeler once more comes into the role of human-computer interaction designer. In this section we outline possible means of explicit specification of dialogues in workflow charts.

It is possible to design a modeling element for immediate server actions with the unique evaluation of conditions at outgoing edges per user. With such modeling elements it should be possible to fix an evaluation order and to specify a fall through edge for each subset of outgoing edges targeting the same user.

When the modeler uses immediate server actions with unique choice to distinguish them from server actions with multiple choice, this extra information can be used to determine the dialogues in a workflow definition, i.e., to identify those parts that should be processed without the worklist client. However, we think it is better to introduce a means to explicitly specify the dialogues in a workflow chart. This could be introduced as a graphical modeling element like a dashed line surrounding a sub diagram of a workflow chart. It could also be introduced for textual specification by a language construct for referencing a bundle identifier or a kind of block structure. The latter must be done with care if modeling elements of workflow charts should be used or re-used in more than one defined dialogue.

If there is a means to specify the dialogues of a workflow chart explicitly this has the following advantage. The user can and should always use immediate server actions with unique choice whenever he knows that the choice is unique and not arbitrary. He can defer the design of the dialogues, i.e., the division of the workflow chart into parts that should be processed only with the dialogue client. He can also re-design the dialogue structure with more freedom and without loss of knowledge concerning unique evaluation, i.e., without loss of knowledge about evaluation orders and fall through edges. It only remains to add that a means to specify the dialogues alone, i.e., without a construct for specifying the unique evaluation order per user, is not sufficient, exactly because the evaluations in a dialogue must be made unique.

A sub diagram specifying a dialogue must not span more than one user. A sub diagram specifying a dialogue must not span more immediate server actions with multiple choice of activation conditions. Both of these requirements can be statically checked. As already mentioned, in the presence of immediate sever actions with unique choices per user dialogues can be inferred and proposed to the modeler. In a sense, dialogues are dynamically recognizable as we have discussed in Sect. 9.2.8. Statically recognizable dialogues are those for which the uniqueness of activation of deferred server actions can be recognized statically. The uniqueness of activation of deferred server actions is non-decidable. Therefore, there is a need for some means of specifying these unique choices. For those dialogues that are statically recognizable, it is, as always with statically recognizable properties like programming language types, a matter of taste whether you want to choose an inference or static specification approach. We think that a mixture might be the best, i.e., an explicit specification of the dialogues, but support by a tool that proposes the different possible dialogues.

9.2.10 Synchronization Issues

In business process modeling languages parallelism and synchronization is introduced by explicit modeling elements, i.e., an 'and'-gateway with multiple fan-out for forking parallel sub processes and an 'and'-gateway with multiple fan-in for joining parallel sub processes. We have discussed the modeling of parallelism and synchronization in Sect. 4.6 . In Sect. 9.2.4 we have explained that there is no need for explicit modeling elements for forking parallel activities in workflow charts and have illustrated this in Fig. 9.5. Similarly, there is no need for explicit specification of synchronization in workflow charts. First, we need to explain what synchronization means in workflow charts.

Synchronization in workflow charts means that the appearance of a deferred server action in a worklist is delayed further until a certain synchronization condition is met. Synchronization shows only in a delayed appearance of a deferred server action in a worklist. In particular it does not show as a resumption after the processing of an immediate server action. After a user has clicked a link on his current client page or submitted a form the triggered immediate server action may take some time to process but after completion of this processing the user is led immediately to his worklist where he can choose some further task. This means the appearance of the worklist is never synchronized against any other event in the workflow system.

Arbitrary synchronization can be implemented by a combination of server action side effects and activation conditions. Figure 9.7 shows how a standard synchronization is specified with a workflow chart. Diagram (i) shows the workflow chart and diagram (ii) shows a corresponding business process model. Each activity in the business model in diagram (ii) corresponds to a starting deferred server action of the same name as the activity with index S like 'start', a client page of same name with index P like 'page' and an immediate server action representing a form of same name with index F like 'form'. The left forking 'and'-gateway in diagram (ii) corresponds to the set of constantly true activation conditions at the edges leading from the immediate server action A_F to its connected deferred server actions. We have explained the realization of the parallel fork connector already in Sect. 9.2.4 and Fig. 9.5.

The synchronizing right 'and'-connector in diagram (ii) is realized by the set of server side and activation condition specifications shown in diagram (i). Two variables b and c are introduced which express whether the deferred server actions B_F and C_F has been completed. Before the parallel activities

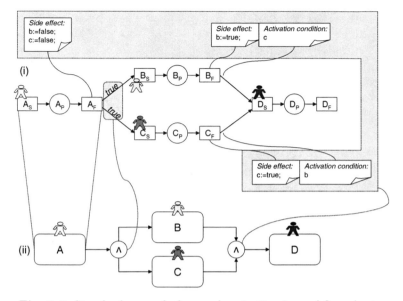

Fig. 9.7. Standard example for synchronization in workflow charts.

B and C are entered, the two variables b and c are set to false. Let us assume that, without loss of generality, the immediate server action B_F is completed first. After its business logic related processing it sets the variable b and tests the variable c. The test of the variable c serves as activation condition. If the test of the variable c evaluates to false, this means that the deferred server action C_F has not yet been completed. As a result, the deferred server action D_S does not occur in the corresponding user's worklist. In Sect. 9.2.4 we have already discussed that it is possible that none of the outgoing activation conditions of an immediate server action evaluates to true. Also, in the current case, the evaluation of the variable c to false does not mean that the current user is blocked. The current user is led to his worklist after the evaluation of the variable c. As we have already mentioned, synchronization shows only as a resumed appearance of deferred server actions in a worklist.

Now, when the immediate server action C_F is also completed eventually, it analogously sets variable c to true and tests the variable b. The setting of the variable c is unimportant – it is only important in the symmetric case. However, the variable b evaluates to true, which means that the deferred server action D_S is now sent to the corresponding user's worklist. As an important detail it is necessary to mention that the two actions of setting the variable b and testing the variable c as well as the two actions of setting the variable c and testing the variable b must be both realized as a compound atomic action.

In Sect. 4.6 we have discussed the semantics of synchronization in business process models. The discussion in Sect. 4.6 fully applies to the synchronization in executable business process specifications. It is important to have a means to realize arbitrary synchronization. In workflow charts it is given by the mechanism of activation conditions. Synchronization can be realized by the interplay of side effects and several activation conditions. No extra mechanism is necessary. No special concurrent activation condition is needed. It is possible to introduce special gateways that express common synchronization patterns as syntactic sugar. This is similar to the possible introduction of a forking gateway as illustrated in Fig. 9.5.

For the synchronization realized in Fig. 9.7 it would be possible to introduce an explicit 'and'-construct with multiple fan-in. This leads to exactly the same discussion that we have had in Sect. 4.6. With the current realization the transition from the immediate server action C_F to the deferred server action D_S is synchronized against the completion of an arbitrary instance of the immediate server action B_F. Therefore, the current realization shows also another odd effect. If a further task A has been finished in the above describe scenario, the variable b is reset to false. So the occurrence of the deferred server action D_S is further delayed and the eventual occurrence of the deferred server action is a synchronization of more than two threads. Actually, this may be the synchronization semantics that has been actually intended. If not, the correct one can be realized by introducing identifiers for sub process instances that are passed around, referencing these identifiers in activation conditions, exploiting further enterprise resource data and so on. The example once more shows the following. The introduction of a concrete synchronization gateway can solve one concrete synchronization pattern. What is needed more than visual representations of concrete synchronization patterns is a means to specify and implement arbitrary synchronization.

9.2.11 Benefits of Integrating Workflow Definitions and Formcharts

With workflow charts we follow a unified workflow and human-computer interaction approach. When we consider workflows we are interested in how workflows materialize as human computer interaction. The worklist paradigm introduces a concrete human computer interaction pattern based on the notion of worklist. We have analyzed the worklist paradigm in Sect. 7. The worklist provides a top-level structure for the human computer interaction of a workflow system and the semantics of the worklist itself can be given in terms of human computer interaction, i.e., in terms of user interaction with the worklist. Workflow charts unify workflow definition and the definition of system dialogues. Workflow charts can be exploited in the following ways:

- Technology independent specification.
- Tpyed automatic programming.
- Flexibility in restructuring the workflow and dialogue design.
- Visibility of dialogue states to workflow technology.

Conceptual Specification versus Automatic Programming

The workflow chart language has been designed for the reason of high-level programming, i.e., as the basis for a high-level programming language as we will discuss further in a second. However, workflow charts can also be used as an abstract or let us say conceptual system modeling language. With conceptual modeling language we mean a non-executable specification language in this section, i.e., a language that serves only for the purposes of system planning and system documentation. Used as a conceptual modeling language workflow charts are technology-independent, i.e., they can be used independent from the implementing technology – the model driven architecture (MDA) [324] community uses the terminology of platform-independent model (PIM) to characterize the considered level of system modeling.

Using a workflow chart as a conceptual system model means that the workflow chart exists as an additional artifact to those descriptions and programs that are used in the implementing technologies. The workflow charts can add value if the description and programs of the implementing technologies are somehow not sufficiently abstract. For example, they can be used, if a plain programming language system is used as the implementing technology. Then, the workflow charts provide the viewpoint which is essential for a workflow-intensive system, i.e., the structure of the system dialogues following the worklist paradigm. They can add value if more than one implementing technology is used. For example, they can be used as an umbrella specification if some parts of the overall workflow system are implemented in another technology than other parts of the system. They can be used in a redocumentation scenario, where it is the target to get the documentation of the functionality of a legacy system or a legacy system landscape under control. They can be used to bridge the gap between business process models and conceptual enterprise application models as outlined in Sect. 5.5. If used as conceptual modeling language, workflow charts grasp the essential structure of a workflow-intensive system.

The workflow chart specification language has been designed with the target to create an executable business process specification language. As presented in this section workflow charts are not yet an executable business process specification language, however, they can be considered the crucial core of such a specification language. A full-fledged executable specification language can be obtained, basically, by elaborating a programming language for the dialogue constraints, the side effect specifications and a concrete specification of the type system. The result of such elaboration is a high-level programming language. In the past, also the term domain-specific language has been used for such specialized high-level programming languages.

With programming language we do not mean only text-based, i.e., ASCII programming language. With programming language we also mean visual programming languages and programming tools that realize a programming interface, e.g., syntax-directed editors and integrated development environments.

For example, in our case it is easy to imagine to integrate workflow charts as the workflow definition language of the workflow tool of an existing workflow management technology. Therefore, it might be better to say programming mechanism instead of programming language. It is another discussion, which programming technology is here to stay, we strictly believe in the future of more and more abstract programming platforms that are oriented towards abstract programming language syntax. We do not delve into the elaboration of an executable business process specification language based on workflow charts. What is important for us is to propose workflow charts as the crucial core of such technologies, i.e., to propose workflow charts as the starting point for the design of such technologies.

Flexibility in Restructuring the Workflow and Dialogue Design

In a workflow technology that fully exploits workflow charts as definition language, the system dialogues and the intermediate workflow states are specified at the same level with the same language. This is different in today's workflow technologies. In today's workflow technologies the system dialogues are programmed in a programming language, often with the help of a rapid development tool. The intertwining of the resulting programs is specified with the usually visual workflow definition language. If you want to restructure the workflows and the system dialogues you have to refactor both the programs of the system dialogues and the workflow definition. With a tool based on workflow charts the redesign of the dialogues amounts to a refactoring of the explicit specification of the dialogues as explained in Sect. 9.2.7.

Visibility of Dialogue States to Workflow Technology

In Sect. 7, we have explained the worklist paradigm and have analyzed it from the viewpoint of human-computer interaction. A user's worklist can be considered a top-level dialogue pattern which wires the rest of the dialogues that the user can experience. In the past, workflow technologies has been products that are either oriented towards rapid development of document flow from scratch or products that have been used for enterprise application integration. The current business process management suites are rather products that are in the tradition of enterprise application integration.

Figs. 9.8 and 9.9 serve the purpose to visualize the typical usage of workflow technology for enterprise application integration. Systems emerge in enterprises. If enterprises are large, more than one IT system is implemented to support the business processes of the enterprise. One, but not the only reason for this can be that the several functional units of the enterprise implement their own IT systems. Other reasons might be that systems are not developed but bought and there is no single product that supports the many business processes of the enterprise or that the enterprise decides to support certain

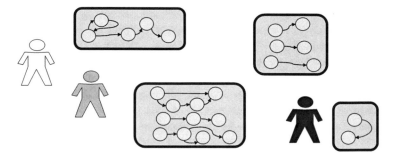

Fig. 9.8. An enterprise system landscape before integration.

businesses by a certain IT systems that yield unique selling points for the enterprise. Therefore business processes are often supported by more than one IT system, for example, if business processes span more than one functional unit. This is the situation depicted in Fig. 9.8.

From time to time the system landscape and the interplay of the several IT systems becomes so complex that there is the need for reconsidering its architecture. In particular, the complexity shows in a poor IT support for the interplay between the several IT systems. One solution is the total refactoring of the whole IT system landscape, i.e., a refactoring of all business processes and a new implementation of the IT support as a single new superior system. Usually, such a total refactoring would be much too cost- and time intensive. The other solution is to analyze carefully the interplay of the existing IT systems and to implement extra IT support for this interplay. Workflow technology can now be used to implement this extra IT support as shown in Fig. 9.9.

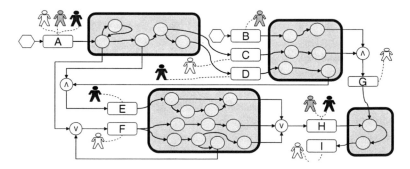

Fig. 9.9. Enterprise application integration with the help of workflow technology.

Business process management suites offer more than workflow definition and rapid development for the integrating of enterprise applications. As depicted in Fig. 9.1 they offer advanced features, e.g. for business process monitoring or business process simulation. With respect to this advanced features the system dialogues in the gray boxes in Fig. 9.9 are actually black boxes. The internal states of these IT systems are not visible to the advanced features of business process management suites without further efforts. If a business process management suite is used for the purpose of enterprise application integration this structural friction is naturally there. If you want to use a business process management suite in order to develop an IT system from scratch, the invisibility of the dialogue states for advanced analytical tools of the platform can be considered unsatisfactory. The usage of a business process technology as the initial enterprise application development platform embodies the trend of making business processes executable. A business platform based on workflow charts unifies workflow states and dialogue states and therefore opens the dialogues for full analysis by advanced features from the outset.

Flexibility Beyond the Limit of Client Page Interaction

We have said that we are not interested here in the elaboration of a concrete executable business process specification language or mechanism. However, we have also said that we believe in the future of abstract-syntax oriented programming environments in the future [226, 227]. In such a platform programs are created and changed by direct manipulation of the abstract syntax of the programs. Direct manipulation of abstract syntax of a program means that the program trees are presented to the user similar to the representation of a file system in a modern GUI-based file explorer. Each programming element has a unique, opaque identifier. Programming elements can be easily created and moved around. Similar to syntax-directed editors it is never possible to create a syntax-violating program.

If the envisioned business process platform is built as an abstract programming platform the above described flexibility in restructuring the system and visibility of items become available at the granularity of client page construction and interaction. For example, with such a technology it would be easy to move a sub part of a report to another client page. As another example, it would be possible to analyze the interaction with a single form and the single elements it consists of.

9.3 Towards Integrating Human Activity and Workflow Definition

Workflow charts can be given a unique, complete semantics in terms of the reaction of an IT system to the action of a human user. In general, a business process model is a mix of human-computer interaction and further, auxiliary activities. It is possible to abstract from the auxiliary activities and try to understand the business process merely in terms of the IT system that supports it. The more a business process is supported by an IT system, the better it can be usually understood in terms of the IT system. However, often the modeler wants to specify further activity explicitly. This further activity can be human activity or automatic activity, i.e., machine-based activity that is hard to grasp in terms of human computer interaction. Basically, we discuss the specification of auxiliary functionality in terms of human activity in this section for ease of understanding.

One ad-hoc manner to describe the way people work is in natural language. The description can be given structure by an underlying workflow chart specification. For example, it would be possible to decompose an overall workflow chart into pieces and sub workflows that naturally correspond to certain human task that are amenable to a meaningful description in natural language. The auxiliary human activity based business process can also be described with a combination of business process modeling language plus comments in natural language as it is best practice in many successful business process documentation projects. The several modeling elements can then be set into relation with the specification elements of the corresponding workflow definition. We call such an approach a tracking approach, because it is similar to the successful usage of tracking tools in tracking requirements against code in today's software engineering projects.

This systematic structuring of an auxiliary specification along the structure of a workflow chart specification can even be generalized to hierarchies built on top of a basic workflow definition. We want to outline a different approach in this section. We have a look at the direct mixture of workflow charts with auxiliary elements and the difficulties in defining possible semantic interpretations. We only look at flat diagrams. This means that all the auxiliary elements are basic elements in the sense of model hierarchies. The flat diagrams discussed in this section can be made subject of building hierarchies with all its aspects as discussed in Chapter 5.

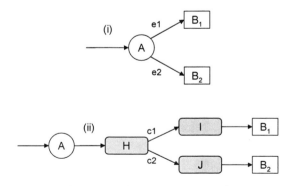

Fig. 9.10. Inserting auxiliary specification between client pages and immediate server actions.

Please have a look at the simple example in Fig. 9.10. Diagram (i) in Fig. 9.10 is a pure workflow chart, whereas diagram (ii) in Fig. 9.10 enriches diagram (i) with further modeling elements that represent human activity. The workflow chart elements are depicted and used as introduced and described in Sect. 9.2 – see Fig. 9.4. The additional activities are grayed in diagram (ii). Diagram (i) expresses that the user sees a client page A that offers two forms B_1 and B_2 as immediate interaction options. In addition to this diagram (ii) is meant to express that the user has to perform some human tasks before he is allowed to submit one of the forms B_1 or B_2. Therefore the business process model given by the activities H, I, J, the connecting edges and the flow conditions c_1 and c_2 should be compatible with the notion of workflow definition.

The problem is to elaborate an appropriate notion of compatibility. If the two flow conditions c_1 and c_2 represent a complete and unique selection the given business process model implicitly specifies how the user selects between the two interaction options given by the two forms. If the two flow conditions c_1 and c_2 represent a multiply choice it is an option to classify the business process model as incompatible with the workflow definition and therefore to classify the resulting whole diagram (ii) as invalid. It is also an option to dynamically interpret the user's selection of the form as independent from the evaluation of the flow conditions in those cases in which none of them or both of them evaluate to true. Questions arise. Should the user wait for completion of both of the activities I and J in the case that both of the flow conditions evaluate to true? Does the evaluation of both of the flow conditions to false represent an early exit from the overall business process and workflow?

Furthermore, it might be requested that the flow conditions c_1 and c_2 are somehow compatible with the enabling conditions e_1 and e_2 expressed in diagram (i). The enabling conditions are evaluated immediately before the client page A is shown to the user. A form is only offered to the user if the corresponding enabling condition has been evaluated to true. The enabling conditions e_1 and e_2 are not yet represented in diagram (ii). The question is whether they can appropriately represented as part of the flow conditions c_1 and c_2. Anyhow, Fig. 9.12 proposes a solution on how to represent the enabling conditions.

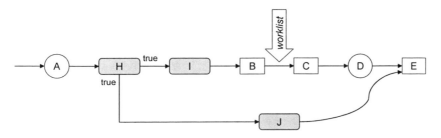

Fig. 9.11. Synchronizing auxiliary activity against form submission.

Figure 9.11 shows a more complex example. After the client page A is shown to the user he starts with activity H. After he has finished activity H he starts with activities I and J in parallel. This parallelism might be a form of quasi-parallelism or even true parallelism, in particular, if the worker of activity J is different from the worker on activity I. After the form B has been submitted it is possible that the worklist reveals even more parallelism to the user. The edge of the human activity J to the form E can be implicitly understood as synchronizing against the submission of the form E via page D represented by the edge between the client page D and the form E. It appears natural to require that it should not be possible to submit a form that does not occur as part of a client page. With this synchronizing interpretation of edges leading from a human activity to a form it is possible to repaint diagram (ii) in Fig 9.10 as the diagram in Fig 9.12.

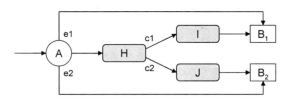

Fig. 9.12. Alternative insertion of auxiliary specification between client pages and immediate server actions.

Similarly, diagrams can be used to express the synchronization of human tasks against the selection of a task from a worklist. Figure 9.13 shows an example for this. The diagram could be interpreted as follows. After completion of activity K the user should proceed with the selection of task C_1 from the worklist and after completion of activity L the user should proceed with the selection of task C_2 from the worklist. Similar questions with respect to the possible semantics arise for the diagram in Fig. 9.13 as has arisen for diagram (ii) in Fig. 9.10. For example, it is possible to interpret the firing of the edge from activity K to task C_1 as an additional activation condition to the activation condition a_1.

The semantics of the combined business process models and workflow charts remains vague in this section. The purpose of the section was to give an impression of the opportunities to elaborate workflow charts further to deal with further phenomena. It also shows that the semantics of the workflow charts form a robust backbone for the understanding of workflow intensive systems.

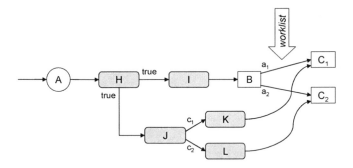

Fig. 9.13. Synchronizing auxiliary activity against worklist selection.

9.4 On Closing the Gaps in Business Process Technology

We have motivated the need for more flexible business process technology. Flexible business process management is hindered by the gaps and tension between today's tools for business process management that can be divided into tools for business process modeling, workflow execution and application programming as indicated in Fig. 1.1. Business process modeling exists in its own right. Workflow definition and application programming together form the level of business process automation. Future business process management platforms will overcome these gaps and tension – see Fig. 9.14. Now is the time to understand the gaps and tensions in business process technologies and to recommend concrete improvements.

In Sect. 9.2 we have proposed a typed workflow definition language, the workflow chart. The workflow chart can be exploited as a domain-specific programming language [349] for workflows. It integrates the definition of workflows with the programming of user dialogues from the outset and in this way overcomes the unnatural separation of workflows and dialogues in today's business process management suites. An integrated development environment based on workflow charts will open up the full design space of dialogues in a workflow system and will significantly improve such important software engineering principles as maintainability, testability [104] and reuse of program artifacts. A prototypical version of such integrated development environment is currently being implemented.

The typed approach can be extended from workflow definitions to business processes in general. Section 5 gives an idea about the options in designing such typed business processes, which are actually leveled data flow diagrams. An elaborated approach of typed business processes can help in mitigating the gap between business process modeling and business process automation. However, a conceptual gap between business process modeling and business process automation, which we have characterized in Sect. 4 and 6, will always remain, because there is a practical need for the informality of business process languages. Nevertheless, with or without a strictly typed approach the gap between modeling and automation can be mitigated significantly. Tracking is the key. Tracking is the systematic establishment of meaningful associations between entities of several kinds of software artifacts, which in this case are on the one hand business process models and workflow definitions and programs on the other hand. Tracking is also about the maintenance and targeted evaluation of this extra information.

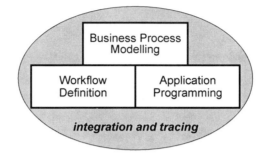

Fig. 9.14. Business process platform mitigating gaps and tensions between business process modeling, workflow control and dialogue control.

The design of an integrated business process platform from scratch is the best means of realizing tracking [12]. Another way of achieving of such tool integration is by realizing a hub-and-spoke tool architecture with a more or less powerful tracking tool as a man-in-the-middle. This alternative of an explicit tracking tool is justified. The clear advantage is a wider, i.e., open usage, because the tracking tool can be designed for the integration of several tools, in particular already existing ones. With explicit tracking tools, software engineers have the opportunity to compose a tool suite that fits their concrete needs best. The currently promising approach for the design of a powerful tracking tool is the multi-dimensional, view based modeling approach called orthographic modeling [11, 9, 10].

Designing a business process platform from scratch obviously has the advantage of unrestricted possibilities in shaping it. For example, it could be oriented strictly towards a typed approach to business processes. We are convinced that in the future we will see both improved fully integrated business process platforms, conceptually well-understood explicit tracking tools as well as a combination of both.

References

1. W.M.P. van der Aalst, A.P. Barros, A.H.M. ter Hofstede, and B. Kiepuszewski. Advanced Workflow Patterns. In: Proceedings of CoopIS 2000 – 7th International Conference on Cooperative Information Systems, Lecture Notes in Computer Science 1901, Springer, 2000.
2. J.R. Abrial. Data Semantics. In: Data Base Management. North-Holland, Amsterdam, 1974, pp. 1–59.
3. L. Aceto, K.G. Larsen. An Introduction to Milner's CCS. BRICS, Department of Computer Science, Aalborg University, March 2005.
4. A. Agrawal et. al. WS-BPEL Extension for People (BPEL4People), version 1.0, Active Endpoints, Adobe Systems, BEA Systems, IBM, Oracle, SAP, June 2007.
5. R. Agrawal et.al. The Claremont Report on Database Research, May 2008.
6. Aristotle. Metaphysics.
7. C. Atkinson, O.Hummel. Supporting Agile Reuse Through Extreme Harvesting. In: Proceedings of XP 2007 – the 8th International Conference on Agile Processes in Software Engineering and Extreme Programming, Lecture Notes in Computer Science 4536. Springer, 2007.
8. C. Atkinson, P. Bostan, O. Hummel, D. Stoll. A Practical Approach to Web Service Discovery and Retrieval. In: Proceedings of ICWS 2007 – the 5th IEEE International Conference on Web Services. IEEE Press, 2007.
9. C. Atkinson, D. Brenner, P. Bostan, G. Falcone, M. Gutheil, O. Hummel M. ,Juhasz and D. Stoll. Modeling Components and Component-Based Systems in KobrA. In (A. Rausch, R. Reussner, R. Mirandola, F. Plasil, Eds.): The Common Component Modeling Example – Comparing Software Component Models, Lecture Notes in Computer Science 5153, Springer, 2008.
10. C. Atkinson, D. Stoll and P. Bostan. Supporting View-Based Development through Orthographic Software Modeling. In: Proceedings of ENASE 2009 – the 4th International Conference on Evaluation on Novel Approaches to Software Engineering, 2009.
11. C. Atkinson and D. Stoll. Orthographic Modelling Environment. In: Proceedings of FASE'08 – Fundamental Approaches to Software Engineering, Lecture Notes in Computer Science 4961, Springer, 2008.

12. D. Auer, D. Draheim, V. Geist. Extending BPMN with Submit/Response-Style User Interaction Modeling. In: Proceedings of CEC'09 - the 11th IEEE Conference on Commerce and Enterprise Computing, 2009

13. E. Babbie. The Practice of Social Research, 8th edition. International Thomson Publishing Servicesm, August 1997.

14. C. Babcock. Data, Data, Everywhere. Information Week, January 2006.

15. S. Balbo, D. Draheim, C. Lutteroth, and G. Weber. Appropriateness of User Interfaces to Tasks. In (Alan Dix, Anke Dittmar, Eds.): Proceedings of TA-MODIA 2005 - 4th International Workshop on Task Models and Diagrams for User Interface Design – For Work and Beyond, ACM Press, 2005.

16. S.K. Banerjee. Methodolgy for Integrated Manufacturing and Control System Design. In A. Artiba and S.E. Elmaghraby (Editors): The Planning and Scheduling of Production Systems, Methodologies and Applications, Chapman & Hall, 1997.

17. M. Barad. Decomposing timed Petri nets of open queueing networks. In: Journal of the Operational Research Society, vol. 45, no. 12, 1994, pp. 1385-1397.

18. M. Barad. Timed Petri Nets as a Verification Tool. In (D.J. Medeiros, E.F. Watson, J.S. Carson, M.S. Manivannan, Editors): Proceedings of WSC'98 – Winter Simulation Conference, IEEE Computer Society Press, pp. 547–554.

19. C.I. Barnard. The Functions of the Executive. Harvard University Press, 1938.

20. K. Beck. Extreme Programming Explained – Embrace Change. Addison-Wesley, 2000.

21. S. Beer. Fanfare for Effective Management – Cybernetic Praxis in Government. The 3rd Richard Goodman Memorial Lecture, Delivered at Brighton Polytechnic, Moulsecoomb, Brighton, 14th February 1973.

22. S. Beer. The Heart of Enterprise – Companion Volume to: The Brain of the Firm. John Wiley & Sons, 1994.

23. S. Beer. The Brain of the Firm – Companion Volume to:The Heart of Enterprise. John Wiley & Sons, 1994.

24. M. Beisiegel et.al. Service Component Architecture – Building Systems using a Service Oriented Architecture. Joint Whitepaper, version 0.9. BEA, IBM, Interface21, IONA, Oracle, SAP, Siebel, Sybase, November 2005.

25. M. Beisiegel et.al. ASCA Policy Framework, SCA Version 1.00. BEA, Cape Clear, IBM, Interface21, IONA, Oracle, Primeton, Progress, Red Hat, Rogue Wave, SAP, Siemens, Software AG, Sun, Sybase, TIBCO, March 2007.

26. D. Bell. The Coming of Post-Industrial Society. Basic Books, 1976.

27. H.D. Benington. Production of Large Computer Programs. In: Proceedings of the ONR Symposium on Advanced Programming Methods for Digital Computers, June 1956.

28. P.A. Bernstein. Middleware: a Model for Distributed System Services. Communications of the ACM, vol. 39, no. 2, February 1996, pp. 86–98.

29. P.A. Bernstein, E. Newcomer. Principles of Transaction Processing – For the Systems Professional. Morgan Kaufmann, 1997.

30. P. Bernstein, M. Brodie, S. Ceri, D. DeWitt, M. Franklin, H. Garcia-Molina, J. Gray, J. Held, J. Hellerstein, H. V. Jagadish, M. Lesk, D. Maier, J. Naughton, H. Pirahesh, M. Stonebraker, J. Ullman. The Asilomar Report on Database Research. ACM SIGMOD Record, vol. 27, no. 4, December 1998.

31. D.H. Besterfield. Total Quality Management. Prentice Hall, 1995.

32. L. Bird. Selecting the Tools to Support the Process. In (P. Barnes, A. Hiles; Editors): The Definitive Handbook of Business Continuity Management. Wiley, 2007, pp. 263–279.

33. M.J. Blechar. Magic Quadrant for Business Process Analysis Tools. Gartner RAS Core Research Note G00148777. Gartner, June 2007.

34. J. Bloem, M. van Doorn, P. Mittal. Making IT Governance Work in a Sarbanes-Oxley World. John Wiley & Sons, 2006.

35. B.W. Boehm. A Spiral Model of Software Development and Enhancement. IEEE Computer, vol. 21, no. 5, pp.61–72, 1988.

36. B. Boehm, H.D. Rombach, M.V. Zelkowitz. Foundations of Empirical Software Engineering: The Legacy of Victor R. Basili. Springer, 2005.

37. C. Böhm, G. Jacopini. Flow Diagrams, Turing Machines and Languages With Only Two Formation Rules. Communications of the ACM, vol. 3, no. 5, 1966.

38. K. A. Bohrer. Architecture of the San Francisco Frameworks. IBM Systems Jouranl, vol. 37, no. 2, Industrial Business Machines, 1998.

39. K. Bohrer, V. Johnson, A. Nilsson, B. Rubin. Business Process Components for Distributed Object Applications. Communications of the ACM, vol. 41, no. 6, June 1998, pp. 43–48.

40. B. Bordbar, D. Draheim, M. Horn, I. Schulz, and G. Weber. Integrated Model-Based Software Development, Data Access and Data Migration. In: Proceedings of MoDELS/UML 2005 - ACM/IEEE 8th International Conference on Model Driven Engineering Languages and Systems, Lecture Notes in Computer Science 3713, Springer, October 2005.

41. D. Box et al. Simple Object Access Protocol (SOAP) 1.1 – W3C Note, May 2000.

42. E. Brinksma, H. Hermanns. Process Algebra and Markov Chains. In: Lectures Notes of the School on Formal Methods and Performance Analysis 2000, Lecture Notes in Computer Science 2090, Springer 2001.

43. British Standards Institution. Business Continuity Management – Part 1: Code of Practice. British Standard BS 25999-1:2006, BSI Group, 2006.

44. S. Brobst. The Future of Data Warehousing. DEXA Keynote at DaWaK'07 – the 9th International Conference on Data Warehousing and Knowledge Discovery, September 2007.

45. F.P. Brooks. The Mythical Man-month – Essays on Software Engineering. Addison-Wesley, 1975.

46. F. P. Brooks. No Silver Bullet – Essence and Accidents of Software Engineering. IEEE Computer, vol.20, no.4, April 1987.

47. J. Browne, J. Harhen, J. Shivnan. Production Management Systems. Addison-Wesley, 1996.

48. A.W. Brown. CASE in the 21st Century – Challenges Facing Existing Case Vendors. In: Proceedings of STEP'97 – the 8th International Workshop on Software Technology and Enginering Practice. IEEE Press, 1997.

49. A.W. Brown, S. Johnston, K. Kelly. Using Service-Oriented Architecture and Component-Based Development to Build Web Service Applications. Santa Clara, CA: Rational Software Corporation, 2002.

50. P. Buneman, S. Khanna, W.-C. Tan. Why and Where: A Characterization of Data Provenance. In: Proceedings of ICDT 2001 – the 8th International Conference on Database Theory, Lecture Notes in Computer Science 1973 Springer 2001.

51. J. N. Buxton, B. Randell. Software Engineering – Report on a Conference Sponsored by the NATO Science Committee, Rome, October 1969. NATO Science Committee, April 1970.
52. F. Buytendijk, D. Flint. How BAM Can Turn a Business Into a Real-Time Enterprise. Technical Report AV-15-4650. Gartner Research, March 2002.
53. R.C. Camp. Business Process Benchmarking – Finding and Implementing Best Practices. Irwin Professional Publishing, 1995.
54. D. Cannon, D. Wheeldon. Service Operation – ITIL Version 3. Stationery Office Books, May 2007.
55. G. Case. Continual Service Improvement – ITIL Version 3. Stationery Office Books, May 2007.
56. Central Computer and Telecommunications Agency. IT Infrastructure Library – Service Support. Renouf, 2000.
57. P.P.-S. Chen. The Entity-Relationship Model – Toward a Unified View of Data. ACM Transactions on Database Systems, vol.1, no.1, pp.9–36, March 1976.
58. L. Chow, C. Medley, C. Richardson. BPM and Service-Oriented Archtiecture Teamed Togehter: A Pathway to Success for an Agile Government. In (L. Fischer, Editor): 2007 BPM and Workflow Handbook. Future Strategies, 2007, pp. 33–54.
59. A. Church. The Calculi of Lambda-Conversion. Annals of Mathematics Studies. Princeton University Press, 1944.
60. M. Colan. Service-Oriented Architecture expands the Vision of Web Services – Characteristics of Service-Oriented Architecture. IBM Corporation, April 2004.
61. B.P. Collins, J.E. Nicholls, I.H. Sørensen. Introducing Formal Methods: the CICS experience with Z. Technical Report TR 12.2777, IBM Hursley Park, December 1990.
62. J. Coplien, D. Schmidt. Pattern Languages of Program Design. Addison-Wesley, 1995.
63. B.Cornu, A.Karpati, A.Strehler, J.Andersen, I.Cortelazzo, D.Draheim, R.Messner, G.Rößling, S.de Vries. Report of the Working Group on Collaborative Learning at SECIII. In (Tom J. van Weert and Robert K. Munro, Editors): Informatics and the Digital Society. Kluwer Academic Publishers, January 2003.
64. J.M. Correia. What BAM Looks Like Now and in the Future. ID Number LE-16-0431. Gartner, April 2002.
65. R. J. Creasy. The Origin of the VM/370 Time-Sharing System. IBM Journal of Research and Development, vol. 25, no. 5, September 1981, pp. 483-490.
66. A.F. Cutting-Decelle, J.J. Michel. ISO 15531 MANDATE: A Standadized Data Model for Manufacturing Management. In International Journal of Computer Applications in Technology, vol. 18., nos 1-4, 2003.
67. K. Czarnecki, U. Eisenecker. Generative Programming – Methods, Tools, and Applications. Addison-Wesley, 2000.
68. T. DeMarco. Structured Analysis and System Specification. Prentice Hall, 1979.
69. W. E. Deming. Out of the Crisis. MIT, Center for Advanced Educational Services, 1982.
70. F. DeRemer, H. Kron. Programming-in-the-Large Versus Programming-in-the-Small. In: Proceedings of the International Conference on Reliable Software. ACM Press, 1975, pp. 114 – 121.

71. P. Derler, R. Weinreich. Models and Tools for SOA Governance. In (D. Draheim, G. Weber, Editors): Proceedings of TEAA 2006 – International Conference on Trends in Enterprise Application Architecture, Lecture Notes in Computer Science 4473, Springer, 2006.

72. J. Desel, W. Reisig. Place/Transition Petri Nets. Lecture Notes in Computer Science 1491, Springer, 1998, pp. 122–173.

73. Deutsches Institut für Normung. Deutsche Industrienorm DIN 66001. Sinnbilder für Datenfluß und Programmablaufpläne. DIN, September 1966.

74. M.E. Dickover. Principles of Coupling and Cohesion for Use in the Practice of SADT. Technical Publication 039. SofTech Inc., 1976.

75. M.E. Dickover, C.L. McGowan, D.T. Ross. Software design using SADT. In: Proceedings of the 1977 Annual Conference. ACM Press, 1977, pp. 125–133.

76. E.W. Dijkstra. Go To Statement Considered Harmful. Communications of the ACM, vol. 11, no. 3, pp.147–148, 1968.

77. N. Dixon. The Organizational Learning Cycle. McGraw-Hill, 1994.

78. B. Dragovic et.al. Xen and the Art of Virtualization. In: Proceedings of SOSP 2003 – the 19th ACM Symposium on Operating Systems Principles. ACM Press, 2003.

79. D. Draheim and G. Weber. Strongly Typed Server Pages. In: Proceedings of The Fifth Workshop on Next Generation Information Technologies and Systems, LNCS 2382, Springer, June 2002.

80. D. Draheim. Learning Software Engineering with EASE. In (Tom J. van Weert and Robert K. Munro, Editors): Informatics and the Digital Society. Kluwer Academic Publishers, January 2003.

81. D. Draheim. A CSCW and Project Management Tool for Learning Software Engineering. In: Proceedings of FIE 2003 - Frontiers in Education: Engineering as a Human Endeavor. IEEE Press, 2003.

82. D. Draheim and Gerald Weber. Storyboarding Form-Based Interfaces. In: Proceedings of INTERACT 2003 - Ninth IFIP TC13 International Conference on Human-Computer Interaction. IOS Press, 2003.

83. D. Draheim, G. Weber. Modeling Submit/Response Style Systems with Form Charts and Dialogue Constraints. In: Proceedings of the Workshop on Human Computer Interface for Semantic Web and Web Applications, LNCS 2889. Springer, 2003.

84. D. Draheim and L. Pekacki. Process-Centric Analytical Processing of Version Control Data. In: Proceedings of IWPSE 2003 - International Workshop on Principles of Software Evolution. IEEE Press, 2003.

85. D. Draheim, E. Fehr and G. Weber. Improving the Web Presentation Layer Architecture. In (X. Zhou, Y. Zhang, M.E. Orlowska, Editors): Web Technologies and Applications, LNCS 2642. Springer, 2003.

86. D. Draheim, C. Lutteroth and G. Weber. Factory: Statically Type-Safe Integration of Genericity and Reflection. In: Proceedings of the 4th International Conference on Software Engineering, Artificial Intelligence, Networking, and Parallel/Distributed Computing. ACIS, 2003.

87. D. Draheim, E. Fehr and G. Weber. JSPick - A Server Pages Design Recovery Tool. In: Proceedings of CSMR 2003 - 7th European Conference on Software Maintenance and Reengineering. IEEE Press, 2003.

88. D. Draheim, G. Weber. Co-Knowledge Acquisition of Software Organizations and Academia. In: Proceedings of LSO 2004 – The 6th International Workshop

278   References

on Learning Software Organ3tions. Lecture Notes in Computer Science 3096. Springer, June 2004.

89. D. Draheim, G. Weber. Form-Oriented Analysis – A New Methodology to Model Form-Based Applications. Springer, October 2004.

90. D. Draheim, M. Horn, I. Schulz. The Schema Evolution and Data Migration Framework of the Environmental Mass Database IMIS. In: Proceedings of SSDBM 2004 - 16th International Conference on Scientific and Statistical Database Management. IEEE Press, 2004.

91. D. Draheim and G. Weber. Specification and Generation of Model 2 Web Interfaces. In (M. Masoodian, S. Jones, B. Rogers, Eds.): Computer Human Interaction. LNCS 3101, Springer, 2004.

92. D. Draheim, C. Lutteroth and G. Weber. Generator Code Opaque Recovery of Form-Oriented Web Site Models. In: Proceedings of WCRE 2004 - The 11th IEEE Working Conference on Reverse Engineering. IEEE Press, 2004.

93. D. Draheim. Book Review: Frank Soltis, Fortress Rochester – The Inside Story of the IBM iSeries. In: IEEE Annals of the History of Computing, vol. 27, no. 4, IEEE Press, October 2005.

94. D. Draheim. Description of the ER2005 Tutorial 7: Modeling Enterprise Applications. In (Jacky Akoka et.al., Eds.): Perspectives in Conceptual Modeling, LNCS 3770, Springer, 2005.

95. D. Draheim, G. Weber. Modelling Form-Based Interfaces with Bipartite State Machines. Journal Interacting with Computers, vol. 17, no. 2. Elsevier, 2005, pp. 207-228.

96. D. Draheim, C. Lutteroth and G. Weber. Robust Content Creation with Form-Oriented User Interfaces. In: Proceedings of CHINZ 2005 - 6th International Conference of the ACM's Special Interest Group on Computer-Human Interaction, ACM International Conference Proceeding Series, vol. 94, ACM Press, 2005.

97. D. Draheim, C. Lutteroth and G. Weber. A Source Code Independent Reverse Engineering Tool for Dynamic Web Sites. In: Proceedings of CSMR 2005 - 9th European Conference on Software Maintenance and Reengineering. IEEE Press, March 2005.

98. D. Draheim, C. Lutteroth and G. Weber. A Type System for Reflective Program Generators. In: Proceedings of GPCE 2005 - Generative Programming and Component Engineering, LNCS 3676, Springer, 2005.

99. D. Draheim, C. Lutteroth and G. Weber. Generative Programming for C#. ACM SIGPLAN Notices, vol. 40, no. 8., ACM Press, August 2005.

100. D. Draheim, C. Lutteroth and G. Weber. Integrating Code Generators into the C# Language. In: Proceedings of ICITA 2005 - The 3rd International Conference on Information Technology and Applications. IEEE Press, 2005.

101. D. Draheim, C. Lutteroth, G. Weber. Finite State History Modeling and its Precise UML-Based, Semantics. In: Advances in Conceptual Modeling - Theory and Practice. LNCS 4231, Springer, November 2006.

102. D. Draheim, G. Weber. ER 2006 Tutorial: Conceptual Modeling for Emerging Web Application Technologies. In: Advances in Conceptual Modeling - Theory and Practice. LNCS 4231, Springer, November 2006.

103. D. Draheim, G. Weber (Editors). Trends in Enterprise Application Architecture, LNCS 3888, Springer, March 2006.

104. D. Draheim, J. Grundy, J. Hosking, C. Lutteroth, G. Weber. Realistic Load Testing of Web Applications. In: Proceedings of CSMR 2006 - 10th European Conference on Software Maintenance and Reengineering. IEEE Press, March 2006.

105. D. Draheim, C. Lutteroth, G. Weber. Graphical User Interfaces as Documents. In: Proceedings of CHINZ 2006 - 7th International Conference of the ACM's Special Interest Group on Computer-Human Interaction, ACM International Conference Proceeding Series, ACM Press, July 2006.

106. D. Draheim, P. Thiemann, G. Weber. A Spreadsheet Client for Web Applications. In Proceedings of NGITS 2006 - The Sixt Workshop on Next Generation Information Technologies and Systems, LNCS, Springer, July 2006.

107. D. Draheim, G. Weber. The Core NSP Type System. In: Proceedings of WMR 2006 – Workshop on Web Maintenance and Reengineering, CEUR Workshop Proceedings, 2006, to appear.

108. D. Draheim, G. Weber (Editors). Post-Proceedings of the 2nd International Conference on Trends in Enterprise Application Architecture, Springer LNCS, June 2007.

109. D. Draheim. Plenary Talk: Towards Seamless Business Process and Dialogue Specification. In: Proceedings of SEKE'2007 – the 19th International Conference on Software Engineering & Knowledge Engineering. Knowledge Systems Institute Graduate School, ISBN 1-891706-20-9, July 2007.

110. D. Draheim, T. Koptezky. Workflow Management and Service-Oriented Architecture. In: Proceedings of SEKE 2007 - The 19th International Conference on Software Engineering and Knowledge Engineering. July, 2007.

111. D. Draheim. Possible Objectives of the RIESCA Project – Kind of Protocol on the RIESCA Kick-Off Workshop, 17th and 18th June 2008, Espoo.

112. D. Draheim, C. Nathschläger. A Context-Oriented Synchronization Approach. Electronic Proceedings of the 2nd International Workshop in Personalized Access, Profile Management, and Context Awarness: Databases (PersDB 2008) in Conjunction with the 34th VLDB Confercence, pages 20-27, 2008.

113. D. Draheim. Frontiers of Structured Business Process Modeling. In (A. Hameurlain, J. Küng, R. Wagner): Transactions on Large-Scale Data- and Knowledge-Centered Systems I, Springer, 2009.

114. D. Draheim, O. Mangisengi. Integrated Business and Production Process Warehousing. In (D. Taniar, Editor): Progressive Methods in Data Warehousing and Business Intelligence - Concepts and Competitive Analytics. IGI Global publication, 2009.

115. D. Draheim, M. Himsl, D. Jabornig, J. Küng, W. Leithner, P. Regner, T. Wiesinger. Concept and Pragmatics of an Intuitive Visualization-Oriented Metamodeling Tool. In: Journal of Visual Languages and Computing, vol. 21, no. 4, Elsevier, August, 2010.

116. N. Drakos. Magic Quadrant for Team Collaboration and Social Software. Gartner RAS Core Research Note G00151493. Gartner, October 2007.

117. H. Dresner. Business Activity Monitoring: New Age BI?, Gartner Research LE-15-8377, April 2002.

118. M.A. Emmelhainz. EDI: A Total Management Guide. Van Nostrand Reinhold, 1993.

119. R. Eshuis, R. Wieringa. A Formal Semantics for UML Activity Diagrams – Formalising Workflow Models. Technical Report CTIT-01-04, University of Twente, Department of Computer Science, 2001.

120. T. Erl. SOA: Principles of Service Design. Prentice Hall, July 2007.

121. A.K. Erlang. Telefon-Ventetider – Et Stykke Sandsynlighedsregning. Matematisk Tidsskrift, 1920.

122. J. Evdemon, D. Jordan (Editors). Web Services Business Process Execution Language Version 2.0. OASIS standard wsbpel-v2.0-OS, OASIS, April 2007.

123. ICT – Information and Communication Technologies – Work Program 2007-08, CORDIS – Community Research & Development Information Service, 2007.

124. H. Fayol. Administration industrielle et générale – prévoyance organisation-commandement- coordination- contrôle. Extrait de la Société de l'Industrie Minerale. Dunod, 1916.

125. J. Fenn. Understanding Gartner's Hype Cycles – 2007. Gartner Research ID Number G00144727, Gartner, July 2007.

126. J. Fenn, A. Linden. Gartner's Hype Cycle Special Report for 2005, Gartner Research ID Number G00130115, Gartner, August 2005.

127. M. Fleury, F. Reverbel. The JBoss Extensible Server. In (M. Endler, D. Schmidt, Editors): Proceedings of Middleware 2003 — ACM/IFIP/USENIX International Middleware Conference, Lecture Notes in Computer Science 2672, Springer, 2003.

128. J.N. Foster, G. Karvounarakis. Provenance and Data Synchronization. In: IEEE Data Engineering Bulletin, vol. 30, no. 4, IEEE Press, 2007.

129. J. Fourastié. La grande métamorphose du XXe siècle. Essais sur quelques problèmes de l'humanité d'aujourd'hui. Paris, Presses universitaires de France, 1961.

130. E. Gamma et al. Design Patterns – Elements of Reusable Object-Oriented Software. Addison-Wesley, 1995.

131. H. Garcia-Molina, K. Salem. Sagas. In: ACM SIGMOD Record, vol. 16 , no. 3, ACM Press, 1987.

132. D. Garlan, M. Shaw. An Introduction to Software Architecture. Technical Report CMU/SEI-94-TR-21, Carnegie Mellon University, Software Engineering Institute, January 1994.

133. Gartner. The Gartner Glossary of Information Technology Acronyms and Terms. Gartner, 2004.

134. D. Georgakopoulos, M. Hornick and A. Sheth. An Overview of Workflow Management: From Process Modeling to Workflow Automation Infrastructure. Distributed and Parallel Databases, 3, pp. 119-153, 1995.

135. W. Gillette. Managing Megaprojects: a Focused Approach. In: Software, vol. 13, no. 4, IEEE, 1996.

136. M. Govekar, R. Schulte. BAM Architecture: More Building Blocks Than You Think. Technical Report AV-15-5070. Gartner Research, April 2002.

137. R.P. Goldberg. Survey of Virtual Machine Research. IEEE Computer Magazine, vol. 7, no. 6, IEEE Press, 1974, pp. 34–45.

138. J. Gray. The Transaction Concept: Virtues and Limitations. In: Proceedings of VLDB'1981 – the 7th International Conference on Very Large Databases. IEEE Press, 1981.

139. J. Gray. An Approach to End-User Application Design. In (A. Whinston, Editor): Data Base Management and Applications. D. Reidel Publishing Company, 1981.

140. J. Gray. The Cost of Messages. Tandem Technical Report 88.4, Part No. 14661. Tandem Computers, March 1988.

141. J. Gray, A. Reuter. Transcation Processing: Concepts and Techniques. Morgan Kaufmann, 1993.
142. J. Gray et al. The Lowell Database Research Self Assessment, June 2003.
143. J. Grudin. Computer-Supported Cooperative Work: History and Focus. Computer, vol. 27, no. 5, IEEE Press, May 1994, pp. 19–26.
144. L. Gulick. Management is a Science. Academy of Management Journal, no. 1, 1965, pp. 7–13.
145. C.A. Gunter. Semantics of Programming Languages – Structures and Techniques. The MIT Press, 1992.
146. G. Guta, W. Schreiner, D. Draheim. A Lightweight MDSD Process Applied in Small Projects. In: Proceedings of SEAA 2009 – the 35th Euromicro Conference on Software Engineering and Advanced Applications, IEEE Computer Society 2009.
147. L. Haas. Building an Information Infrastructure for Enterprise Applications. In (D. Draheim, G. Weber, Editors): Trends in Enterprise Application Architecture, Lecture Notes in Computer Science 3888, January 2006.
148. P.J. Haas. Stochastic Petri Nets – Modelling, Stability, Simulation. Springer, 2002.
149. B. Hahn, C. Ballinger. Tpump in Continous Environment – Assembling the Teradata Active Data Warehous Series. Active Data Warehouse Center of Expertise, April 2001.
150. M. Hammer. Beyond Reengineering: How the Process-Centered Organization is Changing Our Work and Our Lives. HarperCollins Publishers, 1996.
151. M. Hammer, J. Champy. Reengineering the Corporation: A Manifesto for Business Revolution. HarperCollins Publishers, 1993.
152. M.J. Harry. The Vision of Six Sigma, 8 volumes. Tri Star Publishing, 1998.
153. M.J. Harry. Six Sigma: A Breakthrough Strategy for Profitability. In: Quality Progress, May 1998, pp. 60–64.
154. M.J. Harry, R. Schroeder. Six Sigma – The Breakthrough Managment Strategy Revolutionizing the World's Top Corporations. Doubleday, 1999.
155. R. Hayes, S. Wheelright. Restoring our Competitive Edge: Competing Through Manufacturing, John Wiley and Sons, 1984.
156. A. Hess, B. Humm, M. Voss, G. Engels. Structuring Software Cities A Multidimensional Approach. In: Proceedings of EDOC 2007 – the 11th IEEE International Enterprise Distributed Object Computing Conference. IEEE Press, 2007.
157. A. Hiles. The Definitive Handbook of Business Continuity Management, 2nd edition. Wiley, January, 2008.
158. J.B. Hill, M. Cantara, M. Kerremans, D.C. Plummer. Magic Quadrant for Business Process Management Suites, 2009. Gartner RAS Core Research Note G00164485. Gartner, February 2009.
159. M. Himsl, D. Jabornig, W. Leithner, D. Draheim, P. Regner, T. Wiesinger, J. Küng. An Iterative Process for Adaptive Meta- and Instance Modeling. In: Proceedings of DEXA 2007 – 18th International Conference on Database and Expert Systems Applications. Springer, September 2007.
160. M. Himsl, D. Jabornig, W. Leithner, D. Draheim, P. Regner, T. Wiesinger, J. Küng. Intuitive Visualization-Oriented Metamodeling. In: Proceedings of DEXA 2009 - 20th International Conference on Database and Expert Systems Applications. Springer, September 2007.

161. C.A.R. Hoare. An Axiomatic Basis for Computer Programming. Communications of the ACM, vol. 12, no. 10, pp. 576–580, 1969.
162. A. Holl, G. Valentin. Structured Business Process Modeling. In: Proceedings of IRIS 27 – Information Systems Research in Scandinavia, 2004.
163. K. Holley, J. Palistrant, S. Graham. Effective SOA Governance. IBM White Paper, IBM Corporation, March 2006.
164. D. Hollingworth. The Workflow Reference Model. Technical Report TC00-1003, Workflow Management Coalition, Lighthouse Point, Florida, USA, 1995.
165. R. Hull, R. King. Semantic database modeling: Survey, applications, and research issues. ACM Computing Surveys, vol. 19, no. 3, pp.201–260, 1987.
166. IBM Corporation. Smart SOA: Best Practices for Agile Innovation and Optimization. IBM White Paper. IBM Corporation, November 2007.
167. M. Imai. Kaizen: The Key to Japan's Competitive Success. McGraw-Hill, 1986.
168. Industrial Business Machines. On Demand Business Executive Guide. IBM Corporation, 2004.
169. Institute of Electrical and Electronics Engineers. IEEE Standard 830-1993, Recommended Practice for Software Requirements Specifications, Software Engineering Standards Committee of the IEEE Computer Society, New York, 1993.
170. The Instrumentation, Systems, and Automation Society. Enterprise-Control System Integration – Part 1: Models and Terminology. American National Standard ANSI/ISA-88.01-1995. ISA, October 1995.
171. The Instrumentation, Systems, and Automation Society. Batch Control – Part 1: Models and Terminology. American National Standard ANSI/ISA-95.00.01-2000. ISA, 2000.
172. The Instrumentation, Systems, and Automation Society. Enterprise-Control System Integration – Part 3: Activity Models of Manufacturing Operations Management. American National Standard ANSI/ISA-95.00.03-2005. ISA, 2005.
173. International Organization for Standardization. International Standard ISO 1028:1973. Information processing – Flowchart symbols. ISO, 1973.
174. International Organization for Standardization. International Standard ISO 9735. Electronic Data Interchange for Administration, Commerce and Transport (EDIFACT) – Application Level Syntax Rules. ISO, 1988.
175. International Organization for Standardization. International Standard ISO 9000-3:1991(E). Quality management and quality assurance standards – Part 3: Guidelines for the application of ISO 9001 to the developement, supply and maintenance of software. ISO, 1991.
176. International Organization for Standardization. International Standard ISO 9241-10. Ergonomic Requirements for Office Work with Visual Display Terminals (VDTs) – Part 10: Dialogue Principles. ISO, 1991.
177. International Organization for Standardization. International Standard ISO 9001:1994(E). Quality systems – Model for quality assurance in design, developement, production, installation and servicing. ISO, 1994.
178. International Organization for Standardization. International Standard ISO 9000:2005(E). Quality Management Systems – Guidelines for Performance Improvements. ISO, 2000.
179. International Organization for Standardization. International Standard CEI/IEC 62264-1:2003. Enterprise-Control System Integration – Part 1: Models and Terminology. ISO, March 2003.

180. ISO Technical Committee TC 184/SC 4. ISO 10303-1:1994 Industrial Automation Systems and Integration – Product Data Representation and Exchange – Part 1: Overview and Fundamental Principles. International Organization for Standardization, 2004.

181. International Organization for Standardization. International Standard ISO/IEC 20000-1:2005(E). Information Technology – Service Management – Part 1: Specification. International Organization for Standardization, 2005.

182. International Organization for Standardization. International Standard ISO 9000:2005(E). Quality Management Systems – Fundamentals and Vocabulary. ISO, 2005.

183. International Organization for Standardization. International Standard ISO/IEC 20000-2:2005(E). Information Technology – Service Management – Part 2: Code of practice. International Organization for Standardization, 2005.

184. ISO Technical Committee 184/SC 4. ISO 15531-32:2005. Industrial Automation Systems and Integration – Industrial Manufacturing Management Data: Resources Usage Management - Part 32: Conceptual Model for Resources Usage Management Data. International Organization for Standardization, 2005.

185. International Organization for Standardization. International Standard ISO 9241-110. Ergonomics for Human-System Interaction – Part 110: Dialogue Principles. ISO, 2006.

186. International Technical Support Organization. The Solution Designer's Guide to IBM On Demand Business Solutions, 3rd edition. Redbook SG24-6248-02, Industrial Business Machines, September 2005.

187. IT Governance Institute. COBIT 4.1 – Framework, Control Objectives, Management Guidelines, Maturity Models. ISBN 1-933284-72-2, IT Governance Institute, 2007.

188. IT Governance Institute. COBIT Quickstart, IT Governance Institute, 2007.

189. M. Iqbal, M. Nieves. Service Strategy – ITIL Version 3. Stationery Office Books, May 2007.

190. G. Jalloul. UML by Example. Cambridge University Press, 2004.

191. K. Jensen, L.M. Kristensen, L. Wells. Coloured Petri Nets and CPN Tools for Modelling and Validation of Concurrent Systems. International Journal on Software Tools for Technology Transfer, vol. 9, Springer, 2007, pp. 213–254.

192. J. Johnson, T.L. Roberts, W. Verplank, D.C. Smith, C. Irby, M. Beard, and K. Mackey. The Xerox Star: A Retrospective. Computer 22(9), pp. 11-26, 28-29, September 1989.

193. V. Johnson, B. Rubin. The San Francisco Project: Business Process Components and Infrastructure. ACM Computing Surveys, vol. 32, no. 1, March 2000.

194. R.S. Kaplan, D.P. Norton. The Balanced Scorecard: Translating Strategy into Action. Harvard Business School Press, 1996.

195. A. Kay. The Reactive Engine. PhD thesis, University of Utah, September 1969.

196. L.F. Kenney, D.C. Plummer. Magic Quadrant for Integrated SOA Governance Sets, Gartner RAS Core Research Note G00153858. Gartner, June 2008.

197. S. Kent and O. Patrascoiu. Kent Modelling Framework Version – Tutorial, Computing Laboratory, University of Kent, December 2002.

198. S. Khoshafian. Business Process Management for Six Sigma Projects. In (L. Fischer, Editor): 2006 BPM and Workflow Handbook. Future Strategies, 2006.

199. S. Khoshafian. BPM Center of Excellence Manifesto. In (L. Fischer, Editor): 2007 BPM and Workflow Handbook. Future Strategies, 2007, pp. 73–84.

284   References

200. B. Kirkerud. Object-oriented Programming with Simula. Addison-Wesley, 1989.
201. B. Kirwin. CIO Update: To Control TCO, It Must Be Measured and Managed. ID Number IGG-04162003-02. Gartner Group, April 2003.
202. J. Kletti. Manufacturing Execution System - MES. Springer, 2007.
203. M. Kloppmann, D. Koenig, F. Leymann, G. Pfau, A. Rickayzen, C.v. Riegen, P. Schmidt, I. Trickovic. WS-BPEL Extension for People – BPEL4People. IBM, SAP, 2005.
204. D.E. Knuth. Structured Programming with go to Statements. Computing Surveys, vol. 6, no. 4, Association of Computing Machinery, December 1974
205. D.E. Knuth, R.W. Floyd. Notes on Avoiding 'go to' Statements. Report No. 148, Computer Science Department, Stanford University, 1970.
206. D.E. Knuth, R.W. Floyd. Notes on Avoiding 'go to' Statements. In: Information Processing Letters, vol. 1, no. 1, February 1971, pp. 23–31, 177.
207. J. Kolbitsch, H. Maurer. The Transformation of the Web: How Emerging Communities Shape the Information we Consume. In: Journal of Universal Computer Science, vol. 12, no. 2, 2006, pp. 187–213.
208. S. Rao Kosaraju. Analysis of Structured Programs. In: Proceedings of the 5th Annual ACM Symposium on Theory of Computing, 1973, pp. 240–252.
209. P. Kruchten. The Rational Unified Process. Addison-Wesley, 1999.
210. S. Lacy, I. Macfarlane. Service Transition – ITIL Version 3. Stationery Office Books, May 2007.
211. P.J. Landin. The Next 700 Programming Languages. Communications of the ACM, vol. 9, no. 2, pp. 157–165, March 1966.
212. J. Lara , H. Vangheluwe. Using AToM as a Meta CASE Tool. In: Proceedings of the 4th International Conference on Enterprise Information Systems, Universidad de Castilla-La Mancha, Ciudad Real (Spain), April 2002.
213. Y. Lee, Y. Kim, H. Choi. Conflict Resolution of Data Synchronization in Mobile Environment. In: Proceedings of ICCSA 2004 – the 4th International Conference on Computational Science and Its Applications, Lecture Notes in Computer Science 3044, Springer, 2004.
214. C. Lettner, C. Hawel, T. Steinmaurer, D. Draheim. Complex Event Processing for Sensor-based Data Auditing. In: Proceedings of ICEIS'08 – the 10th International Conference on Enterprise Information Systems, 2008.
215. B. Leuf, W. Cunningham. The Wiki Way – Quick Collaboration on the Web. Addison-Wesley, April 2001.
216. K. Lewin. Resolving Social Conflicts : Selected Papers on Group Dynamics. Harper & Row, 1948.
217. G. Lewis, E. Morris, L. O'Brien, D. Smith, L. Wrage. SMART: The Service-Oriented Migration and Reuse Technique, Technical Note CMU/SEI-2005-TN-029, SEI – Software Engineering Institute, Carnegie Mellon University, September 2005.
218. F. Leymann, D. Roller. Business process management with FlowMark. Proceedings of IEEE Compcon, March 1994.
219. F. Leymann, D. Roller, and M.T. Schmidt. Web Services and Business Process Management. IBM Systems Journal 41, 2002.
220. B.J. Lheureux, P. Malinverno. Magic Quadrant for B2B Gateway Providers, Gartner RAS Core Research Note G00157460. Gartner, June 2008.

221. B. List, B. Korherr. A UML 2 Profile for Business Process Modelling. In: Perspectives in Conceptual Modeling – Proceedings of the ER'2005 Workshops. Lecture Notes in Computer Science 3770, Springer, 2005.

222. B. List, B. Korherr. An Evaluation of Conceptual Business Process Modelling Languages. In: Proceedings of the 2006 ACM Symposium on Applied Computing. ACM Press, 2006, pp. 1532–1539.

223. T.S. Kuhn. The Structure of Scientific Revolutions. University Of Chicago Press, December 1996.

224. Lotus Development Corporation. Domino Workflow – Automating Real-World Business Processes. White Paper. Lotus Development Corporation, 1999.

225. R. Luecke. Creating Teams with an Edge – The Complete Skill Set to Build Powerful and Influential Team. In: The Harvard Business Essentials Series. Harvard Business School Press, 2004.

226. C. Lutteroth. AP1 – A Platform for Model-based Software Engineering. In (D. Draheim, G. Weber, Eds.): Proceedings of TEAA 2006 - 2nd International Conference on Trends in Enterprise Application Architecture, Lecture Notes in Computer Science 4473, Springer, 2007.

227. C. Lutteroth. AP1 – A Platform for Model-based Software Engineering. PhD thesis, University of Auckland, March 2008.

228. J. Lyon. Design Considerations in Replicated Database Systems for Disaster Protection. In: Digest of Papers of COMPCON'88 – the 33rd IEEE Computer Society International Conference. IEEE Press,pp. 428–430.

229. F. Machlup. The Production and Distribution of Knowledge in the United States. Princeton University Press, 1962.

230. C.M. MacKenzie, K. Laskey, F. McCabe, P.F. Brown, R. Metz, B.A. Hamilton (Editors). Reference Model for Service Oriented Architecture 1.0, Committee Specification 1, document identifier soa-rm-cs, OASIS Open, August 2006.

231. Q.H. Mahmoud. Service-Oriented Architecture (SOA) and Web Services: The Road to Enterprise Application Integration (EAI). Sun Microsystems, April 2005.

232. D.E. Mahling, N. Craven and W.B. Croft. From office automation to intelligent workflow systems. IEEE Intelligent Systems 19(3), 41-47, 1995.

233. R. Maier, T. Hädrich, R. Peinl. Enterprise Knowledge Infrastructure. Springer, 2005.

234. Fredmund Malik. Managing Performing Living – Effective Management for a New Era. Campus, 2006.

235. P. Malinverno. Service-Oriented Architecture Craves Governance. ID Number G00135396, Gartner Research, January 2006.

236. O. Mangisengi, M. Pichler, D. Auer, D. Draheim, H. Rumetshofer. An Activity Warehouse Model Based on Business Activity Monitoring Requirements, In: Proceedings of ICEIS 2006 – International Conference on Enterprise Information Systems, June 2006.

237. M. McClellan. Applying Manufacturing Execution Systems. CRC Press, 1997.

238. D. McCoy. Business Activity Monitoring: Calm Before the Storm. ID Number LE-15-9727. Gartner Research, April 2002.

239. D. McCoy, Y. Natis. Service-Oriented Architecture: Mainstream Straight Ahaed. ID Number LE-19-7652. Gartner Research, April 2003.

240. D. McCracken, A. Newell. The ZOG Human Computer-Inferface System – A Renewal Proposal to the Office of Naval Research for the period 1st March

1983 to 1st October 1984, Renewal of Grant N00014-76-0874: ZOG: An Interactive Programming Environment Using a Graph-Structured, Rapid-Response Guidance System. Carnegie-Mellon University, May 1983.

241. M.D. McIlroy. Mass Produced Software Components. In (P. Naur, B. Randell, Editors): Software Engineering – Report on a Conference Sponsored by the NATO Science Committee, January 1969, pp. 138-150.

242. P. McJones (Editor). The 1995 SQL Reunion: People, Projects and Politics. SRC Technical Note 1997-018, Digital Systems Research Center, August 1997.

243. A. McNamara, M.A. Chishti. Business Integration Using State-Based Asynchronous Services. In (L. Fischer, Editor): 2006 BPM and Workflow Handbook. Future Strategies, 2006.

244. Manufacturing Enterprise Solutions Asssociation. MES Explained: A High Level Vision, White Paper no. 6. MESA International, September 1997.

245. D. Merriman. Total Economic Impact: Really Understanding the IT Cost/Benefit Equation. Giga Information Group, 2003.

246. MetaCase. Domain-Specific Modelling: 10 Times Faster Than UML. White Paper, MetaCase Consulting, Finland, January, 2001.

247. D. Miers, P. Harmon and C. Hall. The 2006 BPM suites report. Business Process Trends, 2006.

248. J. Miller, J. Mukerji. MDA Guide, Version 1.0.1, Object Management Group, 2003.

249. R. Milner. A Calculus of Communicating Systems. Lecture Notes in Computer Science 92, Springer, 1980.

250. R. Milner. Communication and Concurrency. Prentice Hall, 1989.

251. C. Moore, C. Teubner. Making Sense Of The Business Process Management Landscape. Forrester Research, May 2006.

252. R. Morel, D. Draheim, M. Pilloud, M. Farooq. Recommendations of the Working Group on Social Issues and Power Shifts at SECIII. In (T.J. van Weert and R.K. Munro, Editors): Informatics and the Digital Society. Kluwer Academic Publishers, January 2003.

253. P.M. Morse, G.E. Kimball. Methods of Operations Research. MIT Press, 1951.

254. National Institute of Standards and Technology. Integrated Definition for Functional Modeling (IDEF0), Draft Federal Information Processing Standards Publication 183. U.S. Department of Commerce, December 1993.

255. Y.V. Natis. Service-Oriented Architecture Scenario, Gartner Research ID Number AV-19-6751, Gartner, April 2003.

256. P. Naur, B. Randell (Editors). Software Engineering – Report on a Conference Sponsored by the NATO Science Committee, Garmisch, October 1968. NATO Science Committee, January 1969.

257. M. Nguyen, A. Tjoa. Zero-Latency Data Warehousing for Heterogeneous Data Sources and Continuous Data Streams, iiWAS'2003 - The 5th International Conference on Information Integrationand Web-based Applications Services, p. 55 - 64, 2003.

258. M. Nicolett, K.M. Kavanagh. Magic Quadrant for Security Information and Event Management. ID Number G00147559. Gartner, May 2007.

259. S.P. Nielsen, C. Easthope, P. Gosselink, K. Gutsze, J. Roele. Using Domino Workflow, IBM SG24-5963-00, IBM International Technical Support Organization, May 2000.

260. O. Nierstrasz, S. Gibbs, D. Tsichritzis. Component-oriented Software Development. Communications of the ACM, vol. 35, no. 9, September 1992.

261. D. Norton, M. Blechar, T. Jones. Magic Quadrant for Business Process Analysis Tools, 2010. Gartner RAS Core Research Note G00174515. Gartner, February 2010.

262. K. Nygaard, O.-J. Dahl. The Development of the SIMULA Languages. The 1st ACM SIGPLAN Conference on History of Programming Languages, pp.245–272. ACM Press, 1978.

263. Object Management Group. OMG Unified Modeling Language Specification, version 1.5, March 2003.

264. Object Management Group. Common Object Request Broker Architecture: Core Specification, version 3.0.3, formal/04-03-12, Object Management Group, March 2004.

265. Object Managament Group. Business Process Modeling Notation (BPMN) Specification, Final Adopted Specification, dtc/06-02-01, February 2006.

266. Object Managament Group. CORBA Component Model Specification, OMG Available Specification, version 4.0, formal/06-04-01 dtc/06-02-01, April 2006.

267. Office of Government Commerce. ICT Infrastructure Management. Bernan, 2002.

268. Office of Government Commerce. Official Introduction to the ITIL Service Lifecycle. Stationery Office Books, August 2007.

269. OPC Foundation. OPC Common 1.10 Specification, OPC Foundation, 2006.

270. Oracle. Adding Mobile Capability to an Enterprise Application With Oracle Database Lite. White Paper. Oracle, June 2007.

271. T. O'Reilly. What Is Web 2.0 – Design Patterns and Business Models for the Next Generation of Software. O'Reilly Media, September 2005.

272. N. Palmer. Workflow and BPM in 2007: Business Process Standards see a new Global Imperative. In (L. Fischer, Editor): 2007 BPM and Workflow Handbook. Future Strategies, 2007.

273. D. Park. Concurrency and Automata on Infinite Sequences. In: Proceedings of the 5th GI-Conference on Theoretical Computer Science, Lecture Notes in Computer Science 104, Springer, 1981, pp. 167–183.

274. M.C. Paulk. How ISO 9001 Compares with the CMM. IEEE Software, vol. 11, no. 1, pp. 74–83, January 1995.

275. M.C. Paulk, B. Curtis, M.B. Chrissis, C.V. Weber. Capability Maturity Model, Version 1.1. IEEE Software, vol. 10, no. 4, pp.18–27, 1993.

276. M.C. Paulk, C. Weber, S. Garcia, M.B. Chrissis, M. Bush. Key Practices of the Capability Maturity Model Version 1.1. Carnegie Mellon Software Engineering Institute, Technical Report CMU/SEI-93-TR-025, February 1993.

277. D.L. Parnas. A Technique for Software Module Specification with Examples. Communications of the ACM, vol. 15, no. 5, 1972, pp.330–336.

278. D.L. Parnas. On the Criteria To Be Used in Decomposing Systems into Modules. Commun. Communications of the ACM, vol. 15, no. 12, 1972, pp. 1053–1058.

279. D.L. Parnas. Software Aspects of Strategic Defense Systems. Software Engineering Notes, ACM Sigsoft, vol. 10, no. 5, ACM Press, 1985.

280. M. Pedler, J. Burgoyne, T. Boydell. The Learning Company: a Strategy for Sustainable Development. McGraw-Hill, 1991.

281. C.A. Petri. Kommunikation mit Automaten. Dissertation. Schriften des Rheinisch-Westfälischen Institutes für instrumentelle Mathematik an der Universität Bonn, 1962.

282. M. Pichler, H. Rumetshofer, W. Wahler. Agile Requirements Engineering for a Social Insurance for Occupational Risks Organization: A Case Study. In: Proceedings of RE'06 – 14th IEEE International Requirements Engineering Conference, IEEE Computer Society, pp. 246–251.

283. R. Pirinen, J. Rajamäki. Rescuing of Intelligence and Electronic Security Core Applications (RIESCA). Working Draft, Laurea University of Applied Sciences, June 2008.

284. R. Pirinen, J. Rajamäki, L. Aunimo. Rescuing of Intelligence and Electronic Security Core Applications (RIESCA). In: WSEAS Transactions on Systems, vol. 7, no. 10, October 2008.

285. G. Plotkin. LCF Considered a Programming Language. Theoretical Computer Science, vol. 5, 1977, pp. 223–255.

286. M. Pohlmann, M. Schönefeld. An Evolutionary Integration Approach using Dynamic CORBA in a typical Banking Environment. Case Studies Workshop of the 6th European Conference on Software Maintenance and Reengineering, March 2002.

287. K. Popper. Logik der Forschung, Springer, 1934.

288. K. Popper. The Logic of Scientific Discovery, Routledge Publishers, 1959.

289. M.E. Porter. Strategy and the Internet. Harvard Business Review, March, pp.63–78, 2001.

290. Plato. Cratylus.

291. Project Management Institute. PMBOK Guide – A Guide to the Project Management Body of Knowledge, 2000 Edition. Project Management Institute, 2000.

292. J. Pyke. BPM in Context: Now and in the Future. In (L. Fischer, Editor): 2007 BPM and Workflow Handbook. Future Strategies, 2007.

293. E.S. Raymond. The Cathedral and the Bazar. O'Reilly & Associates, 1999.

294. M. Reichert, P. Dadam. ADEPTflex-Supporting Dynamic Changes of Workflows Without Losing Control. Journal of Intelligent Information Systems, vol. 10, no. 2, Springer, 1998 pp. 93-12.

295. W. Reisig. Petri nets: an Introduction. Springer, 1985.

296. S. Rinderle, M. Reichert, P. Dadam, P. Flexible Support Of Team Processes By Adaptive Workflow Systems. Distributed and Parallel Databases, vol. 16, no. 1, Springer, 2004, pp. 91-116.

297. R. Revans. What is Action Learning ? In: The Journal of Management Development, vol. 1, no. 3., pp. 64-75. MCB Publications, 1982.

298. R. Revans. The ABC of Action Learning. Lemos & Crane, 1998.

299. I. Robinson (Editor). ACID Transaction Policy in SCA, SCA Version 1.00. BEA, Cape Clear, IBM, Interface21, IONA, Oracle, Primeton, Progress, Red Hat, Rogue Wave, SAP, Siemens, Software AG, Sun, Sybase, TIBCO, December 2007.

300. D.T. Ross. Structured Analysis (SA): A Language for Communicating Ideas. IEEE Transactions on Software Engineering, vol. 3, no. 1, pp. 16–34, January 1977.

301. D.T. Ross, J.W. Brackett. An Approach to Structured Analysis. Computer Decisions, vol. 8, no. 9, September 1976, pp. 40–44.

302. D.T. Ross, K.E. Schoman. Structured Analysis for Requirements Definition. IEEE Transactions on Software Engineering, vol.3, no. 1, pp. 6–15, January 1977.

303. W.W. Royce. Managing the Development of Large Software Systems. Proceedings of the IEEE WESCON Conference, August 1970, pp.1–9. IEEE, 1970.
304. B. S. Rubin, A. R. Christ, K. A. Bohrer. Java and the IBM San Francisco Project. IBM Systems Journal, vol. 37, no. 3, Industrial Business Machines, 1998.
305. C. Rudd, V. Lloyd. Service Design – ITIL Version 3. Stationery Office Books, May 2007.
306. J. Rumbaugh, M. Balaha, W. Premerlani, F. Eddy, W. Lorenson. Object-Oriented modeling and design. Prentice Hall, 1991.
307. N. Russell, A.H.M. ter Hofstede, W.M.P. van der Aalst, N. Mulyar. Workflow Control-Flow Patterns: A Revised View. BPM Center Report BPM-06-22, BPM Center, 2006.
308. N. Russell, W.M. P. van der Aalst, A.H.M. ter Hofstede, D. Edmond. Workflow Resource Patterns: Identification, Representation and Tool Support. In: Proceedings of CAiSE 2005 – the 17th Conference on Advanced Information Systems Engineering, Lecture Notes in Computer Science 3520, Springer, 2005, pp. 216-232.
309. A. Sankaramurthy. Oracle MES Solution for Discrete Manufacturers – Lower Your Costs and Improve Visbility Through a Single Integrated ERP/MES Solution. Oracle Corporation, November 2006.
310. SAP. Manufacturing Strategy: an Adaptive Perspective. SAP White Paper, SAP 2003.
311. A.-W. Scheer. Embedding Data Modelling in a General Architecture for Integrated Information Systems. In: Proceedings of ER'92 – the $11^{7}th$ International Conference on the Entity-Relationship Approach. Lecture Notes in Computer Science 645, 1992.
312. A.-W. Scheer. ARIS – Business Process Modeling. Springer, 1999.
313. A.-W. Scheer, O. Thomas, O. Adam. Process Modeling Using Event-Driven Process Chains. In (M. Dumas, W.M.P. van der Aalst, A.H.M. ter Hofstede, Editors): Process-Aware Information Systems – Bridging People and Software through Process Technology. John Wiley & Sons, 2005, pp. 119–146.
314. B. Scholten. Integrating ISA-88 and ISA-95. ISA, 2007.
315. R.W. Schulte. "Service Oriented" Architectures, Part 2. Gartner Research ID Number SPA-401-069. Gartner, 1996.
316. R.W. Schulte, Y.V. Natis. "Service Oriented" Architectures, Part 1. Gartner Research ID Number SPA-401-068. Gartner, 1996.
317. D.S. Scott. Data Types as Lattices. In: Society for Industrial and Applied Mathematics (SIAM) Journal on Computing, vol. 5, no. 3, pp. 522–587, 1976.
318. John R. Searle. Speech Acts: An Essay in the Philosophy of Language, Cambridge University Press, 1969.
319. W.A Shewhart. Economic Control of Quality of Manufactured Product. D. Van Nostrand Company, 1931.
320. W.A. Shewhart. Statistical Method from the Viewpoint of Quality Control. The Graduate School of Agriculture, 1939.
321. S. Shlaer, S.J. Mellor. Object-Oriented Systems Analysis: Modeling the World in Data. Pearson Education, Yourdon Press Computing Series, March 1988.
322. A. Silberschatz, M. Stonebraker, and J.D. Ullman. Database Research; Achievements and Opportunities into the 21st Century. SIGMOD Record 25(1): 52–63, 1996.

323. A. Smith. An Inquiry into the Nature And Causes of the Wealth of Nations, Book 1 – Of the Causes of Improvement in the Productive Powers of Labour, And of the Order according to which its Produce is Naturally Distributed among the Different Ranks of the People. The Glasgow Edition of the works of Adam Smith, vol. II, edited by R.H. Campbell and A.S. Skinner. Oxford University Press, 1976.

324. R. Soley. Model Driven Architecture. Object Management Group, November 2000.

325. F. Soltis. Fortress Rochester . The Inside Story of the IBM I series. 29th Street Press, July 2001.

326. C.W. Stern, M. S. Deimler. The Boston Consulting Group on Strategy: Classic Concepts and New Perspectives. Wiley & Sons, June 2006.

327. J.E. Stiglitz, The Roaring Nineties: A New History of the World's Most Prosperous Decade. September, 2003.

328. J.E. Stoy. Denotational Semantics: The Scott-Strachey Approach to Programming Language Theory. MIT Press, 1981.

329. C. Strachey and C.P. Wadsworth. Continuations: A Mathematical Semantics for Handling Full Jumps. In: Higher-Order and Symbolic Computation, vol. 13, no. 1–2, April 2000.

330. C. Strachey and C.P. Wadsworth. Continuations: A Mathematical Semantics for Handling Full Jumps. Technical Monograph PRG-11, Oxford University Computing Laboratory, Programming Research Group, Oxford, England, 1974.

331. J. Sugerman, G. Venkitachalam, B.-H. Lim. Virtualizing I/O Devices on VMware Workstation's Hosted Virtual Machine Monitor. In: Proceedings of the 2001 USENIX Annual Technical Conference. The USENIX Association, 2001.

332. L.H. Sullivan. The Tall Office Building Artistically Considered. In: Lippincott's Magazine, no. 57, March 1896, pp. 403–409.

333. Svensk Standard. Databehandling – Programsprak – SIMULA, SS 636114, 1987.

334. K.E. Sveiby, T. Lloyd. Managing Knowhow – Add Value by Valuing Creativity. Bloomsbury, October 1989.

335. Clemens Szyperski. Component Software: Beyond Object-Oriented Programming. ACM Press, 1998.

336. A. Tarski. A Lattice-Theoretical Fixpoint Theorem and its Application. In: Pacific Journal of Mathematics, vol. 5, pp. 285–309, 1955.

337. O. Taiichi. Toyota Production System: Beyond Large-Scale Production, Productivity Press, 1988.

338. F.W. Taylor. Scientific Management – Comprising: Shop Management, The Principles of Scientific Management, Testimony Before the Special House Committee, Harper & Row, 1911.

339. F.W. Taylor. Shop Management. In (F.W. Taylor): Scientific Management – Comprising: Shop Management, The Principles of Scientific Management, Testimony Before the Special House Committee, Harper & Row, 1911.

340. F.W. Taylor. The Principles of Scientific Management. In (F.W. Taylor): Scientific Management – Comprising: Shop Management, The Principles of Scientific Management, Testimony Before the Special House Committee, Harper & Row, 1911.

341. F.W. Taylor. Hearings Before Social Committee of the House of Representatives to Investigate the Taylor and Other Systems of Shop Management Under the Authority of House Resolution 90. In (F.W. Taylor): Scientific Management – Comprising: Shop Management, The Principles of Scientific Management, Testimony Before the Special House Committee, Harper & Row, 1911.

342. R. Ten-Hove, P. Walker. Java Business Integration 1.0 Final Release, Specification JSR 208. Sun Microsystems, August 2005.

343. T. Thalhammer, M. Schrefl, and M. Mohania, M.: Active Data Warehouses: Complementing OLAP with Analysis Rules. Data & Knowledge Engineering 39, 2001.

344. S. Thatte (Editor). Specification: Business Process Execution Language for Web Services Version 1.1, May 2003.

345. TPC. TPC Benchmark W (Web Commerce). Transaction Processing Performance Council, 2000.

346. TPC. TPC Benchmark H (Decision Support), Standard Specification, Revision 2.6.0 Transaction Processing Performance Council, 2006.

347. UN/CEFACT. UN/CEFACT's Modeling Methodology (UMM): UMM Meta Model – Foundation Module Version 1.0, Technical Specification. UN/CEFACT, 2006.

348. UN/CEFACT and OASIS 2001. ebXML Business Process Specification Schema, Version 1.01. Business Process Project Team, UN/CEFACT, OASIS, 2001.

349. van Deursen, A., Klint, P., J. Visser. Domain-Specific Languages: An Annotated Bibliography. ACM SIGPLAN Notices, vol. 35, no. 6, ACM Press, 2000, pp.26–36.

350. D. Wackerow. MQSeries Primer. IBM MQSeries Enterprise Application Integration Center, October 1999.

351. C.P. Wadsworth. Semantics and Pragmatics of the λ-Calculus. Ph.D. Thesis, Oxford University, 1971.

352. G.H. Watson. Strategic Benchmarking – How to Rate Your Company's Performance Against the World's Best. Wiley, 1993.

353. J. Waldo. The Jini Architecture for Network-Centric Computing. Communications of the ACM, vol. 42., no. 7.

354. R. Weaver. The Business Value of the Service Component Architecture (SCA) and Service Data Objects (SDO). Business Value White Paper, version 0.9. International Business Machines, November 2005.

355. P. Westerman. Data Warehousing – Using the Wal-Mart Model. Morgan Kaufmann Publishers, 2001.

356. Workflow Management Coalition. Workflow Management Coalition Terminology & Glossary, Document Number WFMC-TC-1011, WfMC, February 1999.

357. O. Weiß. Integrated System Modelling Using the Form-Oriented Analysis: Focusing SOA and Model-Driven Techniques on Simple System Usage. Vdm Verlag Dr. Müller, 2008.

358. Windows User Experience Team. Microsoft Windows User Experience: Official Guidelines for User Interface Developers and Designers. B&T, 1999.

359. L. Wittgenstein. Tractatus Logico-Philosophicus. Kegan Paul, Trench, Trubner & Co., 1922.

360. P. Woodman. Business Continuity Management. ISBN 0-85946-480-6, Chartered Management Institute, March 2007.

361. E. Yourdon. Modern Structured Analysis. Yourdon Press, Prentice Hall, 1989.
362. T. Ziebermayr. A Framework for Enhanced Service Reuse in an industrial SOA-Context. Dissertation, Institute for Application Oriented Knowledge Processing, Johannes-Kepler-University Linz, March 2010.
363. T. Ziebermayr, R. Weinreich, D. Draheim. A Versioning Model for Enterprise Services. In: Proceedings of WAMIS 2007 - 3rd International Workshop on Web and Mobile Information Services. IEEE Press, May 2007.

Index

Breinigsville, PA USA
24 August 2010
244134BV00006B/25/P